LISETTE A

Lig Up

Illustrated by
Valentina Toro

PUFFIN

PUFFIN BOOKS

UK | USA | Canada | Ireland | Australia
India | New Zealand | South Africa

Puffin Books is part of the Penguin Random House group of companies
whose addresses can be found at global.penguinrandomhouse.com

www.penguin.co.uk www.puffin.co.uk www.ladybird.co.uk

Penguin Random House UK

First published 2024

001

Set in 12.5/17.5pt Bembo Book MT Std
Typeset by Jouve (UK), Milton Keynes
Printed and bound in Great Britain by Clays Ltd, Elcograf S.p.A.

The authorized representative in the EEA is Penguin Random House Ireland,
Morrison Chambers, 32 Nassau Street, Dublin D02 YH68

A CIP catalogue record for this book is available from the British Library

ISBN: 978-0-241-63765-4

All correspondence to:
Puffin Books
Penguin Random House Children's
One Embassy Gardens, 8 Viaduct Gardens, London SW11 7BW

MIX
Paper | Supporting responsible forestry
FSC® C018179
FSC www.fsc.org

Penguin Random House is committed to a sustainable future for our business, our readers and our planet. This book is made from Forest Stewardship Council® certified paper.

PUFFIN BOOKS

Lights Up

Lisette Auton is a northern disabled writer, activist, poet, novelist, spoken-word artist, actor, film- and theatre-maker, and creative practitioner. She's an award-winning poet who has performed at Northern Stage, ARC, the Southbank Centre and the Sage, in pubs, in a crypt, at festivals, indoors, outdoors, on a bridge and in a launderette.

Books by Lisette Auton

THE SECRET OF HAVEN POINT

THE STICKLEBACK CATCHERS

LIGHTS UP

Follow Lisette online

@lisette_auton

lisetteauton.co.uk

#LightsUp

This book is dedicated to Harper Lee, rescue dog and my beloved editor-in-chief.

And to all the Very Good Dogs: those still with us, and those playing for all eternity at the farm in the sky – especially Milly, Drummer, Ralph, Django, Woody, Aldo, Captain Pugwash, Fraggle, Barney, Maizie, Nyssa, Romana, Ren, Jake, Daisy and Rex.

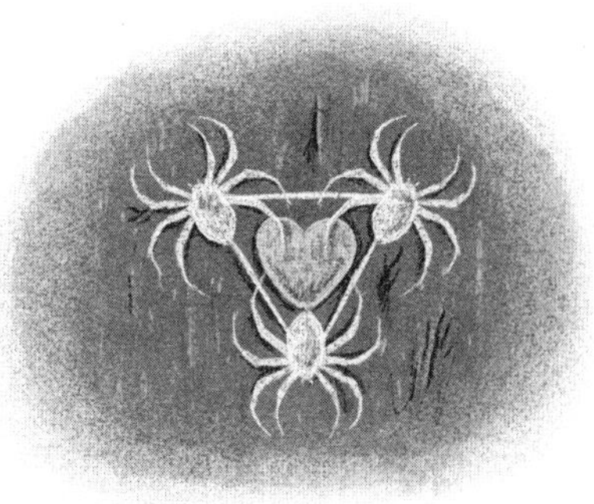

Chapter One

Way Back When, 1767

'Some villages have a beautiful waterfall, wild ponies in meadows, and what do we have?' Araine Redwood asked her little sister.

'Spiders,' replied Nora. 'Urgh, why does it have to be spiders? I think we got the worst option. The last one left!'

'Exactly,' agreed Araine.

'Girls!' said their mam. 'They've been here since the world was born, weaving their webs under our village, keeping us safe, linking us from this world to the next by invisible strands. Turning dew into diamonds,' she added, trying to get them both tucked up on the straw mattress they shared in the eaves of their cottage's little attic, at the other end of the room to their parents' bed.

A chicken settled next to Nora and she patted its head absent-mindedly.

'Nonsense – we'd know about that if it was true! That's even worse than some of Nora's fibs,' said Araine. 'You do tell some whoppers.'

'I do not!' Nora tugged her big sister's long curly blonde hair and stuck her tongue out. She scooched down to the end of the bed, so that Araine couldn't reach to tug her pigtails in return. 'Anyway,' she retorted, 'if there really were dew diamonds, then Dad wouldn't have to work so hard for Lord Machiavelli.'

There was a heavy pause as they tried not to think about their father curled up downstairs, unable to climb the ladder to the loft any more.

'Mam, is it true that the spiders let folk say goodbye?' asked Araine, trying to change the subject when she saw her sister's face crumpling. But then asking about saying goodbye to dead people probably wasn't the best idea. Luckily, Nora didn't seem to notice – she was too excited and bouncy.

'Can the spiders really do that? Tell us the story, Mam!'

Mam glanced at the spiders in the corner of the room, watching them, keeping them safe. 'You'll know the answer to that when your time comes and you need them. Just make sure there's three of you together. Now, hop into bed!'

'Oh, Mam!' whined Nora.

'You'll not be able to get up in the morning otherwise, and none of us wants to live with Madam Grumpy.'

'Aye, Nora,' said Araine with glee, siding with her mam.

'Me? Araine, you're the worst!'

Araine could see that Nora was on the verge of tears. She couldn't bear her sister being upset, and knew she loved the tales about their mam once saving the spiders so they were now in her debt, and had promised they'd always look after her two daughters in return.

She looked at Mam. 'Tell us about the spiders' diamond that lets you say goodbye to the dead!'

The spiders all scuttled over and sat by Mam's feet. One harvestman spider with spindly legs and a body like a seed even settled itself on her foot. The spiders loved their mam and this story, just as much as the sisters did.

Nora curled up in bed, watching a tiny money spider beginning to weave a web above her.

'Tell us! Tell us! Tell us!' yelled the sisters between giggles as their mam began to recount the tale of Attercop, their village. It was said that the spiders lived beneath Attercop. They had a precious diamond made from dewdrops, the spiders' heart, which could link with the villagers for a brief moment, allowing them to say goodbye to their loved ones before they departed for the next world. The spiders' web filled a cavernous catacomb, weaving out from below the church and reaching to the very edges of the village, keeping all those above it safe.

'The diamond only works with three, just like the points of the triangle carved above the church door. Three people who have loved and lost – they can hold the spiders' heart to say their last goodbye, to know that their loved ones are safe on their final journey.'

The sisters drifted off to sleep as their mam's familiar words soothed and lulled them.

Araine rolled over, whimpering, as her dream shot her into a memory of her little sister watching the performance tent being set up. Nora was as excited as the troupe of actors, who'd just arrived in Attercop. It was a blue-sky day and Araine and Nora, in their matching dresses, were sitting next to each other on a hay bale with their best friend, Lucie Lightfoot. They laughed and pointed as some of the players acted out stories while others did somersaults and danced.

The blue faded to grey and Araine moaned in her sleep, pulling her blanket further round herself, desperately trying to keep warm. In her dream, the grey sky transformed into the grey of their dad's skin. And when she ran towards him, dream-running slow, when she finally hugged him, instead of strong muscles, he felt like a twig and she had to be careful not to snap him.

Araine's eyes flew open as she called out for her father. The space beside her was empty – where was Nora? She was nowhere to be seen. And this wasn't their blanket.

Araine sat up in fright, bringing her knees towards her and flinging off the blanket of cobwebs that she'd pulled about herself to keep warm. Looking around, she realized she was in the village bakery, not her bedroom. Then she saw the spiders in the corner, all standing guard, and she screamed.

The panic lasted for just a moment. 'Calm yourself, Araine,' she muttered, trying to get her breathing under control. Mam would tell her off for upsetting the spiders.

They had obviously kept their promise to her mam: they were the ones who had got Araine through the night, their web keeping her warm. Araine hadn't always known what was real and what was story when Mam told her the tales about the spiders, but maybe her mother had been telling the truth . . .

Mam . . . Everything came flooding back to her, and Araine dissolved into sobs that she thought would break her heart in two. Her dying dad had been working long hours in the fields, even though he could barely stand, because Lord Machiavelli did not like anything to fall behind schedule.

The thought of evil Lord Machiavelli was like poison in Araine's heart; it brought out all the bad bits in her, like when she was mean to her sister if she didn't want to share or was being annoying. Araine knew that everyone had *some* nasty bits inside, but that could be forgiven if you said sorry and walked into kindness. That's what her mam said. Whatever that meant.

But Araine couldn't forgive Lord Machiavelli. Not ever. She tried to shut out her thoughts of revenge, like putting a broom between the spokes of his carriage's wheels so it would overturn when he was inside. No! She was doing it again!

'Stop thinking about him!' she scolded herself. And yet there he was. In her mind, playing over and over again, was a conversation between him and her dad, which she'd watched while hiding behind a barn.

That had been the beginning of the end.

'What would the world be like if we all stopped working?' Lord Machiavelli had said pompously to her father.

His Lordship was dressed in silks and velvet. He was plump with rich food and was sitting on a horse he could barely ride – a horse that was worth more than their cottage and all the houses in the village put together, their homes that they lived in and paid for with their service. Araine had watched as her dad had tried to pick up the scythe, but it was too heavy for him, and he stumbled and fell. Their giant of a dad, now withered and broken.

'Back to work – stop wasting time!' Lord Machiavelli had yelled at the villagers who were trying to help her father. She'd have run to him too if Nora hadn't appeared at that moment and tugged her away.

That was the night the villagers carried Araine and Nora's dad back to their cottage and Mam made a bed for him downstairs by the fire, instead of him climbing the ladder to where they all slept with the chickens.

He didn't get up again.

'You're the elder sister,' he'd said to Araine.

'Only by thirteen months,' she'd said sulkily, suspecting that she was going to be asked to do something she didn't want to do.

Her dad had ruffled her hair. 'That makes all the difference: you're ten and Nora is only nine. It's your job, as the eldest and strongest, to always keep her safe.'

Araine had felt really grown up when he said that. She *was* so much older than her sister, and she promised her father she'd take care of Nora.

But now look at me, she thought. She couldn't even do that right.

'There's still a chance for her,' Araine told herself. 'Don't give up.'

However, she couldn't forget the image of Nora asleep yesterday, before Araine had left her, not waking despite Araine's efforts. And her little sister's fingers, blue and freezing cold.

Not long after their dad's death, fever had struck the village, and Lord Machiavelli had escaped in a convoy of snorting and galloping horses and carriages, leaving the villagers to either starve or catch the illness that poisoned the air.

First the fever took their mam. In a daze, Araine and Nora had buried her in their garden and placed her favourite lavender on top of the mound of earth. Then they went inside the cottage and barred the doors. When Nora became sickly and pale, when the breath began to catch in her chest, Araine knew the sickness had found her too.

'No! I can't think like that. I just need to get back to her and everything will be all right,' Araine said to herself, and gave her head a little shake to try to get rid of the thought. But it was a very gnarly one and wouldn't let go of her heart.

Surely Nora would be all right? She *had* to be. Araine had promised her father!

But they had desperately needed food. If she was too weak to look after Nora, what would become of them? So, yesterday, Araine had made the difficult decision to leave her little sister and had hurried across the bridge over the river dividing Attercop from the town of Cawlington, all set to barter anything she had for food. What if the baker had no bread? Should she steal some flour?

When she'd got to Cawlington, she didn't have to worry whether thieving was a bad thing or not, because there was nothing to take: the place was deserted. The streets were usually bustling, full of people yelling and selling things, pickpockets, people getting in the way, stray dogs and children begging for food, especially on the corner by the Travelling Duck pub where she'd sit outside when her dad had business in town.

But there was no one.

The silence was so unexpected that Araine had had to stop for a moment and wiggle her fingers in her ears to make sure they weren't playing tricks on her.

Everyone had fled, and she couldn't find a single scrap of food. The bakery had been ransacked: bare shelves, a cold oven and empty flour sacks by the door.

As she'd been sitting on the pavement outside the bakery, trying to decide what to do next, the sky had suddenly darkened and a warm wind picked up, then thunder crashed in the distance. By the time Araine spotted where the storm was coming from, the sky had split open and huge drops of rain had begun to fall. Within seconds, horizontal rain was lashing and it soaked her to the bone before she'd had the chance to find shelter in the bakery, leaving her shivering.

When rain like this came down, the river swelled and the bridge linking Cawlington and Attercop was too dangerous to cross. Araine was trapped. She kicked out in anger. She'd have to leave Nora all alone in their cottage until the rain stopped.

Lightning struck the timber-framed building opposite. Araine had watched the spark ignite, and she'd screamed and huddled in a corner. No candles or matches, no way to get dry or to have any light.

That's unless lightning strikes here, she'd thought, and then immediately decided not to dwell on that.

She'd curled up in a ball, and sang the songs she would sing at home when Nora was being annoying and wouldn't go to sleep. She'd thought there was no way she'd have been able to sleep, but her eyelids were so heavy that they had soon begun to close.

Now, the next morning, after she'd shaken off the spiders' blanket, as well as her dreams, Araine peered out of the bakery door, the spiders keeping a respectful distance behind her. The sun was creeping up in the watery sky; she held her hand out and caught no rain. Wasting no time, she ran.

She'd only gone a few paces when she heard a distinct pattering behind her. Araine stopped and looked over her shoulder. The spiders were following her.

'Do you want to help me? Then find us some food!' she yelled at them. 'You were supposed to keep us safe, but you didn't save Mam or protect Nora! If you can't help us, leave me alone!'

They paused as she stared at them, and as soon as she sped off again they followed once more, gathering in number, tumbling over one another, growing in size like the swollen river.

Araine raced over the bridge to her village, stumbling as her tired legs gave way but hauling herself back up.

No food. A wasted journey.

'I'm coming, Nora – hold on!'

How could she have thought that leaving her little sister was the right idea?

The wind howled and Araine pulled her shawl tight round her long curly blonde hair as she stopped in her tracks and stared at the red cross that the villagers had painted on the lopsided wooden front door to her cottage.

She knew what that meant. She was too late.

Araine threw herself to the ground, pounded her fists into the earth and sobbed for Nora, for her baby sister.

All of a sudden, a spider dropped on to her arm. She screamed and brushed it off, but then there came another and another, falling out of the sky, raining down on her, getting tangled in her long hair. The ones that had followed her home surged towards her.

'You were meant to keep her safe! Get off me! *Get off me!*' Araine shrieked into the wind, and they did. She watched as the spiders jumped into the air and tumbled towards the ground, some of them securing themselves with silk lines before they leaped.

As she looked down, she saw that they had formed themselves into a wriggling, churning line, crawling over one another to form an arrow on the stony ground behind her. An arrow that pointed away from her front door with the flame-red cross and towards the ancient stone church in the centre of Attercop. Her mouth dropped open.

Her mam said the church had been built before the world was fully formed, when only spiders existed. The steps that ran round and round up the church tower were worn and smooth, and even on the hottest day the stone was always cold. Araine had often felt that the church was watching over them, keeping them safe.

Not any more.

I can't leave Nora behind!

There were no grown-ups around to help her decide what to do, and the pain in her heart squeezed so tightly she thought it would explode. Then the sky burst open with more rain and lightning.

Her mam had always told her that spiders weren't something to be afraid of: they were there to help the villagers. So she did the only thing she could do. Araine followed the spiders.

'Hello?' Araine called as she pushed open the great door of the stone church. 'Anyone here?'

Her voice echoed back, swooping down from the high roof space, but there was no reply.

She jumped as the door closed behind her with a deep thud. The air was mossy and damp, thick, as though you could cut it. A tear threatened to leak out of her eye, but she angrily wiped it away. This was not the time to grieve – she could do that later. She needed shelter and food first. Her dad would be proud of how practical she was being.

Her dad! She'd let him down so badly.

Araine pressed her lips together and refused to cry.

The spiders poured under the door into the cool of the church, and swirled round her feet. Araine rubbed her eyes, closing them tight. How could any of this be happening? She was seeing things – because of how sad and lost she felt. Maybe she'd made it up about the spider blanket and the cross on her door and the arrow? Maybe Nora was absolutely fine, wondering where Araine was, waiting for her to come home! If Araine opened her eyes and the spiders were gone, she'd know it had all been a horrible trick her mind was playing on her.

She slowly opened her eyes.

The spiders were still there.

Anger flashed inside her, the bright red bubbling kind that her mam told her to keep in check, and she screamed into the cool quiet of the church, her shout bouncing off the walls and returning to her like a ghost's unearthly cry.

She was now shivering so hard her teeth clattered together. When the spiders began their march over the thick stone slabs up the aisle towards the centre of the church, she didn't know what else to do but follow them.

They passed the altar and came to a halt at the entrance to the tower that took you up and up, round and round the smooth, narrowing steps until you burst out into the light of the roof.

Araine took a step up and then immediately stopped as a formation of spiders broke off and formed a large X in front of her foot.

'Not this way?' Her voice felt too big in the silent church, with all the stone saints looking down on her. 'What was that?'

Her voice bounced back again, but underneath her feet she was sure she could hear voices that *weren't* her echo. Someone else was here! She knelt down on the cool stone, next to where the spiders had stopped her climbing, and examined the thick wall: not a gap in sight.

But a symbol carved in the floor caught her eye. It was the one on the front of the church that their mam always told them about before bed, but Araine had never noticed it here before. Carved into the stone slab was a triangle, with a spider at each of its points, and in the centre of the triangle was the outline of the diamond-dew heart.

There it was again! She could definitely hear a voice! And was that warmer air she could feel? Where was it coming from?

Araine bent down further to examine the floor. Then she watched in shock as the huge army of spiders, all different shades of brown and grey, some fluffy and some sleek, a few with what looked like hard shell armour, began to balance on top of each other around the edge of the slab with the strange triangle symbol in its centre.

Despite her sadness, Araine laughed out loud; they reminded her of the players she and Nora had seen last summer, who'd come from the big city of York to perform on the village green.

The dreams she'd had in the bakery floated back to her. Araine shook her head to get rid of the image of her grey skin-and-bone dad; that's not how she wanted to remember him. Then she said a very bad word out loud when she thought about Lord Machiavelli and how he must be enjoying his pampered life, away from all this death and suffering. She whispered an apology to her mam for saying it, especially in church.

The last few spiders climbed on top of the others. Were Araine's eyes playing tricks? No! The stone slab with the symbol was slowly starting to sink. She leaned forward, holding her breath, and gently put her hand in the centre of the wriggling mass, trying not to crush any of them. She pressed her weight on the slab too, but it didn't budge any further.

The spiders looked at her accusingly as if she should know what to do next, their little bulbous eyes – hundreds of them – staring at Araine.

'I don't know!' she exclaimed, and then realized grief mixed with anger was a very peculiar thing, and that sadness and fear left you lost and muddled up and made you believe that spiders were acrobats.

Araine closed her eyes and took a breath. When she opened them again, the spiders were still staring at her.

She reached carefully down to the small symbol of the triangle carved in the centre of the stone slab and traced her finger along the edges of the heart shape in its centre. It was cool to the touch and the grooves were deep. She realized she'd expected something to happen and nothing had, but she looked up and saw that the spiders at the edges, forming a circle round her hand, were leaning forward intently, as if willing her on.

She pressed her fingers in turn on each of the spiders carved into the stone at the points of the triangle.

Nothing.

'Tell me what I'm supposed to do next!'

But the spiders just kept staring at her.

'You're no help at all,' she muttered.

Araine traced the triangle, and when her finger reached the corner where she had begun there was a sharp cracking noise that made her jump. Suddenly the stone dropped a little way, then slid underneath the slab next to it, and she had to pull her hand back to stop herself tumbling downwards. She peered into the darkness below, and as her eyes got used to the light a spiral staircase revealed itself, curling into the black.

She couldn't wait to tell Nora about this!

Then her heart trembled and tightened again when she remembered she couldn't. It was as though little chunks of her heart were becoming stone each time she thought about what she'd lost.

Before she could think about it any further, the spiders began to march down the stone staircase, and the sounds that Araine had heard became loud and clear voices.

'Who's there?' someone cried out from below. 'Have you brought our mam?'

The question was followed by the sound of crying, and Araine could hear another voice, a little bit older and less squeaky, trying to give comfort. It sounded familiar, but with all the echoing in the church she couldn't quite place it.

Two voices, thought Araine. *And with me that makes three – a triangle!*

She cast one last glance at the familiar church, and then took a step into the unknown.

Chapter Two

Then, 1878

Jack leaped back as a carriage nearly mowed him down. He'd never seen Cawlington so busy! He waited until his heart had stopped pounding violently from his near miss, and his messy mass of golden hair had come back down from being startled by the blast of air. Then he looked both ways properly and stepped carefully out between a steady stream of carriages.

He dashed to the other side of the road where there was a huge crowd of people who couldn't afford tickets, but, like him, weren't going to miss out on the free spectacle of seeing the rich people arrive – and hopefully getting a glimpse of Araine Machiavelli herself!

Jack was excited to see her, but really it was Harcus Machiavelli he was waiting for. His head buzzed with excitement and he felt a little dizzy. He'd read about Harcus in the papers that his big brother Matthew collected from the streets – they couldn't afford to spend precious money on a new copy – and he now had a little scrapbook of all of Harcus's exploits, Matthew carefully tearing them out and bringing them home for him. But if Jack could see Harcus for real, it would be incredible! Maybe Harcus would do backflips down the street!

Jack burrowed his way through the crowds, trying to make his way to the front by the barrier, and he nearly got squashed up against two people arguing. He managed to move just in time to avoid barrelling into them, but someone bent to pick up a dropped glove and Jack tripped and fell, then someone stood on his hand.

'Ow!'

But his voice was lost in the shouts of the folk eagerly waiting, pushing and shoving each other, and the street vendors trying to sell their matchbooks, programmes, smelling salts, candied nuts and anything else they'd thought might prove popular at the grand opening of the new theatre. This one was even more modern than the one that had been there before. Araine Machiavelli had swooped in when the old Lightfoot Theatre had been destroyed, building this brand-new one in its place. Rumour had it that the stage was now so large you could fit an elephant on it, and there was a water tower so that *full-sized* boats could have battles! Jack wished he could go inside. He'd never been in the Lightfoot either, couldn't afford to even come close. This would have to do.

He wished, too, that Matthew could be here with him, but he wasn't and Jack couldn't quite remember why. It must have been something really important for Matthew to miss this.

Jack used his size to his advantage and crawled between legs and skirts until finally he had the best view right at the front of the crowd. The newspaper had said that the whole town and beyond would be here for the grand opening of the Machiavelli Empire. And they were right!

'Was that Lord Hazlebrook?' a woman beside him asked as she scratched her leg and nearly pulled out a handful of Jack's hair by accident.

'He's the one from the paper!'

'Is that real gold on the carriage?'

'They'd best not stay long round here – someone will nick it!'

Jack held steady in his position cross-legged on the kerb opposite the theatre, pinching anyone's ankles who came too close or tried to stand in front of him, as carriage after carriage pulled up outside the grand entrance and the great and the good were helped down from their carriages and into the opulence beyond his view.

He craned his neck. Surely it must be time?

There! He craned his neck to the right, and coming down the street towards the theatre was a troupe of acrobats, all in red-and-gold leotards, leaping and flipping towards them. This was even better than Jack could have possibly imagined! At last, they were here! He thought his face would break in two from grinning so hard.

Jack couldn't contain his months of excitement any longer; he finally had a chance to glimpse his hero! He began to whisper, then, as he grew in confidence, to chant, 'Harcus! Harcus! Harcus!' The crowd joined in. The noise was thunderous – he could feel it beating inside his chest and had to cup his hands over his ears.

The acrobats leaped and twirled towards him. Again, Jack craned his neck to see, but he still couldn't spot Harcus. Then there was a scream from the crowd and someone pointed, and soon everyone was yelling, 'Look, look!'

Jack followed the excited gazes to the top of the theatre. The new Machiavelli Empire dominated the street and the skyline, overshadowing all other buildings around it. At the very top was Araine's signature symbol carved into the stone: a triangle with a spider on each point and a heart at its centre. His eyes came back to the pavement and worked upwards from the awning-covered entrance with the red carpet leading the way inside, round the statues of spiders adorning the corners of the building, up over the arches and white stone colonnades, following the lights running from the huge water tower high up on its roof.

He squinted – it couldn't possibly be. Right on top of the roof was Harcus Machiavelli! How did he get there? Skinny and tall with a twisted fine moustache that twirled out from his pointy face by a good five inches, he was suddenly dangling from the stonework on the edge of the roof as the whole crowd gasped and held their breath. The acrobats gathered below, unfurling a safety net.

Jack could barely breathe, his chest was so tight.

Then, in the blink of an eye, Harcus was leaping down towards the crowd, rolling and tumbling the length of the building, just in control, looking as though he might fall and then righting himself in time. All the while, the crowd screamed in fear and delight. One moment he was in one position and then, before your eyes could keep up, he was elsewhere. Suddenly he was on the ground and leaning against the elegant column of a lamp post, smoking his tortoiseshell pipe with the bowl in the shape of a deck of fanned-out cards that

Jack recognized from the playbills outside the building. Then he was high-kicking along the top of the barrier to the delight of the cheering crowd. He dived into the air and somersaulted, landing in a bow with his arms outstretched towards the carriage that was now pulling up outside the theatre as the acrobats lined its route.

The carriage was pulled by six pure white horses, all with plumes of ostrich feathers standing proud from gold bands around their heads. The air filled with white puffs from their snorts and whinnies. There was no driver: it was as if they had arrived by magic. The crowd, including Jack, gasped as all six horses drew to a halt, bent their necks into a low bow and then continued down on to one knee. The crowd's chant changed from '*Harcus*' to '*Araine*' – the 'Queen of Spiders' as the newspapers called her, due to the embroidered webs on every outfit she wore.

Slowly, the carriage door opened, the crowd screaming by now with the tension.

Harcus leaped on to the barrier once more and now he sported a red-and-gold top hat. As he raised it, a spotlight beamed above his head, throwing his shadow across the ground. The tip of his shadow moustache and hat rested against the barrier on the ground, right by Jack, who was still sitting cross-legged, his hands tight over his ears because the crowd was so loud he thought his eardrums might burst. He removed his left hand to carefully touch the ground and check whether the shadow was real. It rippled over his hand as he reached out and then stayed in place as he held it there. There was a tap on his shoulder and he looked up into the laughing face of Harcus, holding his real hand out to the boy.

'But . . .!' said Jack to his hero. 'Your shadow!'

'I can never trust it to behave,' said Harcus with a wink.

Jack watched as the man's disobedient shadow began to shrink and stalk across the street, completely independent of its owner. The moment it disappeared at the door of the carriage there was a huge explosion of rainbow lights and stars against the deepening dusk sky, and Araine Machiavelli appeared before the crowd. Not at the carriage door, where everyone was expecting, but in the centre of the street directly in front of the theatre doors, in a dress of deepest red velvet covered in golden spiders and webs. Her arms were outstretched, and Jack was even more in awe and amazement – because she was standing on the back of an elephant!

An actual, real-life elephant, with a striking feathered headdress. Magically appearing from nowhere in the middle of the street.

Jack turned to look back at Harcus, but he had gone.

A sparkle of dancing light drew Jack's attention and he followed it to its source – the spectacular heart-shaped diamond that Araine wore around her neck. As Jack laid his eyes on it, his body gave a great involuntary shudder, and it felt as though something had pierced his chest, like when he ate too fast and Matthew had to rub his back to make the pain go away.

'Welcome to the Machiavelli Empire!' Araine called out, and now somehow Harcus was by her elephant, no longer in his tight acrobat clothes but in evening dress to match Araine's gown.

'How did they do that . . .?'

'Did anyone see . . .?'

'He was just beside me!' cried Jack, joining in with the astonished shouts of the crowd.

Everyone cheered triumphantly and the crowd could no longer be contained, rushing and breaking down the barrier, scrambling over it to get to their idols.

Jack curled himself into a tiny ball, holding his hands over his head to try to avoid being trampled.

Police in their oversized black coats and helmets struggled to hold back the crowd as they fought to get closer, to touch the stars of the theatre. Just as Jack thought he'd be crushed, the elephant raised its trunk into the air and trumpeted. The crowd were so shocked they fell silent and stood still, at the very same moment that the theatre burst into lights in front of them. Gas lamps exploded in a rushing rectangle surrounding the theatre and, when the flashes stopped, the theatre's name was revealed in lights above the entrance:

MACHIAVELLI EMPIRE

Jack scrambled to his feet and looked towards where the elephant had been, where Araine and Harcus had stood.

They had vanished, along with the the elephant, the carriage and horses, and the troupe of acrobats.

Jack shook his head and laughed with delight, then went to reach for the handkerchief in his pocket to wipe his forehead. He looked at his fingers in puzzlement as he realized he was holding a piece of paper in his hand.

Show this to the stage-door hand. Welcome to the Machiavelli Empire, Jack Redwood.
Araine Machiavelli

'How do you know my name?' whispered Jack to the piece of paper.

Could this really be happening? He looked around, but he couldn't see Araine, just a crowd beginning to disperse, none of them wanting to catch the eye of the police officers on the prowl. Jack was suddenly afraid, not of the letter in his hand but of being too scared to do something about it.

He said to himself the phrase he often did: 'What would Matthew do?'

He faked the courage of his older brother, straightened his back, held his head high and marched to the side of the theatre.

At the stage door, a giant of a boy with a bright green beard looked him up and down. 'So you're the half-life, are you? Yes, I can feel the sadness in you too.' Then he reached out and gently squeezed the top of Jack's arm and smiled at him. 'Let's see what you're made of – follow me!'

His voice was so much softer and kinder than Jack was expecting that it gave him a surprise and he forgot how his legs worked.

The green-bearded giant-boy laughed at Jack in a way that put him at ease. 'My name is Tattie, and I know who you are. We've all been waiting for you. Are you coming? We haven't got all day.'

Jack didn't have time to think about the mysterious note he was clutching tightly, what on earth a half-life was and why they'd been waiting for him, as he had to run to keep up with Tattie. He strode through doors, along narrow corridors, ducked under ropes, passed open dressing rooms full of limbs reaching for powders and potions.

'Is that a –'

'A giant man made of wood? Yes, that's Snod – you'll meet him properly later. He's a Harcus special,' replied Tattie as they marched past a wardrobe room brimming with costumes on rails, where a wooden man was jerkily shaking the creases out of one of them.

'But that's –'

'Impossible, yes! Welcome to the theatre, Jack. Keep up!'

Jack was dizzy with everything going on around him. One moment he was stepping over acrobats stretching and the next he was avoiding a monkey shrieking in a cage. It was hot, sweaty and noisy, and cluttered with too many people. There was nothing of the richness and wealth he'd just seen outside. This was messy and mucky, with peeling paint and unfinished surfaces.

'This is backstage,' explained Tattie. 'Where the real magic happens.'

Backstage, mouthed Jack to himself, absorbing the new word.

He was so awestruck, trying to take it all in, that he didn't realize Tattie had stopped and he ran straight into his back. The boy with the green beard was so huge and muscly it was like hitting a wall at top speed.

Tattie turned round and grinned at him. 'These are the wings.'

Then he gently grabbed Jack by the shoulders, moving him into position at the side of the stage. He put his face so close to Jack's that Jack could smell the gravy he must have had on his dinner, could see bits of meat in his teeth.

'The audience is out there, behind that curtain, waiting for magic, and we can't disappoint by being in the wrong place at the wrong time and breaking the spell. Do not move from this spot!'

'I w-won't,' stammered Jack. 'I promise!'

And why would he? This was the best view in the whole house. He could feel it: the tension in the air, the knowledge that something was going to happen but not knowing quite what.

To check he wasn't dreaming, he pinched his arm.

He didn't wake up.

Jack could hear the audience behind the curtain settling into their seats. Whispers of goosebumps ran up and down his arms. There was a tingling in the back of his neck, and he felt light-headed. This had to be a dream! This time he pinched his arm *and* scrunched his toes tight: he still didn't wake up.

This was definitely truly real!

He watched from the shadows as forty dancers silently glided into position on the stage in the dark behind the curtain, arms held ready. He could hear the chatter from the audience. Tattie silently appeared behind him and tapped him on the shoulder. He pointed to a tiny peephole in the curtain. Up close, Jack could see that Tattie's beard was patchy and a bit fluffy, which suggested that he wasn't as old as he was trying to look. But he seemed a lot older, as though he'd seen a lot, maybe a bit too much. He looked eleven, like him? A little bit older? Thirteen at the most. It was confusing that it was so hard to tell. Younger than Matthew, for sure.

Jack peered through the hole in the curtain. Standing on tiptoe, he could see the audience.

'That's called the auditorium,' said Tattie. 'And those things that stick out, where the really posh people are, they're called boxes.'

Jack had never seen anything so beautiful, so dripping in wealth. The whole interior was red and gold, just like Araine's dress – from the cherubs adorning the high ceiling to the patterned carpets and the chairs. There was gold leaf on the boxes, and even the lamps seemed to burn gold. Everything was decorated in wisps of gold spiderwebs that floated in the breeze made by the ladies fanning themselves.

Jack's scalp prickled as a hush descended.

'You can feel the quiet tumbling towards you, can't you?' whispered Tattie. 'From right up in the gods, the highest-up seats, down to the next level, the dress circle, rushing like a silent tidal wave until it stops at Row A down there, nearest to the stage, right at the front of the stalls.'

Tattie dragged Jack back from the curtain and into the wings, then clicked his fingers at the dancers, who tightened their poses.

Jack held his breath. He'd never, ever felt like this before, as if magic was about to begin. He couldn't believe how lucky he was. Matthew would think he was telling fibs when he told him. Backstage!

The light at the edges of the curtain disappeared as the auditorium went dark. The curtain was raised at the exact same time that the orchestra struck their first note. Jack could just about see into the gloom beyond the dancers. A long rectangular hole opened up at the front of the stage, then as if by magic a long row of lit gas lamps rose from the trapdoor, bathing the dancers in a golden glow.

Jack trembled and gasped.

Tattie whispered in his ear, 'Welcome to the theatre, Jack Redwood, our final piece of the triangle. This is lights up!'

Chapter Three

Now

'Hettie Lightfoot, your Free Spirits are here for a lift to the theatre for the auditions. Are you ready? They're eating me out of house and home! Hurry up!'

'We're not the Free Spirits any more – I've told you that a million times! And I'm not coming!' I yell back at my mam as she stands outside my bedroom door.

I finish testing the lights, then sit back in the chair at my desk and look at the miniature Arts Centre that I've just finished making. I can imagine my Free Spirits causing carnage and nicking biscuits in Mam's kitchen. We're a trio, best friends – me, Gift and Nikesh. We met at the Arts Centre, the real building that this model is based on. *Was* based on? Anyway, it doesn't exist any more, and so the Free Spirits shouldn't either. That's what our theatre group is called. *Was* called. We were the founding members and came up with the name.

Nikesh swears they found the name 'Free Spirits' in an old Victorian theatre programme, Gift says she thought she heard it on the radio, and I had this dream where spiders spelled out 'FREE SPIRITS' on a wall, all in capital letters. Yes, horrible, crawling, slinking, scary spiders wiggling their hairy, disgusting bodies to form the letters. I had to wash my face three times after I woke up and get my mam to check I didn't have spiders in my ears. We all showed up by the fountain outside the Arts Centre, RIP, and said the name at exactly the same time.

My grandad started the miniature version. I can tell which bits he did because they're precise; the bits I've done are wonky. I hope he won't mind.

I can feel my tummy lurch when I remember that I can't ask him.

I've finished the model as a memorial to Edward Redwood, my grandad. I don't have the same surname as him because my mam married a Lightfoot. Which is hilarious because my feet are stompy, and you can definitely hear me coming, especially if I honk the horn on my scooter.

My grandad loved that his name rhymed.

He loved lots of things, like bruised bananas, getting the last bits out of a ketchup bottle, writing and directing plays, making scenery, our Arts Centre and, most of all, me.

That's not me being big-headed; that's just a fact I know is true because he would actually say, 'Hettie Lightfoot, I love you best of all.'

And I would say, 'Even more than . . .' and fill in the blank with all the things I knew he loved, and he'd always say yes. Then I'd joke and tell him I didn't love him more than salt-and-vinegar crisps.

I use my tweezers to glue down a little bit of grass that's poking out and annoying me, then sit back in my chair and take a good look, twirling the tweezers in my fingers as I do.

Is it finished? I have a checklist in my head. I love ticking things off, in my brain or on epic stationery. My current favourite notebook has a rainbow on the cover that lights up when you press a button, and I've been using a sparkly pink unicorn pen. I scratch my head with it while I think. My pen gets stuck and I have to tug it out. My hair is thick and ginger-coloured, and when it's down it goes into a kind of triangle shape. I look at my pen. The lid's gone – it'll be stuck in my ponytail somewhere. Gift will pick it out for me when I see her; my arms get tired and wobbly if I hold them up for too long, so she can do some digging.

I can't believe it. No boxes left to tick.

The model is definitely, finally finished.

I grab a tissue from the box on my desk and wipe the tears escaping from my eyes. They're red-raw these days. I thought it would get easier as time went on, but it's nearly fourteen months since Grandad died, and as everyone moves on, and I don't, the weight inside me where my heart should be gets heavier and heavier.

I shake my head; this is meant to be a happy bit – I've *finished*!

Grandad was a miniaturist. Which means a maker of tiny things. I tried to help him sometimes, but – as with the fence in front of me covered in glue splodges – my body isn't really made for intricate work. My brain is though. Planning and labels and sorting: yes, that's my thing!

When he retired from being a plumber, Grandad started out doing ships in bottles, then progressed to fancy kits off the internet, and then he went on to make his own from scratch: wooden buildings and rooms and all the furniture to go in them. He'd use the bits and bobs I found for him around the house and from school, and recycle them into something new and teeny. Teamwork. I spotted that the little contact-lens holders

Mam gets free with her bottles of lens-cleaning solution could be turned into an excellent tiny double sink or set of tom-toms.

I touch my pocket. Two pens, a crisp-packet triangle and my grandad's round-nosed pliers. Mam gave them to me when he died. Having them there feels like he's with me. I know that's silly, but that's the way it is.

This miniature of the Arts Centre is what he was working on when he died. The first time he went there was with Mam and Dad to see a show I'd produced. Basically, being a producer for a show means being the Queen of Organization, and that's why I'm brilliant at it, with my loads of lists and highlighter pens and making sure everything gets done when it's meant to. Grandad thought I did a very good job of organizing the show but that the set was terrible, so I told him I bet he couldn't do any better, and then he did, just to prove me wrong.

His set was *lots* better.

Then he started writing and directing, and we couldn't get him out of the place, which would be awful if your grandad was the sort of person who embarrassed you in front of your friends, but he was brill. So brill that my friends tried to steal him. They even made him Artistic Director of the Free Spirits.

They called him Ed Red and it made him beam every single time he heard it. All my best memories with him are in the Arts Centre.

When he got sick, he made us all promise that we'd hold a party there for him after he'd gone.

I told him that he wasn't allowed to die.

A little sob pops out of my mouth without me realizing it was going to, and I have to try to hold my bottom lip still. I can't cry again. I'm too tired from crying.

I'll never forgive him for doing that and leaving me. For dying.

We couldn't hold the party for him that none of us wanted to have anyway, because the council detonated the Arts Centre. Actually *blew it up*, said it was condemned, unsafe, not worth saving.

I'll never forgive them for doing that either.

My chest goes tight and I have to do a huff to keep the cry inside me that's threatening to explode right out. Not as a little sob but as a mighty roar – and, when it feels like that, I have to keep it inside because if it comes out I'm not sure it will ever stop.

I used to be cool as a cucumber – a Grandad phrase for being unflappable in a crisis – but at the moment all my emotions feel big and like fireworks, and I'm never quite sure what's going to come out of my mouth. I like being in control, but now my heart and whole body feel wobbly. As if my foundations have come loose.

I miss Grandad.

I miss him so much.

I miss a lot of things. Like the bit of me that just feels like a hole. I wish I could fill it up with something and then it wouldn't hurt as much, but I don't want to fill it up with something because then I'll forget him and I won't do that.

My head is very confused.

I try to tell Gift, my *best* best friend, but she hasn't had any reason yet for feelings this big, and I just feel silly and like I'm not explaining it well but I know she's trying to understand, and then I stop and go quiet because my words aren't big enough to match the missing bit of me.

See, I can't get it to make sense out loud.

One of the things that I know could fill up the empty bit of me is theatre stuff, but that's on my number one No Way In The Universe Ever Again list. And if there's one thing I can be, just like my grandad was, it's ruddy stubborn.

Anyway, we put on plays in a place that was blown to smithereens, so I can't do that even if I wanted to. And even if it hadn't been, it was a theatre, and I've banned me from that, so I couldn't anyway.

'Are you actually up, Hettie?'

'Yes!' I yell back to Mam, who's now yelling at me from the kitchen.

We live in a bungalow in Cawlington, on an estate called Attercop, on the shabby side of town. My mam has ginger triangle hair too, and works as a dental hygienist, which I think is gross but she really loves. Cawlington is big enough to have a twelve-screen cinema. I love the cinema. Not as much as I loved theatre, which is live and you're wondering whether something might go wrong and you're there in person with the actors and the set and . . . well, it's just blimmin' magic.

Not any more though – nope! It's dead to me.

I stroke my finger along the miniature path Ed Red made on the Arts Centre model, with its grooved paving slabs that he'd chiselled out with a toothpick. Luckily, one he *hadn't* used. He could be gross like that. I follow the path past the fountain on the right. In summer, in the real fountain, not this miniature one with water made from crinkly plastic, we would dance and chuck water at each other and get soaked. I trail my finger up the big steps to the double-arched front door. Gift, Nikesh and I used to sit on those big grey steps, worn smooth from all those bums and feet, watching people coming and going, listening out for gossip, learning our lines, sharing bags of the out-of-date crisps Gift's mam brought home from work each Friday.

I still can't believe our theatre is gone.

And I definitely can't believe that I'm being forced to go to the monstrosity that's now in its place.

'But you can't call it a monstrosity,' said Gift yesterday. 'Because (A) that's a grown-up word so you should use summat like "horribleness" or "ugly", and (B) you can't call it that because you've never actually *seen* it.'

'You were the one that told me it was!'

'I *know*,' said Gift as she tied her braids up in a tartan scarf. 'But I'm allowed to use words like that because I'm more mature and older than you –'

'By two weeks!'

'And because I've actually *seen* it. Your knowledge is second hand and therefore an inferior source, as reinforced by last week's history lesson on first-hand and second-hand sources. And which one is most valid and to be relied upon?'

'Have you swallowed Nikesh?' I asked her. Nikesh is brainy and an excellent researcher and historian, and a massive biscuit thief. 'That's the sort of stuff they'd spout!'

Gift is very good at telling you off while loving you at the same time, and it's usually enough to gently kick my bum into action and make me forget whatever it was I was grumpy about.

But not recently.

It annoys me that they've all given up too easily, forgotten that Ed Red wanted to save our Arts Centre, and they've all been stolen away by the shiny new theatre that was built on the ground where it once stood. They both want to go to the auditions for a new theatre troupe. We got a brochure through the letterbox about it a few weeks ago. Mam thinks she was being subtle leaving it on my desk for me to read, but I couldn't bear to, so I shoved it in the drawer.

Well, they can be stolen away by it. I won't be.

I bend forward to ease back the lid of the cardboard box that sits on the floor by my desk. It will safely house Grandad's miniature until I can get a glass case to keep the dust off it.

There's a brilliant ghost story about the Arts Centre, from when it was an old theatre, that I kept thinking about when I was finishing off the model. Grandad used to always tell it at Halloween. It's about magic spiders and a spooky heart-shaped diamond that can turn people into ghosts! I wrote it down in my swirly notebook when I first heard it, but then I had to hide the notebook in the airing cupboard and sleep with the light on for a fortnight because it felt too real, and I kept having nightmares where I was trapped in a web.

If there was a diamond, *and* we'd found it, I bet we could have saved our Arts Centre. The council people were right though: it was falling down and seriously mouldy, and you weren't allowed to go in parts of it because bits kept dropping off and nearly landing on people's heads. But the town loved it; me and Grandad loved it. It was ours! The council could have at least *tried* to save it! They didn't even listen properly when we told them how much it meant to all of us.

I smack my hand on the desk so hard that the box jumps, and something wafts out from beneath it. I need the tweezers to pick it up, it's so small – a teeny little paper rectangle. I'm about to chuck it away when I turn it over and realize there's something scribbled on it. I hold it up to the light, but I still can't make it out, so I grab Grandad's magnifying glass.

And nearly drop it.

It's actually a little envelope, a billion times smaller than the cute stationery set I got in my stocking one year.

Written on the front in scratchy, ink-blobbed writing is my name, except they've used Grandad's too: Hettie Lightfoot-Redwood.

Where there should be a miniature stamp, there's a symbol. I nearly drop the envelope again. *Ugh!* I shudder. It's a triangle, with a heart in the centre. That bit's fine, but then they go and spoil it with disgusting little spiders at each point of the triangle.

I quickly look over my shoulder, as if the person who put it here might still be behind me. But there's just Snod and Walls watching over me as usual. I swear Snod has a scared look on his face, but I blink and it's gone.

Wallish Walls is seven feet tall and made entirely of metal. His feet are shiny and smooth; all the rest is made up of riveted-together tin cans, a bin lid, and he has a colander as a hat. One of his arms is made out of washing-machine parts and the handle of a whisk, and it makes a massive bang when it falls off, which it does a lot. Grandad made Walls as a brother for Snod's Edge.

We were doing one of our famous twenty-four-hour shows at the Arts Centre, where we put everything together from scratch in one day. I was producing and had at least seven tabs open on my spreadsheet, as well as two notebooks and a flip chart. I'd just sent Gift off to raid the cupboards under the stage for fairy lights when there was a massive bang and I heard her scream. I saw Grandad dashing to the trapdoor to help her. I went too, but I couldn't get up on to the stage because of the steps.

There were more screams and bangs, then finally Grandad came back into my view carrying the shoulders of something huge and heavy and loads of kids were dragging it by its feet and holding its sides.

Gift came running over and plonked herself down on the edge of the stage. Her face was all sweaty and she had cobwebs stuck in her braids.

'Are you spider free?' I asked.

'Is that all you want to know? I just fell through a door into a secret room and found a giant wooden man!'

'Yes, but –'

'I'm spider free! I don't know why you don't like them. They're –'

'Far more scared of me than I am of them, et cetera, et cetera, et cetera,' I finished as my skin crawled.

'Bring it over here so Hettie can see!' yelled Gift, and Grandad reversed towards me, pulling the wooden man by its giant clogged feet. Something flashed and caught my eye.

'Wait!' I yelled, and he stopped still.

One of the kids tripped and fell so that a big wooden arm he'd been supporting crashed on to the stage. I peered at the bottom of one of the giant wooden clogs.

'Whoa,' I whispered.

'That's mega spooky, Hettie,' said Gift. 'That's your name!'

'Why is *your name on it*?' whispered Nikesh, doing their research pose, their finger to their chin.

Engraved on a tiny brass plaque, which had been screwed into the sole of the clog, was H. LIGHTFOOT.

'Well then, it must be yours!' said Grandad. 'Happy birthday!'

'It's not my birthday,' I said, and laughed as they managed to manoeuvre the wooden man so that it sat upright on the edge of the stage, staring at me.

I remember the feeling I had in that moment, because it was like those goosebumps that warn you that what you're about to do is a bad idea. Like when Gift wondered out loud if her braids were flammable while we were sitting next to the Bunsen burner in chemistry, and I just knew if I didn't turn it off she'd have one of her twit moments.

But then Nikesh spoke in their *I-know-things* voice and the moment passed. 'It's an automaton.' They traced their fingers along its carefully carved teeth. 'There will be a lever, springs, a key to wind it somewhere and it will do, well, something. Maybe wave?'

'Automa-what?' I asked.

Why wasn't anyone else freaked out by the fact that my name was on a wooden giant pulled from a secret cupboard that probably, definitely had spiders in it?

'Like olden-day robots,' explained Nikesh.

'Cool!' said Gift.

'There was one made for an exhibition in Paris in the mid eighteen hundreds: a duck that everyone thought was magic because it could eat bread and then poop it out,' added Nikesh.

'Gross,' I said. 'I hope this one's got better manners.'

'There's another plaque on the back of its neck,' said Grandad. '*My name is Snod's Edge.*'

Gift nearly wet herself laughing. 'What kind of name is *that*?'

'We know it,' I said quietly, feeling those goosebumps again. 'Don't we, Grandad? It's a place name. We drive past there on the way to the bookshop in Corbridge when we have a run-out.'

'Good to give you an airing,' said Grandad.

Grandad and I loved driving around and spotting weird place names. I kept a list in my notebook that has film quotes on the front.

'And what's next door to Snod's Edge?' Grandad set up our joke.

'Wallish Walls!' I yelled, and although it wasn't very funny I was suddenly really nervous without knowing why, so I fake-laughed so much I thought I was never going to be able to breathe again. Then everyone was laughing, and I went back to my desk and someone brought a chair over and sat Snod's Edge beside me and I stroked his cool rosewood hand.

The thought of spiders still freaked me out, and that he had my name on him, but there was something kind about him, like I knew him already. Stupid, I know, but it felt just as real as a packet of half-price crisps.

For my next birthday, Grandad made me Wallish Walls, wooden Snod's metal brother. They lived at the Arts Centre – well, until the council announced they were going to blow the place up. And then they lived at Grandad's. But then he died and the council took back his house, so now they live next to my wardrobe. I've got rid of everything that's to do with the theatre – it makes me too sad and angry – but I can't get rid of them. Grandad called them family. That's what they feel like.

I focus back on the teeny-tiny envelope and use the tweezers again, this time to open it. My hands shake even more than usual, desperately trying not to tear the paper.

I slide out the little card that's inside and read it.

You've got to be kidding me. What can this mean? Why me?

I'm one hundred per cent not going – you can bet all the crisps in the world on that! I place the tiny card and envelope carefully on the desk, then glance over my shoulder again.

How did it get here? Who delivered it? I imagine a little spider postman and shake my head to get rid of the horrible image. I read it once more. In the same scratchy writing as the envelope, it says:

You are invited to the Renaissance Machiavelli Empire, Hettie Lightfoot-Redwood.

We will welcome you soon. You are expected.

Jack Redwood, Artistic Director

They can expect me as much as they want – I'm not going! My hands still shaking, I pull out the brochure for the Renaissance Machiavelli Empire from where I shoved it in the drawer. It's printed on very shiny and expensive paper. I feel like a traitor even looking at it, but I want to find out who this Jack is that has the same surname as Grandad. That can't be a coincidence, can it?

The inside cover tells the brief history of how it's built on the site of a legacy of theatres:

> The Lightfoot Theatre was built in 1779 and was highly successful until an explosion occurred and it was destroyed. Next came the Machiavelli Empire, which was the brainchild of Araine Machiavelli. It opened in 1878 and burned down in 1906. Eventually, the Arts Centre was built in its place in 1920 and served the town faithfully until it was condemned and demolished, and then replaced by the Renaissance Machiavelli Empire.

My name again, my actual name! I stroke my finger over 'Lightfoot'. There's a vague memory about Nikesh telling me this before, and Lightfoot and Redwood are names that go way back in Cawlington, but still? It's a little goosebumpy when you add that to the creepy invitation.

I turn the page and there he is: Jack Redwood. In his photo, he's haughty-looking, with messy golden hair that has flecks of grey in it.

I realize I've scrunched up the brochure where I've been holding it at the edges. I steady my breath as I try to smooth it back out.

'There is a distinct habit of theatre destruction around here. I think they're cursed,' I say to the brochure. 'I wouldn't get too comfy, or you may find yourself going *poof* in the night!'

I flick to a double-page spread with opera photos on one side and ballet on the other. It's not only the paper of the brochure that's expensive. The ticket prices are massive. Amazing opportunities to see incredible shows! says the brochure in a fancy font. Yup, I think, but for who? Mam and Dad couldn't afford them.

No. Spooky spider invitation or not, the last thing I am ever doing is going to that ruddy theatre that's replacing Grandad's and my special place. Never ever!

I slam the brochure down and the air whips up the teeny notecard and flips it over. There's more writing on the back:

We are the only ones who understand the
fire burning deep in your heart. If you
want to see your grandad for one final
time, come to our theatre.

My hand shakes as I read it over and over again.

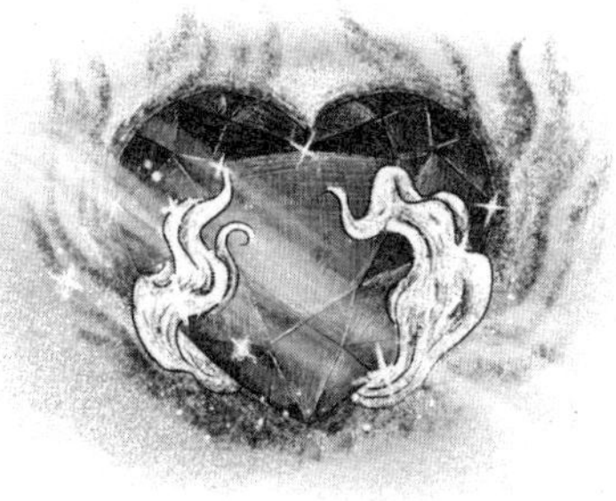

Chapter Four

Way Back When

The underground tunnel Araine walked along was mossy and damp; the same stone from the church above lined the floor down here, aged and smoothed. She could see passages leading off in other directions – it was like a web – and it would be easy to get lost. She wondered where they all led to. Curiously, every other stone in the floor had the triangle symbol carved into it, with a spider at each corner and the heart at its centre. Who had found this place and walked this tunnel before her? Who had carved the stones?

The spiders?

Was this the place Mam had told them about, where the spiders could help you say goodbye to loved ones?

Her head felt strangely light and floaty from not having eaten for days, from trying not to think about what had happened to Nora, but also, and she was embarrassed by this, with the excitement of what she might find. The voices she'd heard from above were now a steady muttering and mumbling. Araine couldn't make out any words, but the sobbing continued, quieter now with breathy gasps.

Lamps flickered in sconces on the tunnel walls, some with moss and ferns threatening to engulf them. The spiders tumbled across her feet and scuttled over one another, and she gave herself over to them and followed. What else could she do? There was nothing, *no one*, to go back to. And she was sure she'd get lost without them in so many passages with twists and turns.

Suddenly the spiders stopped by a huge door, double the size of the one to her cottage.

'Don't think about home,' Araine muttered to herself, wrenching her shoulders back from the slump she'd found herself in.

The door handle was a little brass fist and she felt reassured by it, even though she didn't know why.

She took a deep breath and a last look back down the tunnel and then pushed the door open.

Inside it was bright white, gleaming. She blinked rapidly, then had to put her hand over her eyes, gradually opening her fingers to get used to the light.

The light! The beams coming out of the glass balls

on the walls didn't flicker like a flame should; it was pure and strong and blazing white. She walked over and held her hand out towards it. The light didn't move with the breeze from her hand. No heat came off the glass. Magic!

Now that her eyes were accustomed to the brightness, Araine could see that the room was a perfect cube, with the floor, walls and ceiling all touching at neat right angles. The walls were uncannily smooth, as if they'd been buttered with a knife. She touched the closest one to her: no brickwork, or stone, or wood. Where were the joins? The triangle symbols were still on the floor, this time just three of them.

She wanted to ask the spiders where she was, but they stayed in a line just outside the door, as if there was an invisible barrier that wouldn't let them past.

Suddenly a sob caught her attention, and she spun round.

'Hello?' she called, her voice more wobbly than she would have liked. 'Who's there?'

There were two short pillars, both about her height, in the centre of the room, each topped with a glass dome with something inside them. Had the noise come from there?

Araine hugged herself as she walked slowly towards one of the pillars and peered on top, having to stand on her tiptoes. She gasped at the model encased within. The detail was extraordinary, exactly how she remembered it from the summer the players came to Attercop. Excited now, she dashed over to the second pillar and peered into the other dome. In it was a tiny brick building and she had to sound out the word hand-painted on a sign on the outside of it.

'*Thee-at-ree*,' she said, the unfamiliar word not feeling quite right in her mouth, and sounding too noisy in the crisp white space.

A tiny voice hidden from Araine's view behind the pillar said, '*Theatre*, actually. That's how you say it out loud.'

Araine jumped in surprise and fright.

'I *thought* it was you,' said a very familiar voice.

Araine peered round the pillar and found her best friend, Lucie Lightfoot, curled up against one of the walls, trying to comfort her little brother, Harcus, who'd just had his fourth birthday two months ago, when Nora had made him one of her famous lemon cakes.

Araine leaped across the room and wrapped her arms round them, the relief making her feel lighter than she had in days, giving them the biggest hug she could manage, trying not to crush Harcus. 'You're here too!'

Lucie's tightly curled short black hair was covered in cobwebs and her pale-blue dress was in tatters.

Araine could see that her friend's knees were covered in cuts.

'How did you get here?' asked Araine when they finally pulled away from each other.

'We followed the spiders,' said Harcus with a big grin. Araine watched it dissolve on his face as he started wailing again. 'I want Mam!'

Araine looked at Lucie, who shook her head.

'Nora?' Lucie asked.

Araine shook her head in return, and the two girls hugged each other once more, tighter this time, as though they would never, ever let go of each other.

When Araine finally loosened her grip on Lucie, she tried to talk about anything but the people they'd both lost.

'What's a theatre?' she asked Lucie.

'I overheard Lord Machiavelli talking to the landlord of the Travelling Duck about it. They put on shows like the players we saw last summer did, but it's in a building not a tent and there's a red velvet curtain, and people pay lots of money to watch, and they have folk who do these things called seances and pretend they can talk to the de–' Lucie stopped mid-sentence and lowered her eyes.

Araine didn't know what to say, so she changed the subject. 'The spiders brought you here too?' She looked over at them all waiting behind the line between the stone passage and the white floor, at the very edge of the strange room.

'Yes,' replied Lucie. 'After, well, after I found Mam, and the villagers put the crosses on the doors, I saw them painting one on yours and I thought that you were . . . Anyway, all these spiders appeared at our house and they made an arrow, but the wind was howling and we were so hungry.'

Araine nodded again and this time her tummy gurgled in response.

'Oh,' said Lucie. 'I'm sorry. I was so shocked to see you . . . I thought no one else . . . I didn't think! Here!'

She pulled out a basket from behind her, filled with bread and apples. Araine wanted to say thank you, but instead her hand darted out and grabbed some bread. She ripped off chunks and shoved them into her mouth, so fast that even Harcus stopped sobbing long enough to watch her.

'See how the basket is woven together,' said Lucie.

'Is that a web?' said Araine, her eyes wide. The basket was slightly tacky and covered with dew like when the sun comes up on a morning and you can see the spiderwebs in the hedges.

'I think so. Isn't it amazing?' said Lucie. 'The spiders made it so we could gather food before we followed them.

They stared at it in silence for a while.

Araine thought about the stories her mam used to tell about the spiders and the church. She dropped a crumb of bread and found it next to one of the symbols on the floor between the two pillars. 'Did you see the triangles in the tunnels?' she asked.

Lucie looked up. 'Yes! Did you have to solve the puzzle with it to get down here?'

'The spiders helped me,' replied Araine as she studied the triangle. Three sides. Three spiders. Three symbols in the room. 'Mam said it only worked to say goodbye to your loved ones when there were three people, like a triangle.'

'You don't believe those old tales, do you?' said Lucie, laughing.

Araine shook her head. 'Of course not.' But she crossed her fingers and hid them under her skirt. 'Do you think it's like this everywhere?' she asked quietly, so Harcus couldn't hear. 'With everyone sick?' Her bottom lip began to tremble.

'Not wherever Lord Machiavelli is,' Lucie said bitterly. 'Money makes you safe. He'll be fine.'

She curled her lip and spat on to the floor. Araine did too. And when Harcus saw what they'd done he joined in, but it was more of a dribble that he wiped off his chin.

'I bet he's got money to go to the theatre.' Araine looked at Lucie to make sure she was saying the word right, and Lucie nodded. 'I bet he's at one now, laughing away without a care in the world.'

Lucie opened her mouth to reply, but then Harcus let out a piercing scream. 'I miss my mam!'

No matter how much Lucie and Araine tried to comfort him, he wouldn't stay still, arching his back and writhing out of their grasp.

'I miss Nora too,' Araine said to the little boy, trying to stop him from crying. 'I'm not very good at making people laugh – I'm far too serious – but Nora, she would have had you giggling by now. I wish I could see her. Just one more time.'

As she spoke, Araine realized her fingers were following the indentation of the triangle in the floor. Her anxiety and grief and absolute fear about what would happen to them now that everyone they had ever loved had gone was soothed by the repetitive motion of tracing the cool lines in the stone. Harcus saw what she was doing and copied her. Lucie found the final triangle on the floor and traced it as well.

'Can you feel that?' asked Araine, sitting bolt upright as what felt like a huge burst of static energy rippled through her. As soon as her finger left the stone, the feeling stopped.

Araine's heart beat faster and faster. If the stories her mam had told were true, and there were three of them like Mam said the spiders needed, is this how she'd get to see Nora one final time, to say goodbye?

Harcus was wide-eyed, his tear-stained face alert.

'What do I know? Try it again,' said Lucie. 'All together.'

And Harcus and Araine moved their fingers, tracing the triangles next to them faster and faster.

'There!' cried Lucie. 'I can feel it!'

The room was charging up with energy. It crackled like when Araine used to get out of bed in the night, and she and Nora could see sparks on her nightdress in the dark that her little sister thought were sprites.

Oh, Nora. Why wasn't she here now? Araine felt her chest tighten and seize.

Her finger moved to the heart in the centre of the triangle, tracing that instead. She concentrated her thinking on Nora and her laughter in the darkness.

A tear rolled down Araine's cheek and landed on the stone. She looked over to the door where the spiders were all still standing in a line, watching. Leaning forward, willing her on to something she didn't yet understand.

She drew her finger over her tear, blending it into the outline of the heart. She glanced over at Harcus and Lucie. They looked as if they were in a trance, tears rolling down their faces too, landing on the hearts, tracing their tears into the stone.

All three of them jumped as the room crackled and sparked, and then there was an enormous bang.

Lucie's eyes widened at something behind Araine, and Harcus pointed.

Araine wriggled round and saw that a drawer had popped out from the wall. She didn't remember seeing it there before – the walls were so smooth and white.

Harcus leaped up to investigate, but Araine grabbed him round the middle.

'It might not be safe!' she said.

Harcus tried to wriggle out of her grasp as Lucie pushed herself up from the floor and crept slowly over to the open drawer.

Araine saw the spiders rustling on the edge of the doorway, eagerly scrambling over each other. 'They definitely want us to look,' she said, pointing to them.

Lucie stood on tiptoes and peered inside the drawer, with Araine holding Harcus on her hip as she scrambled to look too.

'Oh, flippin' heck,' said Lucie.

As she leaned further over, Araine could see sparkles of rainbows dancing across her friend's face. Harcus tried to grab them as they played on the walls and ceiling.

'You have to see this!' Lucie whispered.

Araine took a step nearer as Lucie reached into the drawer.

'Wait!' Araine cried out. 'Are you sure it's safe?'

'Safe?' replied Lucie. 'Is anything?'

Araine didn't know how to answer that, so instead she peered inside. And her eyes bulged at what she saw. She placed Harcus on the floor, his little pudgy arms tugging at her to be lifted back up. She'd never seen anything like it in her entire life.

Lying in a woven silk nest was a diamond in the shape of a heart. It was the size of an egg from their best layer Betty.

'That can't be real!' said Araine, and reached out to touch it. When her finger met its cold surface, flames seemed to erupt inside it and she felt a spark running through her.

She carefully lifted it out of the drawer, its weight heavier than she'd imagined, and as she did, it was as if the splinters of cold and loss in her heart knitted together a little. She felt warm.

She held it lower so that Harcus could see it too, his chubby little fingers reaching out at the same time as Lucie's.

The moment that all three of them touched the diamond, the room exploded into light.

Chapter Five

Then

'Good, innit?' whispered a voice in Jack's ear, snapping him back out of the world of the dancers and the costumes and perfume and sweat in the air on the stage, and into the dark of the wings where someone's face was far too close to his. 'Close your mouth or you'll catch flies.'

Jack jumped and clamped his jaw closed, almost falling over some of the ropes hanging in the wings from the gantry above.

Tattie caught him and smiled. 'Shhh! The show must never be interrupted. Don't worry though,' he continued, somehow reading Jack's mind. 'It took Araine ages to find us, and she *really* needs us. You could wander on to the stage naked with a chicken and she still wouldn't chuck you out! Though I wouldn't recommend it.' He gave Jack a huge grin and his green beard wiggled. 'My real name is William Lightfoot, but everyone calls me Tattie. Cos I like spuds. And the hairy beast over there with the ruff is Rex.'

Jack peered into the shadows and his eyes adjusted until he saw a brown-and-white Staffordshire bull terrier, stocky with short dumpy legs, a big head, and a giant gold-and-red concertinaed ruff round his neck.

The Staffy dog lifted his paw and Jack waved shyly back at him.

'Oh, and the big wooden automaton in the corner behind me, wanting a formal introduction but trying to hide and pretend he's not being nosy, is Snod's Edge. Don't you have some work to do, Snod?'

'The big wooden what?' asked Jack, spotting the giant man he'd seen from the corridor earlier.

'I am not a big wooden what,' replied Snod in a voice that was like falling into velvet, rich and deep. 'I am an automaton. Harcus's greatest invention: a walking, talking wooden man!'

'Of course you are,' said Tattie, slapping Snod on the back. 'The very finest, in fact the one and only ever wooden man!'

'He can't really be made out of wood? That has to be a costume . . .' Jack whispered to Tattie as the wooden man, Snod, bowed at Tattie's compliment and walked jerkily away with a wave.

'What do you think?' asked Tattie, winking at Jack.

The conversation stopped as Jack tried to work out whether wooden men actually existed, if he'd ever meet his hero Harcus, who'd also made Snod, and what Tattie meant and why he was here and . . .

Tattie gave Jack a knowing smile. 'Your head feels like it's about to explode, eh? I've been there – it's a lot to take in. We've been waiting for you, Jack Redwood. You're the last piece of the triangle.'

Chapter Six

Now

Mam knocks on my door, opens it and steps inside before I can yell at her not to come in, but I manage to just shove the envelope into my desk drawer before she spots it.

She shrieks. For the nine hundred billionth time.

'Surely you must know they're there by now, Shirley,' I say at the exact same time that my dad yells it from the kitchen. I giggle and shout, 'Jinx!'

'Every ruddy time,' my mam says. 'And what are they wearing now?' She goes over to Wallish Walls and Snod's Edge, who are standing like sentries on either side of my wardrobe doors.

'Walls, in order to keep his metal rust free, is tastefully modelling my waterproof, while Snod, to fend off a chill in his wooden bones, is absolutely loving wearing my dressing gown.'

Mam tugs at the dressing gown to make it hang better round Snod's massive carved legs. 'I really wish you'd let us put them in the garage. Don't you find them creepy, staring at you when you sleep?'

'If they go in the garage, I'm going with them! Grandad –'

'Yes, I know, pet. Grandad said they were family, and brought them back to life for you.'

'Not back to life, Mam! He *restored* Snod! Now that would be creepy if he'd brought Snod to life.'

'What have you got there?' Mam asks.

'Nothing,' I say as I try to stuff the brochure for the new theatre back into the drawer, but then I remember that I even more so don't want her to see the tiny envelope, so I hand over the brochure instead.

'Oh, look at this costume!' says Mam. 'I'd love to see that.'

'Seen the prices?'

Mam squints at them. She usually nicks Dad's glasses, but he hasn't left any in here. 'Ouch,' she says, and breathes out slowly. 'Maybe we could go to a show instead of a birthday present?'

She takes one look at my stubborn face glaring up at her over my model and hands me back the brochure without me saying anything. She places her hand gently on my shoulder and screws up her face in the way that makes her eyes crinkle.

'Oh, Hettie, love. I know it's not what you wanted, not what any of us wanted –'

I raise an eyebrow at her.

'It's not!' Mam exclaims. 'OK, I didn't always agree with some of the militant tactics you and your grandad deployed –'

'Militant!' I burst out. 'Waving some placards and shouting was hardly getting an army together!'

'There was the stand-off with the bulldozer,' she says. 'You've got to admit that was brilliant.'

Mam tries not to smile and rearranges her face while she pretends to look at one of the photos of me and Gift on my dresser. 'But there's no use in cutting your arm off to spite . . . well, something. How does it go?'

I can't help myself laughing, and I hold out my intact arms for a hug. Mam always bumbles sayings. It's one of the things I love most about her.

'Your Mean Machine is fully charged,' she tells me, 'and I now have a kitchen with two Free Spirits stealing my chocolate digestives. Hurry up!'

'I'm not going,' I say. But I can sense the envelope inside the drawer, as if it's throbbing. I don't move but look at the model of the Arts Centre instead.

Mam follows my gaze. 'This is incredible, pet. You doing this for him. Your grandad would be so proud of you.' She does a big sniff, and I hand her a tissue. Once she's blown her nose, she says, 'Can I help you get it in the box?'

'Yes please.' My hands go a bit shaky as we lower it into the box on the floor, and the weathervane on top starts to wobble a little.

'That's an amazing likeness,' says Mam. 'I thought you couldn't work out how to cut it that small?'

'Cut what?' I'm concentrating on trying to make my hands stop wobbling, but it's just making them wobble more.

Mam notices and takes the weight off my side and gets the model into the box. I shake out my hands to stop the twitching, and Mam says, 'The dog. I'm so impressed!'

I get the goosebumps feeling again. It crawls up my legs until it's reached my scalp and it's as though I have spiders writhing in my stomach. I reach out to touch the tiny replica of the dog that is now on top of the miniature Arts Centre.

Grandad didn't make that.

Neither did I.

Suddenly it begins to spin. Mam and I stare at it.

'How did you make it do that?' she whispers. 'It's like magic!'

There's no wind blowing it, but it's whizzing round and round.

'Can you see it too?' I ask Mam, and she slowly nods, unblinking, unable to take her eyes off the little dog, which looks as if it's running and barking, then catching something sparkly and heart-shaped in its mouth, then stopping for a second and running the other way.

'It's incredible, Hettie!'

There are many old town stories as to why our Arts Centre had a dog on the weathervane on its roof, but none of them seemed to have any grounds in reality or research, no matter how much Nikesh investigated. Grandad was going to write a play about the Arts Centre's myths and legends, including the dog and the diamond heart. We even had a date booked to perform it – but it's kind of hard to perform in a theatre that's been exploded.

The moment is broken by Gift and Nikesh coming along the corridor with their usual clatter.

'Shirley, she still in a mood about coming today?' says Nikesh to my mam as they stand by the bedroom door, assessing my mood, one hand on their hip.

'She says she's not coming,' Mam tells them.

Gift shoves past Nikesh and leaps on to my bed.

Nikesh stays in the doorway, eating a biscuit from a

stash in their hand. They chuck one to me like a frisbee when they see me eyeing them up.

Gift grabs one of the cushions from my bed and thwacks me with it. Gift can't keep still and I'm rubbish at moving, so we sort of balance each other out.

The backdraught from the cushion makes the tiny weathervane spin again, and the movement catches her eye. 'Hettie, that's proper mint!'

I try to tell her I didn't make it as she unfolds the lid of the box and a giant spider crawls out from under the flap and I scream.

'GET IT, GET IT NOW! GET IT AWAY FROM ME! Now! Arghhhh!'

Mam grabs the box and moves it to my bed, to stop me flipping it over in my panic and destroying the little theatre I've worked so hard to complete. Gift reaches out and cups the hideous creature in her bare hand. I'm nearly sick.

'It's tiny, Hettie!' says Gift. 'Don't be such a drama queen. Look how small it is!'

'Don't you dare open your hand!' I shriek at her. 'Kill it!'

'I will do no such thing, you evil overlord. Imagine how much more scared of you it must be! You're a giant in comparison.'

'I've told you, I don't care – kill it!' I yell again.

'Chill it out, Hets!' Gift says, tutting.

Ever since that bloomin' ghost story, I can't cope with the thought of those little furry legs crawling all over me. I shudder and go cold.

'We have over six hundred and fifty species of spider in this country,' says Nikesh. 'And only twelve of them bite.' They say it to me like that's supposed to be calming information.

I shake my head. 'I bet this is a bitey one!'

Gift opens my window, gently holds the spider out and pops it on to the sill, then closes the window. 'It's gone!' she declares.

'It's not gone though, is it?' I say as I scratch myself all over. 'It's waiting there and it will summon its spider army and before I know it they'll launch an attack!'

'Course they will – spider armies are everywhere,' says Nikesh.

'Will they?' I ask in horror. 'Are they?'

'Course not!' Gift says, and then she smiles. 'Now stop flapping – we're late!'

'She says she's not coming,' says Mam again.

'I, erm –'

They all stare at me as I think about the tiny note. It has to be some sort of hoax. But who would do that? If there's any possibility of seeing Grandad again, or finding out who'd send such a sick message . . .

'Look, Hettie, I didn't want to have to do this, but here goes,' says Mam. 'You *are* going. Stop shaking your head at me, young madam. Otherwise –' she pauses for dramatic effect – 'I'm withdrawing your stationery allowance.'

Gift and Nikesh draw their breath in so loudly I can hear it.

'And I know your pink highlighter is fading fast, so I've got you over a bucket here.' She looks triumphantly at me.

Nikesh leans forward. 'I think you mean *barrel*, Shirley.'

She humphs at them. 'On the van in two.'

I open my mouth to speak.

'No arguments!'

I look at the pink highlighter pen on my desk and whisper, 'Thank you!' That got me out of explaining why I've changed my mind.

So no one will suspect a thing, I act like I'm in a proper mood.

'Help me with this then,' I say to Gift and Nikesh as I struggle to grab the Arts Centre in its box off my bed. My wheelchair rams into the side where the drawers are – there's no gap for me to slot in like with my desk, and my arms aren't long enough to reach. I could stand to get it, but that's precious energy wasted, and who needs to do that when you've got two mates at your command?

If I'm going, I will make it worth my while. I'll take Grandad's miniature Arts Centre and make a fuss until they let me put it on show!

I wheel myself out of my bedroom, the mysterious message running over and over in my head.

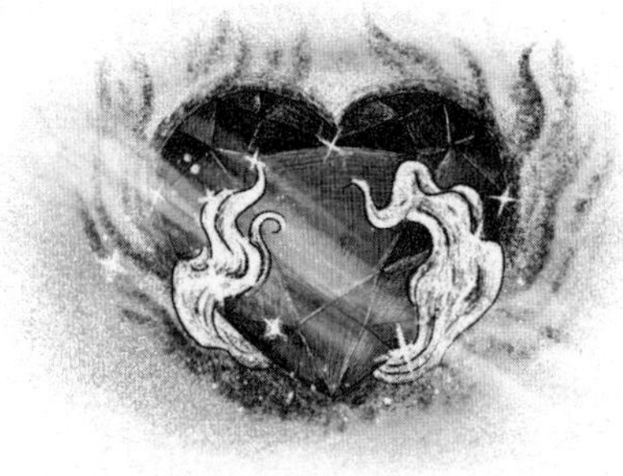

Chapter Seven

Way Back When

Araine could hear Lucie screaming as the room filled with white light firing out from the centre of the heart-shaped diamond. Araine couldn't tell whether her eyes were open or closed: it was like when you stared at the sun and everywhere afterwards had blobs of light that cut out bits of your vision.

In the brightness, Araine thought she could make out two outlines, reverse shadows, the traces of two people. Her eyes must be playing tricks on her.

It couldn't be.

Could it?

'Nora?' she whispered.

Out of the light stepped her sister, faded as if

she'd been bleached by the sun, her outline hazy and shimmering like the ground on a baking-hot day.

'Araine, is that you? Where am I? What happened?'

Araine went running towards her and swept her up in a tight hug.

'Mam!' yelled Harcus, and rushed over to the figure stepping out from behind Nora. He leaped at his mam, who caught him in her arms. 'You're cold,' he said, 'and you feel fuzzy.'

'That's because I think I'm not quite here, love,' said Mrs Lightfoot, holding him tight.

Lucie hadn't moved. 'Is that really you, Mam?'

'Hey, pet lamb,' said her mam, holding out the arm that wasn't hugging Harcus. Without hesitation, Lucie dived at her.

Araine opened her arms, and her little sister fell into them. Harcus was right: she was cold, and it was like trying to hug a cloud.

'Can you touch things?' Araine asked Nora as the two of them sank to the floor between the short pillars, while Lucie and Harcus went to sit in a corner of the white room with their mam.

'Yes,' said Nora, tracing one of the triangles on the floor. 'But it's all very floaty, like I can feel and see through here to somewhere else too.'

'Where?'

'I'm not sure – I can't really see there either. It's as though I'm stuck in between, but I can hear people.'

Araine looked over at Harcus, who was chatting away to his mam and sitting in her lap.

'No, I don't mean them,' said Nora. 'Other ghosts – I can hear them all blathering on, telling their stories.'

'Ghosts?'

'Isn't that what I am?'

Araine didn't know how to answer Nora. She was worried her mind was making it all up and she'd wake up in a cold, damp corner of the church and everyone would be dead and she'd be all alone. That she was even imagining Lucie and Harcus being here. *Stop thinking, brain!*

'Who can you hear, Nora?' asked Araine, trying to ignore her own doubts.

'Everyone!'

'Everyone? You mean it's noisy?'

Nora shook her head. 'No! I mean *everyone*. It's like I can jump around in my head and listen in to all the ghosts and have a conversation with them while I'm still talking to you. It's as if I have a huge encyclopaedia in my head of all the facts any other dead humans have ever known.'

'You're making that up.'

'I'm not! Really, it's wondrous! Oh, and Mam says she hopes you've had something to eat.'

Araine gasped. 'You can speak to Mam? I don't believe you – you're the biggest fibber ever!' She narrowed her eyes at her little sister. 'Tell me something only Mam and I would know.'

'Like what?'

Araine thought for a moment, and then said, 'Mam would whisper something, only to me, every night before I fell asleep. What was it?'

She watched as Nora's eyes flickered, the whole of her becoming even more translucent, before she grew more solid again and said, 'I love you, my eldest pea.'

Araine began to cry, and her whole body shook. The enormity of her mam and sister being dead finally hit her, but it was muddled up with the awe and excitement of talking to Nora. 'You really can talk to her? And you're really dead.'

'A ghost,' said Nora with a cheeky grin. '*Woooooo!*'

'That's not funny,' said Araine, but strangely she found herself trying not to smile.

'It is a little bit funny,' said Nora, and both of them burst out laughing. Once they'd calmed down, Nora whispered, 'Why do you think I'm here?'

Araine looked over her shoulder to the spiders still gathered in a row at the door. 'Because everything that

Mam ever told us was true. The spiders are giving us a chance to say goodbye.'

Lucie and Harcus with their ghost mam came to join Araine and ghostly Nora. They sat down together, laughing and joking about past times, sharing stories, but all the while the ghosts became fainter.

'The magic's fading now,' said Mrs Lightfoot. 'The spiders have done what they promised, what they always do when a triangle of humans, bound together by loss, visit this room and hold the diamond. It's their gift to the village for us keeping them safe. They've given you your last goodbye. It's time to put their diamond back. Time to let us go.'

The spiders bowed solemnly as they awaited the return of their diamond to the open drawer.

Araine gripped Nora's hand tightly; her sister was fading in front of her eyes. She was going to be all alone again. Saying goodbye was impossible. They deserved more time. Even just a little. She couldn't let Nora leave her. How could she keep her promise to her father if she was gone?

'No!' Araine screamed at the spiders. 'You promised! Our mam said she once saved you and you promised her you'd keep us safe! I won't give the diamond back – you can't make me!'

The spiders wriggled and writhed, stepping over each

other, starting to squeal, but they could not cross into the room.

'I need more time!' shrieked Araine, and she grabbed the diamond from a startled Lucie and slammed the drawer shut.

'So what do we do now?' Lucie asked Araine, trying to get her to listen as Araine paced back and forth, muttering to herself, clutching the diamond to her chest. Meanwhile, the two ghosts cowered in the corner of the room, and the spiders continued to scrabble in agitation at the doorway. It was as though the spiders were conferring: this wasn't how the magic was meant to work. The diamond needed to be returned to the drawer.

Araine whipped round and glared at her best friend. 'If we put the diamond back in the drawer, it will be closed to us forever and our chance to see Nora and your mam will be over. You don't want that, do you?'

Araine watched as Lucie glanced at them and then hesitatingly shook her head.

'We need one,' said Araine, looking at the spiders.

Araine sighed as Lucie blinked in confusion. 'One what?'

'A plan,' said Araine decisively. Something about holding the diamond was making her feel stronger, braver, more connected, as if her brain was a spider's web. She liked the feeling.

'We do one last thing, all of us together – you, me, Harcus and the ghosts,' Araine continued. 'It has to be the three of us. It only works with three, a triangle.'

'And then you'll put the diamond back?' asked Lucie. 'Araine, you don't sound like you. I don't think you're meant to keep it this long.'

The spiders all skitter-scattered their feet on the stone as if they were agreeing with Lucie.

'Who ran away when people started to get sick? Whose fault is it that our families are now ghosts?' asked Araine, spittle forming on her lips.

'I-I-I don't know, Araine. You're scaring me – just put the diamond back. We'll look after each other. You, me and Harcus. See, a triangle, just like you want!'

'*Lord Machiavelli*, that's who,' said Araine, ignoring Lucie. 'He had the money to buy medicine, to bring us food and clean water. Instead, he *left* us all to get sick and die.' Araine's eyes glinted like the diamond and she gave a little laugh. 'Let's take the ghosts and pay him a visit. Give him the fright of his life! Make him atone for what he did.'

'And *then* you'll put the diamond back?' Lucie asked again.

'Yes, and then I'll put it back,' replied Araine,

nodding. 'Come on, Lucie. You're usually the one with the wild plans. Surely you can see that this is worthwhile? It could even be fun! And don't we deserve one final adventure together, all of us, just like old times? Please?' She grabbed Lucie's hands and begged her. 'I can't let Nora go, not yet. And I don't think you want to say goodbye to your mam either. Harcus definitely doesn't.'

They looked over and saw that Harcus had joined Nora and his mam in the corner. Nora was telling Harcus a joke and he was laughing.

'Maybe that's really why the ghosts are here,' added Araine. 'For their revenge? And after that they'll just fade away. It's Lord Machiavelli's fault that they died, because he'd abandoned us all, so surely that must be it?'

Lucie looked unsure, peering over at her mam, studying Harcus's face. A little more time together couldn't hurt, could it?

'All right, one final adventure. Then we return the diamond.'

Chapter Eight

Then

'What do you mean by *the last piece of the triangle*?' Jack asked Tattie.

'No time! We'll be late. And also I don't know. I've been waiting for you to find out!' said Tattie as he hauled Jack away from the wings, leaving behind the view of the dancers and the audience.

Rex the dog licked Jack's leg as they ran into the shadows.

'Sorry about that,' said Tattie. 'Got a thing for legs, he has, daft dog. Better wear long trousers from now on unless you want him to give you a bath!'

Jack grinned and bent down to make a fuss of Rex with his one white eyebrow, who pointed his ears up, in the hope that Jack would scratch behind them.

'We need to get a shuffle on,' said Tattie, pulling Jack along.

For a moment, Jack thought that Tattie was going to crash into a black wall before he realised Tattie was pushing open an equally black door. Tattie didn't let go, towing Jack by the wrist along an unlit corridor, the only light coming from a high window at the end of it.

They pushed through another door and suddenly the world erupted into noise and colour. Now, as they dashed down narrow corridors, they were squeezing past people arguing and clowns stomping in big shoes and a parrot flapping about, while a woman in a mermaid costume tried to catch it. Snod waved from a doorway, where he was holding a stack of top hats, and Jack waved shyly back.

The tang of sweat, cigarette smoke and cheap perfume was getting stuck in the back of his throat, making him want to cough. Everyone parted to let them through, almost leaping back. Jack could swear some of them looked scared.

Turning left at the end of a corridor, Jack was surprised by the silence, which was loud in his ears. Unbelievably, there was no one else in this part of the theatre but them. Backstage had seemed too small for the players and theatre crew, with everyone squishing and tripping – and now all this free space!

Why is no one using it? Jack wondered. Then he had a sudden feeling that hairy feet were creeping up and down the back of his neck. He turned round, suddenly expecting his brother to be there, but the passageway was empty.

They made their way along the corridor more slowly now. Tattie let go of Jack's wrist and it was as though he was trying to make himself shrink a bit. For the first time, Jack began to feel not nervous excitement, but like he needed to make a run for it.

What was he doing here? A mysterious note had appeared in his hand and he'd followed. No one knew he'd gone to the theatre – not even Matthew. How would Jack's brother rescue him if he got into trouble?

As they walked further along the corridor, the black wall became a huge wall hanging: a deep midnight-blue curtain with a gold-embroidered moon and stars. Jack couldn't take his eyes off it. The gold thread sparkled in the lamplight, making the stars look like they were moving.

Hold on. Not stars, spiders, Jack realized. And they *were* moving. He scratched the back of his neck and stopped in front of the hanging.

'What are those spiders?' said Jack to Tattie, transfixed by the constellations made as the spiders came together and then broke apart.

'It's magical, isn't it? Anyway, we're here,' said Tattie. He reached up to catch the trail of a shooting spider-star, which unravelled in his hand and became thread.

Jack watched in awe as Tattie wiggled the thread on the palm of his hand to make it into the shape of a key. When he lifted it up, it was solid and made of brass! Then he parted the wall hanging at a practically invisible split in the fabric, to reveal a door. Tattie slid the key into the door's keyhole and turned it.

'Don't worry,' he said to Jack whose jaw had dropped wide open. 'You'll get used to it.' Then he patted Rex on the head and told him to sit and stay.

'Come on in, Jack Redwood,' announced Tattie, as a door creaked open in front of them.

It took Jack's eyes a while to accustom themselves to the gloom. There was a single flickering gas lamp in the corner, and in the centre of the room was the lace-covered table, on which stood a teapot and four teacups. More hangings adorned the walls, this time in rich reds and purples and golds, also covered in spiders, though Jack couldn't tell if they were real or made from thread. It was as if the room had been wrapped up in a velvet hug, but it didn't feel warm like it should have, and for the first time Jack realized just how cold he was. He looked down to find his fingers were blue and he began to shiver then shake.

He was overwhelmed by a sudden urge to run, but his legs wouldn't let him.

Out of the gloom, hidden among the wall hangings, stepped Araine Machiavelli, and behind her, in her shadow, was Harcus.

'Can't you smell it, Harcus?' she whispered. 'Grief always smells like lemons, just like Nora's favourite cake.'

What did she just say? Jack forgot to try to run. He couldn't believe he was actually seeing the Machiavellis close up.

He straightened his shoulders, just like his brother would.

A spider scuttled towards Jack, and Araine clicked her fingers and it leaped back to her. 'Not quite yet, little friend!' She turned to Jack. 'Though it is good that you're already thinking about your brother.'

'How did you know I was . . .?' mumbled Jack.

Nobody answered.

Jack looked closely at Araine, and he could see what hadn't been obvious before, from a distance. Her eyes were cold. Dead. There was no spark of warmth or kindness in them; they didn't match the smile she held somewhat painfully on her face.

'Welcome, my Free Spirits,' Araine Machiavelli said.

Jack looked around.

'Yes, you, little one,' said Araine. 'You and me and Tattie. The Free Spirits, that's who we are now. The head of our little theatre family.'

The head? Jack could feel himself almost bursting with pride. Just wait until he told Matthew.

'And now, after all this rebuilding and searching and hoping, we are once more three. With bloodlines intact, the triangle is complete and we can begin again,' said Araine, who stared deep into Jack's eyes.

Jack held her gaze and he couldn't help but sense that there was something creepy about her – and that feeling took away a little of his pride and excitement, only to be replaced with fear.

'About that,' said Tattie, completely breaking the spell. 'I know we've been waiting for Jack, and it's excellent that he's here now, but *why* exactly have we been waiting for him?'

Harcus looked worried, as though he didn't really want to be there, but he stepped forward and said, 'We have something to offer you both. Only extremely special people get this opportunity.'

Jack watched Tattie smooth down his beard. Why were Harcus's hands shaking if it was such a good offer?

'We know who you are missing, which of your loved ones have moved on, and we know how to let you see them again,' said Harcus.

Jack watched as Tattie crumpled beside him.

'Priss? My little sister?' Tattie said in a whisper. 'But she's dead! I know you hold seances, pretend to talk to the other side, but they're not real.' He looked from Araine to Harcus. 'Are they?'

Araine held her arms out wide and drew herself up to her full height. 'How could I build an empire this magnificent on lies? Every rumour that you've ever heard about me is true. I *can* talk to the dead. I can let them back into your lives – if you'll join me.'

Jack watched in puzzlement as Tattie's face dissolved into tears.

'I'm so sorry your sister has passed, but surely you can't believe any of this? And why am I here? I haven't lost anyone,' said Jack, but the room felt like it was closing in on him, that something was gnawing at his brain. He loosened his collar; it was suddenly hard to breathe.

'My powers are immense,' said Araine. 'I've kept Tattie busy around the theatre these past years since I found him. We've been waiting for you, Jack. And now it's time for you both to step into the roles you were born to have!'

Tattie was looking at Araine as though she was a god, but Jack couldn't wait to escape. What on earth was she talking about? It made no sense, but he could tell that Araine and Harcus believed in what she was saying. Tattie too. If he could just edge towards the door . . .

'In order for my powers to flourish to their full extent once more,' Araine declared, 'I need to find precious half-lives to make up a triangle.'

She held up what looked like a slab of stone, and on it was the same triangle-spiders-heart symbol from the front of the theatre. Jack's mind raced. What were half-lives? That was the phrase Tattie had used. He wished he'd asked him what it meant when he'd had the chance.

Araine went on: 'I can offer you riches beyond your wildest dreams, but, most importantly, the opportunity to be with the one you have lost.'

Jack watched Harcus out of the corner of his eye; he'd shuddered at Araine's last few words. What was going on? He must get away and find Matthew, but where was he? That thing Jack needed to remember . . .

Araine stepped forward, her skirts swishing, and she stroked Jack's face. He tried not to shrink from her touch.

'Matthew's not going to rescue you, Jack. It's *you* who must rescue *him*! Together we will bring him back, bring them all back!'

She began to laugh and Jack felt all the blood in his veins turn to ice.

'Wh-who?' he asked. 'Bring who back?'

'Matthew,' replied Harcus, stepping towards him. 'Jack Redwood, it's time to remember.'

Chapter Nine

Now

I make sure our miniature Arts Centre is safely fastened into its own seat on our minibus.

Dad has his own business doing exercise bootcamps. He specializes in making sure that everyone can take part, so the minibus is accessible and has a ramp at the back for wheelchairs and scooters. Just like mine, my Mean Machine that I use when I leave the house, who is a she because Grandad told me ships are usually a she, and I like the thought of sailing in her.

She's a scooter that's bright pink with black leopard print. Not the sort of scooter you stand on and push with your foot. The Mean Machine is a mobility scooter with a top speed of eight miles per hour. Which is mega fast. I usually travel at three, because that's the average walking speed and it's cruel to make my friends run. Also, the security guard in the shopping centre really does not like it when I go faster than that, though he can't catch me to tell me off! But he does when I get home because he's our next-door neighbour. His name's Alan and he also directs the am-dram panto.

'Wave to Alan!' yells Mam from the passenger seat, and we all wave.

I hold on tight to Grandad's pliers in my pocket or I might actually thump something if I don't. There's too much going on inside my head. I really don't want to be in the minibus heading to the auditions because I made a promise to myself I would never go to the new theatre. But the invitation! Jack same-name-as-Grandad Redwood says I can see my dead grandfather if I come to the theatre. Why would anyone send something like that? It's cruel. And the dog on the weathervane? I didn't do that! And now I'm suddenly carrying out a one-person protest to plonk our miniature theatre right in the middle of the new one, but I haven't planned it out. I haven't even made a spreadsheet!

Gift sits next to me and drapes her arm round my shoulder as Mam slams in the showtunes cassette.

'Cheer up, it might never happen,' she says, and then her face falls as she realizes what she's just said and, even though I know she didn't mean it like that, my mouth spits words out even though I don't tell it to.

'It *did* happen,' I reply as I pat the lid of the theatre's box in the seat in front of me.

'Aw, Hets, man. You're right, it did. I know it's really hard, but don't you think he'd want you to have fun? Wouldn't he want you to move on?'

'Move on from him?' I blurt out, then I turn away from Gift.

Her arm flops off my shoulder. I feel awful. I know she loved him as well. I know they all feel sad for me, but I don't have the words to tell them how much it hurts. I just want them to get it without me having to explain it *every single time*.

I watch a cat stalk a pigeon on a wall up the back alley of one of the rows of terraced houses as we crawl through heavy traffic to get to the town centre.

'Gift, you going to try out for actor or dancer?' asks Nikesh, turning round to face us.

Gift sticks a smile on her face and gives my hand a squeeze. She's so nice to me, even when I'm horrible to her. 'Both. Obviously,' she says. 'What about you?'

'Historian, writer and researcher,' says Nikesh, and does a deep bow.

'Get you!' says Gift, and she stands up to do a little dance, her braids swaying with her.

'Sit down!' yells my mam. 'Seat belt!'

'Sorry, Shirls!'

Mum lets out a sigh. 'It's Shirley, not Shirls. Flippin' Free Spirits – ruddy nightmare, you lot.'

Dad laughs and hands my mam a Polo Mint to calm her down and shut her up because he knows she won't speak with her mouth full.

'We'll have Nikesh doing the brain stuff, me acting and dancing,' says Gift, laughing.

Nikesh shimmies in their seat and high-fives Gift who is happy again, which stops me feeling bad about snapping at her. I've turned into an evil Hettie monster and I can't seem to do anything about it.

Dad makes a sharp turn and everyone smooshes up to the window. Gift grabs the box containing the miniature theatre before it zooms off the seat.

'Oops, sorry, folks,' says Dad, and my mam starts telling him off.

'Shirls, you've got your mouth full!' yells Gift.

'Road safety outweighs talking with your mouth full,' says my mam.

'Hands at ten and two!' Nikesh shouts at my dad, knowing my mam will tell him off again.

Dad swerves into a lay-by and slams on the brakes, and this time Nikesh grabs my box.

'That's it!' he calls out in mock anger at us. 'I've had

enough of you lot. Get out here – you can make your own way.' He fake growls at Gift as she looks at him, and she growls back.

'Now, that's not nice,' says Gift with a playful smile – we all know Dad would have stopped here anyway, round the corner from the theatre, because he hates the new one-way layout to get to it. He knows how much the auditions mean to Gift and Nikesh, otherwise there's no way he would have driven us in on a Saturday. The buses are really unreliable at our end of town, and Nikesh can't bear to be late for anything.

Nikesh picks up their laptop bag, which is filled with scripts and research to show off to the new theatre bigwigs, and we're all about to get up when Gift screams, 'Cute dog!' We all smoosh over to the other side to see where she's pointing. Even my mam and dad. Trotting along the pavement, avoiding the steady stream of pedestrians, is a squat brown-and-white Staffy with legs like tree trunks and a massive head.

'It doesn't have a lead,' I say, wondering if it has an owner and if this is the time Mam and Dad will finally let me have a dog.

'In your head, you've already adopted it, haven't you?' says Gift, giving me a hug.

I grin and give her my floppy-arm hug back and hope that she knows that means I'm sorry for being mean to her. She was only trying to help.

'Not a chance,' says Mam, as she gets out of the minibus. 'Hettie, that doesn't half look like the dog you made for the weathervane.'

I'm about to deny making the dog, but then I realize that Mam's right – I can't believe what I'm seeing! I get that creepy déjà vu feeling when you've definitely not seen something before, but it feels like you have.

'May not have a lead, but that's one glorious ruff,' says Nikesh.

The dog has a red-and-gold ruff on that sticks way out from its neck, all concertina-folded like something Queen Elizabeth the First would wear.

Gift wraps her arm round my neck again, in her usual sort-of-a-hug and sort-of-a-strangle. 'Is it just me or does that dog look exactly like the one on top of your theatre?'

'That's what I just said!' says Mam, opening the back doors. 'Anyway, come on, you lot. We can't stop here for long.'

I get on my scooter and steer it on to the little platform that juts out at the back of the minibus, then Mam presses the button to lower me down. Dad stays in the driver's seat, on the lookout for traffic wardens.

I peer ahead to see if I can still see the dog, but it's gone.

I know that it's impossible, but – like I felt when Snod's Edge was found, my giant wooden clothes horse – I'm sure I flippin' *know* that dog.

We all wave goodbye to Mam and Dad as they drive off in the minibus. Dad beeps the horn as they leave.

Nikesh checks their watch and sighs at us. 'So we're late because of the dog, and yet we're still standing here.' Then they go marching off towards the theatre.

Gift follows them, but I hang back, pretending to be interested in a peeling poster for a circus in the newsagent's window. I really don't want to go. I don't care any more about the mystery behind the invitation or displaying the stupid miniature theatre, because once I turn that corner I'll see the Renaissance Machiavelli Empire for real, and then it *will* be real, and then the *next* step will be forgetting what our old theatre was like.

And the next step after that will be forgetting Grandad.

Gift turns back when she realizes I'm no longer beside her. 'No choice, bestie, if you want your pink highlighter.'

'How can you be OK with this?' I ask.

'I'm not,' she says. 'But we lost. And now I don't want to lose out. I don't want *you* to lose out either! We need those brains of yours to be the best producer ever. I bet no one there's as good as you with a wallchart and a bunch of star stickers.' She hugs me tight. 'Found this,' she says, and hands me the pen top that was lost in my ponytail.

I try not to smile. I do love a star sticker. So I press the throttle on my Mean Machine and we go round the corner together.

Across the road from the new theatre, we stand in a row, facing it. Me in the middle on my Mean Machine, Gift on one side, Nikesh on the other. Buses and taxis whizz by in their lane, while the opposite busy traffic grinds to a halt, even though the light is on green.

'Well, that's . . .' I say and stop. Nikesh and Gift shout and take turns to finish the sentence.

'Very swish!'

'Massive!'

'See-through!'

'Posh!'

'Covered in steps,' I say. 'How am I supposed to get inside?'

It's a huge building, and even I have to admit it's breathtaking: a little bit of reclaimed brick from the Arts Centre, but mainly slices of metal, glass and silver panelling encased in stone. Crisp, clean lines. The bottom half of the theatre, on either side of the door with steps up to it, is made of two sections of glass divided by a vertical thin line of Arts Centre bricks. Stacked on top of the bottom layer is a soaring metal-and-glass tower to the right, pointing up like a shard of glass. On the left I can see floors of people inside offices, and some in what looks like a cafe. There's a dome high up on the roof of one brick section, and I'm gutted to see that the dog weathervane is on top. This place doesn't deserve it. Then it makes me realize that the miniature one on mine is absolutely identical. Who could have made it? How did it get on the model?

I get the same goosebumps I had when Gift found Snod; when I saw the same dog in the street just now; when I saw the weathervane that mysteriously appeared on my model; when I turned over the mysterious invitation. Something very strange is happening. Well, if I have to be here, I may as well be the one to put the pieces together and solve all this weirdness.

My eyes fall back to the entrance. The steps outside it are like a piece of art; they're all angled slabs of shiny marble making up a maze of different-height steps. Even if I could make it up them, my legs and brain wouldn't cope with all the different heights. Not a ramp in sight. How can I solve the puzzle of this place if I can't get in? Mean Machine is not welcome there. That means I'm not either.

'Excellent start,' says Gift through gritted teeth.

Nikesh has pressed the button on the crossing. The green person pops up and flashes, and the cars that were just about to set off have to slam their brakes on again. Drivers and passengers glare at Nikesh, and they wave back.

'You coming?' they yell, already halfway across.

'No way! What's the point?' says Gift. 'I'm not coming if Hettie can't get in. So why are you going?'

'I won't go in without you!' shouts Nikesh. 'But we can at least stand outside and complain, can't we?'

'PROTEST, PROTEST, PROTEST!' yells Gift as she runs to catch up, and they both march across the road, waving their arms.

'Because we've got such a great track record doing that,' I mutter to myself as I rush to follow them.

Nikesh points to a tiny sign screwed into the wall next to the steps. There's a symbol of a wheelchair and an arrow pointing to the side of the building.

'Tradesperson's entrance,' they say. 'Very classy.'

'Remember when we had to put you on a pallet and move you on to the Arts Centre stage on a forklift with the scenery?' asks Gift.

Nikesh very quietly says, 'Not everything about our theatre worked.'

I frown. 'But it was an old building. What excuse do they have here?'

'None,' says Gift. Then she bounces around, pretending she's boxing. People step into the road to avoid her.

'Getting ready to protest!' she yells at a bunch of older people all wearing the same colour anorak. 'Steps are rubbish! We want ramps!'

Most of them scuttle past us super speedily, but one gives her a thumbs up. 'Too right. These old pins couldn't manage those wonky steps. Good for you!'

Gift gets even more energetic and has to be dragged back from the edge of the pavement by Nikesh. A bus beeps its horn.

'The side entrance is where the lower-class citizens would have been made to enter in the old days, getting the riff-raff out of the way so they didn't put off all the posh people in their finery,' says Nikesh.

'Nowt changes then,' I say, watching two young people with matching leather jackets and very expensive rucksacks side-eye Gift, before they leap up the front steps and head through the automatic doors, as I make my way round the side of the building where the arrow is pointing. Nikesh and Gift follow.

'I don't ruddy believe it!' shouts Gift.

'I do,' I say quietly.

There are steps up to the stage door, where there's also a lift, one of those where you open the glass door and roll inside. It only goes up about a metre.

'Did no one think a ramp might be easier?' says Nikesh.

I sigh and manoeuvre the Mean Machine so that I can open the lift door. Then I stop.

It's locked.

There's a small handwritten message on it behind layers of clear sticky tape. I reverse, shaking my head.

Gift bounds over and reads it out loud. '*For safetely, this lift is locked and requires a key. Please collect from the reception desk at the front entrance*. Then there's an arrow sending us back where we came from! And what is "safetely"?!'

Nikesh snorts. 'That would be funny if it wasn't. Budge over – let me sit next to you. I'm knackered with all this rage.'

'Get your own scooter!' I protest.

'At least the steps are good for something,' they say, and plonk themself down on them.

'Shall I go get the key?' asks Gift.

'What? Up the steps on the front?' I huff. 'Where I can't go to ask?'

Gift is leaping around now, can't stand still, properly up for a fight.

Nikesh peers at their watch. 'That is all very true and completely valid, but we're also *exceedingly* late now. The welcome meeting started ten minutes ago.'

I let out a big sigh. 'Well, I don't feel very welcome. I'm heading home.'

'What about your protest?' asks Nikesh, pointing to the model theatre in the basket of my scooter.

'How can I protest if I can't get in?'

'I'm coming with!' yells Gift.

I just have time for a fluttery moment to wonder whether Nikesh will stay or leave when the stage door is flung open and the dog we saw earlier with the Elizabethan red-and-gold ruff comes flying out.

'Oi, you lot! Don't just stand there gawping – catch him!'

The dog leaps about, weaving through us as a big burly person with a green beard runs down the steps.

'Whose side are we meant to be on?' squeals Gift as the dog suddenly leaps up into my lap.

It nuzzles my hand, burying its cool, wet nose underneath it, then shakes its head like it's trying to flap its ears off. They make a whipping sound, and despite the shock I laugh.

The dog looks up at me with its deep brown puddles for eyes and one white eyebrow that makes it look like it's asking me a question. I pat its head and it leans in and gives me a slobbery lick right up my left cheek.

'Incoming!' yells Gift as the person with the green beard comes towards me, reaching for the dog. The dog holds one paw up at me, as if waving goodbye, and then elegantly trots off the other side of my lap and leaps at Nikesh, who's still sitting on the steps.

Nikesh screams their head off. 'It's attacking me – help!'

'It's not!' yells Gift. 'Calm down! It only wants a pat!'

Nikesh continues to scream and flail about. Just as Green Beard lunges for it, the dog gives Nikesh's hand a quick lick, then races off down the busy street, disappearing into the distance.

Green Beard manages to come to a stop just in time to avoid face-planting into me. I look down at the heap on the pavement next to me and my scooter.

Gift is whooping and cheering as the dog makes off. I hold my hand out to help Green Beard up.

'I love that dog, but theatre rules say no dogs, so no dogs it is. I'm William.' He points to the nametag on his chest with his pronouns on, and the creepy spider symbol. 'Pleased to meet you.' He grabs my outstretched hand in a handshake.

'Nice beard,' says Gift, and William grins at her as he stands up.

'How did the dog get in?' I ask William.

He brushes down his trousers before pulling out a comb and running it through his beard. For a moment, I think I can see through him to the steps behind, then I blink. I must have imagined it.

'Complete and utter mystery,' he says, and winks in a way that makes me think it's not much of a mystery and William knows exactly how the dog does it, probably encourages it; he just doesn't want to get into bother. 'All I know is that every day, when I start work, that dog's inside waiting by that door for someone, and today I think we all, erm, oops – I mean, *he* . . . it, that being the dog, Rex, found them. Someone to help us – him, I mean – someone that needed help?' William says it like it's a question, then he takes out a hankie and dabs at his face. 'Needs help. That's it.'

'*Who* needs *what*?' I ask, totally confused.

'You,' he says with a massive grin on his face. 'We, he was waiting for you. So we can begin again, hopefully for the final time.' Then he turns to Nikesh and Gift. 'Howay in,' he says, gesturing for them to go through the stage door.

As I watch my two best friends go up the steps, I try to work through what William said, or didn't say, and unravel his riddle. Yet another to add to the pile of puzzle pieces I'm gathering.

Chapter Ten

Way Back When

With the help of Nora and Mrs Lightfoot being able to talk to the rest of the village ghosts, Harcus, Lucie and Araine dashed round Attercop, gathering up the precious items people had squirrelled away before they died.

At first the two ghosts hadn't wanted to be involved with Araine's plan for revenge, but once she explained to them that it was really, definitely, probably the spiders' true reason for bringing them back, to set the whole village at peace, and that then she'd return the diamond, they agreed to help.

'It's like a real-life treasure hunt!' yelled Lucie as she and Harcus left Old Maggie's cottage with a silver thimble.

'Check under Angus's cabbage-seed pot,' said Nora to Araine. 'He thinks he left a coin or two lurking under there.'

'That's a funny place to hide something,' said Araine as she opened the door to his shed.

Nora giggled and turned her face away, as though she was having a conversation with someone who wasn't there. 'He said it was the only place he could think of to put it so that his wife wouldn't spend it!'

Later that day, the humans and ghosts sat on the floor of the church, counting their loot, as Harcus slept on his mam's ghostly knee, exhausted from their search around the village.

'Do you think it's enough?' asked Lucie as Harcus snored.

'I do,' said Araine. 'Nora, can you ask someone if they think all this will cover the price of a carriage ride to York? Someone must have done it.'

Nora's eyes flickered for a moment. 'Shelby from the pub says you'll have enough. He even has Lord Machiavelli's address, just outside York. A huge mansion. He was bragging about getting a new set of gates for it and adding a whole new wing, just before he left us all when the sickness came.'

'We'll frighten him so much he'll give us all his money and he'll never see his gates again!' said Araine gleefully.

'Take his money?' said Lucie. 'I thought we were just scaring him.'

'I was thinking about it as we gathered up our precious titbits. What would be the worst thing that could ever happen to Lord Machiavelli?' said Araine.

'Being poor, like us,' said Mrs Lightfoot quickly, as though she'd been thinking of it too.

Lucie's eyes sparkled. 'We couldn't do that, could we?'

Harcus sleepily bobbed his head up from his mam's lap and answered her question. 'Free spirits,' he said in a dazed voice.

'There aren't three, silly – just two!' said Nora. 'Well, two of us ghosts here.'

'No, you silly billy,' said Harcus. 'Not *three*, I said *free* spirits. That's us. We're a gang now.'

'Where have you got that from?' asked Lucie.

'The spiders whispered it me. They said that's what we're becoming. We need to give the diamond back before we're lost to it forever.' Harcus sighed and, message delivered, fell back to sleep on his mam's knee, his thumb hanging half out of his mouth.

Lucie shuddered. 'Araine, did you hear what he said?'

'He's just talking dream nonsense. Excellent name though, the Free Spirits. Let's use it!'

Lucie went to speak again, but the look on Araine's face scared her. It was hard and pinched, as if she'd aged over the last day, become colder, wilder. If they just did this one thing together, and Araine *was* right that it was what the spiders had intended, then Araine would be sure to put the diamond away and Lucie would get her friend back.

Lucie looked down at her tattered blue dress. If they did take Lord Machiavelli's money, even if it was only a little of it, maybe she could get some fancy city clothes . . .

'Now then, Nora,' said Araine, 'go and find out what you can about Lord Machiavelli. Tell us any of his dirty little secrets, then we'll be ready to go!'

Araine sent Lucie and Harcus off in search of food and water. She waited a while longer for Nora, but there must have been lots of talking to do, secrets to find, so Araine wandered over to the church door. She was about to step outside, but the spiders rushed at her, ambushing her. They scrambled to make sticky threads to glue her feet in place, and blocked the doorway. They spun thicker cords to trip Araine, but she brushed them aside with a determination that scared the spiders.

They couldn't let her leave, not with the diamond. But they'd made a promise to keep her safe. Staying beside her was all they could do until they could win her back, but they knew that the longer she kept the diamond, the more time she had with Nora, the harder it would become for her to give her sister up. But what else could they do? Tearing it away from her would kill her where she stood, and that would surely break their promise. And spider promises are woven forever.

They followed her as she strode angrily through the graveyard. Keeping close was the best they could do.

At the start of their carriage journey, Araine, Lucie and Harcus passed people travelling on foot, with all their belongings on their backs, heading in the same direction as them.

'Poor souls,' said their carriage driver, crossing himself. 'They'll find nowt waiting for them in the city but a trip to the poorhouse. That's why I nearly didn't stop for you. I wouldn't have done if it wasn't for –' He stopped as he took a greedy glance at the items poking out of the bag beside him.

'See,' whispered Araine to her companions, pointing to the desperate people. 'That's what will happen to us if we don't see this through!'

Mrs Lightfoot said yes loudly in agreement, and the three children looked scared. They'd realized straight away that the carriage driver couldn't see their ghosts, only they could, and Nora had great fun making Harcus laugh by pulling faces at him. The ghosts had promised not to speak. But what if the man could hear their voices? To their relief, the carriage driver didn't appear to notice. He had not been keen on taking the three children until they'd shown him the money and jewellery they had stashed about them from the villagers. It made Araine laugh to think that he was blissfully unaware of his ghostly passengers getting a free ride.

Although the coach was bumpy and uncomfortable, their exhaustion soon won out, and the three of them snuggled up together and were quickly fast asleep.

They woke with a start after the carriage pulled up outside the gates to Lord Machiavelli's mansion on the outskirts of York. The children's faces peered out of the window, making smudges on the glass that Araine wiped with her sleeve. 'It's huge!'

The mansion was three storeys high with turrets and a long sweeping driveway lined with lime trees. Huge gates with ornate ironwork kept the riff-raff out. The new gates Lord Machiavelli had had made while they were all suffering.

'He must be worth a fortune,' said Lucie.

'He could have helped us before things got so bad,' whispered Araine, and Lucie gave her hand a squeeze as she recognized the shared sadness in her friend. 'See, I told you this was the right thing to do.' Araine's voice had suddenly turned sharp. She pulled her shoulders back and wiped away her tears. 'We have nothing, and he has all this! Don't you agree, Nora?'

Araine turned round to look at her sister, but the ghosts had vanished.

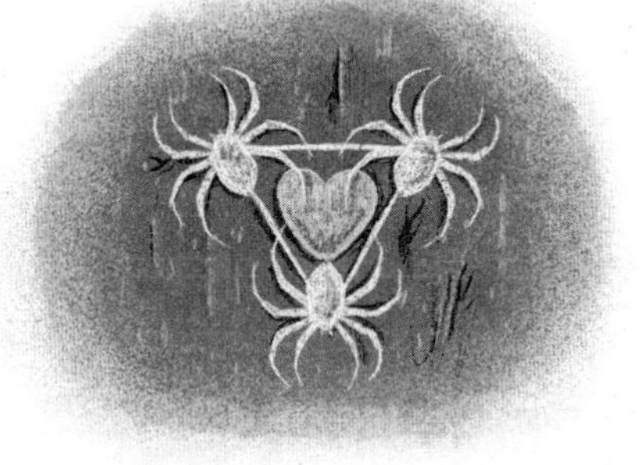

Chapter Eleven

Then

'Time to remember what?' Jack asked Harcus, but he just nodded towards Araine and gave Jack an encouraging smile. This wasn't the brave exuberant man he'd met outside the theatre. Being near Araine seemed to make him shrink.

But Harcus was Jack's hero and Araine's brother. Surely, if he was encouraging Jack, all would be well? Then Jack noticed that Harcus's smile looked a little crooked on his face.

'I can see it, you know, the threads to your lost loved ones. It's one of my many great gifts,' said Araine. 'We had the perfect triangle in the beginning, didn't we, Harcus? You, me and Lucie. But since we split –' Jack noticed Harcus try to hide a shudder when she said this – 'I've tried again and again, countless times, with other half-lives, but they weren't strong enough. Triangles and spiders and heart-shaped diamonds cannot be tricked.' She turned to Jack and Tattie. 'I have lost touch with my precious sister, my Nora! And all the ghosts on the other side! I need strong half-lives, like you two here – not this useless, used-up old one.' Araine glared at Harcus, who bowed his head, not daring to look up.

Jack forgot to be scared for a moment, his brain working furiously to keep up with the words coming out of Araine's mouth. Triangles, spiders, half-lives and ghosts. Surely it was *nonsense*?

'But I know what the secret is now,' Araine declared. 'I know how to get the ghosts back, all of them! The lineage must remain *intact*; the chosen ones must be related to us original three, otherwise the power of the diamond is not strong enough for me to sustain it. The triangle needs *our* bloodline, and here you two are!' She threw back her head and laughed.

Tattie scratched his head and said, 'I'm really sorry, but what has this got to do with me meeting Priss again? With both of us?'

Jack turned to Tattie. 'Why did you stay if you didn't know why you were brought here?'

'Why wouldn't I?' said Tattie as he waved his arms around.

Jack understood completely. He hadn't spent long in the theatre, and he already knew why Tattie never wanted to leave; it was incredible.

'You, dear Tattie, are a Lightfoot,' said Araine. 'And you, dear Jack, are a Redwood. In the past, we were two Lightfoots in Harcus and Lucie, and a Redwood in me, but this time we have two Redwoods and a Lightfoot – and that is a much bolder combination. They will be far braver than you ever were, don't you think, dear Harcus?'

Araine looked at Harcus with such malice that Jack was almost too terrified to question her, even though every word she uttered was baffling to him.

She continued, leaning close to whisper to Jack and Tattie. Despite his fear, Jack could see why she was such a star of the stage – her presence was mesmerizing.

'And, if I'm right,' Araine whispered, 'us forming a triangle will mean that my diamond will shine once more . . . The path to the other side will again reopen, and we shall all be reunited!'

'Well, that makes perfect sense,' muttered Jack, and then clapped his hand over his mouth when Araine glared at him. 'I – I'm sorry . . . I still don't understand why any of this applies to me.'

She reached out a long bony hand and traced her sharp fingernail along his jawline. 'You have the same face as me, the same dark shadow within you.'

'Shadow?' asked Jack, looking for reassurance from Harcus and finding none. Then he turned back to Araine. 'How do I have the same face as you? You're Araine Machiavelli!'

'She stole the name, just like she stole everything, including my sister!' yelled Harcus, unable to restrain his emotions any longer.

'Silence!' screeched Araine, and Harcus immediately cowered. 'You will be silent, and you will respect our guests.'

Jack grabbed Tattie's hand. 'We need to leave, now!'

But Tattie stayed, frozen in terror, no matter how much Jack tried to wrench him from the spot.

Araine turned her attention back to Jack. 'The grief burns bright in you, Jack. He's just behind you!'

Jack looked over his shoulder, but no one was there. 'Who?'

To his confusion, Araine began giggling at him.

'Oh, what fun we will have together!' She laughed as she went over to the little lace-covered table in the centre of the room. The sound was harsh, like a bark.

Jack could hear Rex whining outside the door and he wished he was on the other side of it too. But this was the great Araine Machiavelli! It must all be a performance; he just hadn't understood it yet. Maybe it would all make sense soon? He whispered to himself to buck up.

Matthew wouldn't be scared of an old woman talking about ghosts and spiders.

Araine's eyes met his. Her velvet robes swirled about her, making the embroidered gold spiders on them look as though they were moving. *Were they moving?*

'You think about him a lot, don't you?' she said.

'Who?' asked Jack. *Had she just read his mind?* The playbills said she was psychic, could talk to the dead, do all sorts of magic, but that was all make-believe and misdirection . . . wasn't it?

She stared right into him and Jack could feel an itching and burrowing inside his head. He threw his hands up to protect himself from her. He suddenly knew with complete certainty that she could delve right into his brain, read his thoughts – and steal them.

Suddenly Araine whipped round to Harcus who was still cowering. 'Have you told him anything?' Harcus shook his head. 'You can never be trusted.'

'Not this time, I promise,' Harcus whispered. 'I know the punishment.'

At the word *punishment*, at Harcus's terrified reaction, Jack looked at Tattie and could see that he wanted to flee too, but they were both frozen with fear, unable to escape.

'Good, good,' Araine purred, stretching out the vowels of the last word. Then: 'Sit, Jack, Tattie – sit!

I've made us all tea. Isn't that nice? A little family of Redwoods and Lightfoots sitting together and drinking tea. You be mother and pour, dear Harcus.'

Jack had never, ever wanted to do something less, but he found he'd already taken the few steps across the room and sat at the table, with Tattie to his right, Harcus to his left and Araine at the head. The lamp in the corner flickered and threw shadows.

'I adore how Harcus tries to explain about our little family, even though he doesn't belong any more. It's a delight to listen to! Tattie, you pour the milk.' Tattie looked shocked as his hand reached for the milk jug. 'Let's make ourselves comfortable and listen to Harcus.'

Jack could still hear Rex whimpering and scratching on the other side of the door. Araine clicked her fingers and Jack did a double take as two spiders, tiny and grey with extremely long legs, darted across the carpet from the other side of the room and slid under the door.

Rex stopped making a noise.

'Araine is the Queen of Spiders,' began Harcus in a shaky voice. He couldn't meet the boys' eyes. 'Over a hundred years ago, we lived in the village of Attercop that once stood here.'

'Over a hundred years ago?' exclaimed Tattie. 'But you're only –'

'Have you aged in the years you've been here?' Araine glared at him. 'Even without the diamond I still have traces of power left inside me.'

Tattie's mouth dropped open as if this had never occurred to him.

'Now, do not interrupt again,' snapped Araine, and immediately Tattie's lips slapped back together, as though they'd been glued shut.

Harcus took a deep breath and continued: 'The spiders had made their web under the church, which used to be on this very spot, and it wove through the catacombs below to the outskirts of our village. It was our job to keep the spiders safe and, in return, they allowed us to use their dewdrop diamond, which had the power to grant us a last goodbye.'

Araine pulled the diamond from under her collar, and the boys stared at it as Harcus carried on speaking.

'If there were three of us, a triangle of sorrow, then we could see departed loved ones for a final time. It was only ever meant to be for a brief moment, but Araine stole the diamond to take revenge on those who had hurt us, to keep her sister Nora as a ghost with her always, along with Lucie's and my mam. The spiders tried to stop Araine, to take care of her as they'd promised her mother, and to stop her being corrupted by its power.'

Araine let out a harsh snort.

Harcus glanced at her nervously but kept talking. 'Over time, though, Araine transformed the diamond, which was once full of light and hope, into an instrument of revenge and dark power. As her heart hardened, so did the spiders' hearts.'

Araine beamed with pride, and waved at him to continue the tale.

'For years, we were a success in the theatre, speaking with the dead, but Lucie, my sister and Araine's best friend, grew tired, and eventually the ghosts became paler, more withdrawn. Lucie wanted us to stop – Nora, too, wished it to end. But Araine –' Harcus choked back a sob and refused to say any more.

Araine gave him a disdainful glare, then cleared her throat. 'And so we said goodbye to the wretched Lucie – no backbone, just like her brother. Kept you at my side though, didn't I? Was I not kind? And I can bring her back for you just as I promised, now that you've found me these boys. I control the spiders; I have the heart.'

She paused for a moment and frowned. 'However, I've had to hibernate for periods of time to stay alive, to keep Harcus alive, to conserve our lives. My power has faded to almost nothing, a shadow of what I once could do. To regain the full might of the diamond and summon the dead for you, to step back into my true power once more, I need to complete the triangle with two half-lives that share our original bloodline – you two.'

Jack stared, open-mouthed, and then slowly a smile grew on his face and he began to clap. 'Brilliant, just brilliant. What a show! I can see why audiences come to see you over and over again!' He looked at Tattie, but he wasn't smiling, and neither was Harcus. In fact, Harcus looked as though all the blood had drained from his face, and a quiet moan escaped his lips. Slowly a coldness crept into Jack and he stopped clapping. 'This cannot be real . . . can it?'

'There, there, Harcus,' said Araine. She patted his hand, and he tried to move it out of her reach. 'He always gets so emotional,' she said to no one in particular. 'It's the thought of seeing Lucie again, isn't it?'

'Are you sure this will bring Lucie back?' asked Harcus, his eyes flicking to Jack and Tattie. 'It didn't work the other times. I wouldn't have done it, found the boys for you – I didn't want to – but . . . you promised she'd be safe if I did, that I'd see her again!'

Jack shook his head, trying to sort out the jumble of words. 'Araine, Harcus, why am I here?'

It was Araine who answered. 'Because you are a Redwood, like me. And because you're a half-life, someone living with one foot in the other world because they can't bear their loss, and you don't fully want to be here in this world. You want to say goodbye to your dearly departed loved one – and I have the power to help you. Poor Harcus and Lucie – they're all spent.' Harcus glared at Araine. 'But I have a lot more work to do. We've all lost someone we love, and for me to be at the height of my power I need the three of us.'

Jack tried to take all this in. 'Tattie has lost his little sister. I mean, I don't believe all this hocus-pocus, but at least I can understand why you'd think he was one of your precious half-lives,' he said, once more attempting to get up and leave but failing. He roared at Araine in frustration. 'But I'm telling you – I'm not one of them!'

None of it can be real, he thought, *but they believe it! That's the terrifying thing!*

Jack loved being in the theatre, the thrill of stepping inside and seeing the wonder of backstage, but not when these people actually believed they could talk to the dead! He could see the danger in Araine's eyes. He had to get out, now.

'Stay where you are,' said Araine.

She clicked her fingers and spiders flooded out of drawers, down the walls, from behind the hangings and between the floorboards.

Harcus closed his eyes and moaned to himself. The spiders scuttled towards Jack. Some formed cuffs on his ankles, while others climbed up the chair to bind his wrists until he was pinned in place.

'What are you doing? Let me go!' Jack felt the panic rise in his chest, and his face burned. Try as he might, he could not wrench himself free.

Tattie made a move to help Jack, but Araine clicked her fingers again and a new wave of spiders scuttled over to hold Tattie back.

'Do you not want to see him again?' Araine asked Jack.

'Who?' yelled Jack as he pulled and wriggled to get out of his seat. 'You're not making any sense. You're scaring me! Let me go!'

'It's so much easier if you don't struggle. Tell him!' Araine said to Harcus.

When Harcus didn't answer, she stood up and slammed her fists on the table so that the sugar bowl tipped over. Hunched over, Harcus kept his eyes closed, muttering to himself so that he couldn't hear.

'Tell him!' Araine spat.

At last, Harcus spoke very quietly, rubbing his moustache in a soothing motion. 'You don't want to lose him forever, do you, Jack? If you don't do what Araine says, you will. I would have lost my sister, Lucie, the person I loved most in the whole world, without her. But now that we've found both of you, we'll be able to bring the ghosts back so that they can stay with us forever. Think of the spiders' heart as a bridge, a web between this world and the next, with Araine in control of the ghosts who pass between. We half-lives are on this side, and our ghosts on the other. We can be reunited once more.'

'Look . . .' said Jack, trying to think what Matthew would do in a situation like this.

He slowed his breathing as Araine watched him, and her spiders wound slowly round and round his wrist and ankles, keeping him held in position. Matthew would tell him to stay calm, keep his wits about him, talk his way out.

Araine raised an eyebrow. 'He would, would he?'

'Who would?' said Jack.

'She can hear what you're thinking, Jack,' Harcus hissed.

'And why is that, Harcus?' Araine asked him. 'Do explain to our guest.'

'Because –' Harcus's eyes finally met Jack's. 'Because you're still linked to Matthew, and Araine can feel that, hear those thoughts. But that's all she has the power to do, for now. She's getting weaker with each day that passes and she won't be able to stay here, in this body that has survived so many years. Neither will I – not without you. We've wasted too much of her energy trying to make the triangle work without the right bloodlines. This is her last chance. *Our* last chance. Please help me, Jack!'

'What? What do you mean I'm still linked to Matthew?' said Jack as the spiders kept circling, tightening their grip. 'Because he's my brother?'

The gold embroidered spiders on Araine's robe *were* moving this time. Jack watched as they crept up to her neck, settling on the heart-shaped diamond. Calmly and silently, Araine took the spider-covered jewel and placed it on the table.

'B-but Matthew's alive,' Jack spluttered. 'I'm not a half-life like you!'

'Where is Matthew, Jack?' asked Araine, a hint of menace in her voice. 'Why is he not here with you? Is he at home? Working at the water-pumping station? Tell me – where *is* Matthew?'

Jack looked at Araine, at the diamond heart on the table – the diamond that apparently belonged to the spiders and that was now in Araine's control, allowing her to bring back ghosts. None of this was real . . . surely?

As a thousand thoughts raced through Jack's mind, he couldn't take his eyes off the diamond. The gemstone splintered the light of the gas lamp and refracted it so that dark rainbows danced across the walls.

Suddenly it all came flooding back.

And Jack slumped in his seat as he remembered.

Chapter Twelve

Now

William, the man with the bright green beard, pulls out a key for the lift, unlocks it, then opens the glass door for me to wheel inside so I can press the button to make it rise.

'I'm so sorry,' he says as I reverse in. 'I wanted to tell them it was an awful idea to lock it, but, well, then they'd –'

'No worries. It's hard to say things to people when you know they don't want to hear.'

'It's not that! I can't –' He stops suddenly like he's said too much and just gives me a massive smile instead.

I'm so busy trying to work through everything in my head I forget for a moment that I don't really want to be here. By the time I remember, it's too late – William is at the stage door, and Nikesh and Gift are trotting along a corridor after him. I have no choice but to follow.

'You can complain about the lift and make it better for the next person,' says Nikesh with a smile. 'At the same time that you do your theatre protest.' They point at the miniature Arts Centre in the box in my basket and give me a thumbs up.

As we hurry down the silver-painted corridor lined with portraits of stage stars, I think, *Yes, of course I can!* I complain lots. But why does it *always* have to be *me* telling others what's not working? It would be nice if everything *just worked* without having to play hunt the key or rely on my friends.

'Here we are!' says William, stopping outside a room that says CONFERENCE SUITE in big block capitals, like it's shouting at us. 'I can't go in because Jack can't know I'm back yet. You need to find the –' He pauses and a frown appears on his face – but only for a split second and he's smiling again. 'Well, in you go. Have fun!'

Jack? The one who sent me the note? William must know something. I start to ask him what we have to find, but he's already dashing off along the corridor.

Nikesh quietly opens the door. We peer through and what feels like five hundred faces turn round and stare right back at us. I want to shrink and die. I hate being stared at – that's why I work backstage.

'Not only are you late . . .' says the man with the microphone at the front of the room. He's dressed in faded blue jeans and a purple T-shirt with an outline of the theatre on the front – and he's the same man whose photo was in the brochure, and who sent me the note. *Jack Redwood himself.* '. . . but you are now holding things up,' he continues. 'For heaven's sake, come in! If there's one piece of advice I can give you, it's *never be late*.'

With that, he tuts and spins away from us as he returns to pointing with his laser pen at something on the projection screen. On the back of his T-shirt, in block letters, it says 'ARTISTIC DIRECTOR' with a triangle underneath. I shudder – it's the same symbol from the envelope, with spiders at its corners and a heart in the centre. *Spiders*. I hate spiders.

We make our way into the room and sit in the back row. I can't help but notice that Nikesh gives me the side-eye for us being late. I pull my Mean Machine up at the side, drop my armrests and swivel my seat, and then shift into an aisle chair. Someone turns to face me – it's one of the kids who easily leaped up to the front entrance with their posh rucksacks.

'If you can walk, why the protest about the steps?' he whispers to me.

Before I can even think about replying, the lad's told Nikesh off for dropping their water bottle and being late, and then he turns to face the front with an exaggerated dramatic sigh.

My heart *thump-thump-thumps* in my chest and I look to Gift for support, surprised she hasn't yelled at the boy. But her eyes are fixed on Jack. I go to speak to her and she shushes me. Puts her finger to her lips and actually goes '*Shush!*'

'And in conclusion, and as I was saying before we were so rudely interrupted,' says Jack, standing under a futuristic-looking chandelier that's all spiky metal and spotlights, 'we are proud to set up our youth company, for which you're here today to audition, giving our future theatre impresarios, backstage teams, producers and performers a CV-enhancing kick towards theatrical success.'

He presses a button on his clicker and the projector screen flashes up a burst of confetti. When it stops, the screen shows the same spidery logo that's on his T-shirt and underneath it reads:

ATTERCOP'S CROWN RENAISSANCE YOUTH PARTICIPATORY TROUPE

There's a moment of silence and then the room bursts into applause and cheering. Next to me, Gift is clapping away, gazing around the conference room in awe, at the sleek lines and the plush carpets.

She sees me watching her. 'Incredible, isn't it? It's even got heating!' She shrugs off her hoodie.

Maybe she didn't hear what the lad in front said to me? I lean over to her and whisper, 'But a bit of a mess up there with the name, eh? Did they not spot that the initials of their posh troupe spells out *A Crypt*?'

She shushes me again and goes back to clapping. I roll my eyes and refuse to join in.

So much for Gift protesting with me about the terrible access and the rude company. It's like she's had one sniff of nice chairs and luxurious carpets, and she's under the theatre's – and Jack's – spell.

Which I refuse to be, especially since I need to be on guard and work out why the awful artistic director has invited *me* here. He said I could see Grandad again. I can't even think about that.

I wish I'd told Gift and Nikesh about the invitation.

Once the presentation is over, we're ushered through some double doors, which were concealed behind curtains, into a side room to wait while they 'spin the room', which apparently is posh theatre speak for resetting it for the auditions.

There are tables with white cloths and bottles of water, baskets of fruit and the little packets of biscuits where you only get two. I can see Gift glancing around and then stuffing handfuls into her rucksack. Nikesh is at the other side of the room, looking at framed vintage posters of theatre productions. Once Jack comes in, Gift stops stealing biscuits and starts following him around like a puppy, trying to get him to notice her as he schmoozes from group to group. I shake my head and zoom over to join Nikesh.

'Gift's lost to the smell of new carpets,' I say.

'Can you blame her? Have you seen this place?'

I give Nikesh my best thunder look and they change the subject.

'Look at that necklace on the playbill,' they say. 'How much do you think it's worth now?'

They're staring at a black-and-white poster, drawn by hand, with a pen-and-ink sketch of a woman with a corker of a heart-shaped diamond around her neck. There is ornate lettering proclaiming Araine Machiavelli to be the world's greatest clairvoyant and that tonight she'll be joined by her Free Spirits.

My mouth drops. That's what we call ourselves! But I suppose it's a common thing if you're doing creepy shows. My skin crawls a bit and I have to scratch my hands. All the spooky name coincidences begin to pile up – Jack sharing Grandad's name too. I go to spill everything to Nikesh, but they get in first.

'Araine has an incredible jawline and cheekbones, don't you think?'

The heart-shaped diamond round her neck is huge – and I mean properly massive. But, as I look at it, I get a stabbing pain, like indigestion but in my heart.

'A clairvoyant,' says Nikesh in lecture mode. I won't get a word in when they're like this – I'll have to wait until they've finished. 'That's someone who claims they can communicate with the dead. Something obviously ridiculous. You still get scam artists now taking advantage of people's grief, but in the Victorian age the theatre would have been packed out in the hope that Araine would choose them and send them a message from family who had passed over to the other side.'

'The other side of what?'

'Death. "The other side" just means they've died,' explains Nikesh.

I struggle not to let the tears that have just taken me by surprise escape from my eyes. All of a sudden, I can't talk and have to cough to get my words out. 'Why don't folk just say that then?'

'Death has always been described in other softer words,' Nikesh continues. 'It's to keep people safe from emotions and fear, I suppose. To cushion it. But clairvoyants used that to their advantage. How do you think she got the money to build her theatre?'

Nikesh sighs and I shrug. 'How do you know all this stuff about Araine –' I check the poster to get her surname right – 'Machiavelli?'

'How do you *not* know? She was an incredible force in theatre, across the whole world, and she started here in our town!'

'I don't know because I don't spend all my time in mouldy old libraries!' I retort.

Nikesh rolls their eyes at me. 'She made her fortune from private seances with very rich theatregoers.'

I look baffled and Nikesh rolls their eyes again. 'Seances are expensive meetings to talk to dead people.'

'Why didn't you just say?' I can't help myself and giggle, but Nikesh doesn't find it funny so I put my serious face on. 'Could she really talk to dead people?' I ask, and I get a tiny bit of hope in me when I think about Grandad. If she's linked to this theatre, maybe that's where Jack's hocus-pocus invitation comes from.

I touch Grandad's pliers in my pocket, to keep him close.

'Of course not!' says Nikesh, throwing their head back in disgust. 'But she was excellent at all the tricks to make people believe she could, and Araine's bank balance grew so she could build her own theatre, here in Cawlington.'

'This theatre?'

'No, of course not – keep up! She died in 1906, in a mysterious fire on this very spot. Apparently, they've got an archive here, with all the papers that remained after the fire, or donated by people who've found programmes and things when they've been clearing out attics.'

'Do you think if you ask nicely they'll let you see the archive?' I ask Nikesh, wondering if there could be some information in there that could help me too.

There's a shout behind us and a scuffle breaks out.

'She was nicking!' yells the lad who said we'd made a fuss about the steps. He's holding on to Gift's wrist.

'No, I was not!' shouts Gift as she struggles to pull free from his grasp.

The posh lad stares at her name badge, the ones we were given when we entered this side room. 'What kind of name is Gift anyway? Your parents get you for Christmas?'

I can feel my teeth begin to grind and my fingers curl. No matter how ridiculous she's being now, under the spell of new carpets and a nice paint job, she's my best friend and no one talks to her like that!

The lad laughs, and from where I'm stuck by the wall because I can't get to her through the crush, I can see Jack slowly smile. Gift notices it and her face crumples.

The lad lets go of her. 'Going to cry, are you? A crybaby and a thief. Nice.'

Nikesh swishes through the crowd and leaps in front of Gift, trying to make it all better as they always do. 'Hey, I'm sure it was just a misunderstanding.'

'Did you not hear what he said about my name?' snaps Gift.

Did you not hear what he said to me? Then I feel really mean.

'Now, now,' says Jack, stepping into the centre and holding out his arms. 'Tensions are high; it's a day of drama. That will do. Do apologize to . . . what's your name? *Present?*'

He stares at Gift, who quietly says her name again. I can see how deflated she is. That man sent me a twisted invitation to come here. That *bully*?

'Well, at least it's not Parcel,' says Jack.

Nikesh takes Gift's hand and steers her away.

Jack clears his throat and announces, 'The audition room is now open. Designers, remember your portfolios. Everyone, go through and queue at the table with the name of the role you're auditioning for.' Jack glances over at Gift and Nikesh. 'Let's keep the drama for the stage.'

I've had enough. I'm just getting ready to leave this horrible place, I knew I should never have come here, when Jack's head whips round and he stares right at me.

My skin crawls. He slowly smiles and waves, mouths, *I knew you would come*, and then turns on his heel and walks through to the audition room.

Before I have time to think about what's just happened, I feel a hand on my shoulder.

'He wasn't always like this,' says William, with his green beard, who's suddenly standing next to me.

I jump in my seat.

'What do you mean?' I ask, but he ignores me and, smiling, bends forward to try to read the name on my badge.

'I'm Hettie,' I say, and genuinely smile for the first time since I've been in here – it's impossible not to with his beaming bearded face. 'Hettie Lightfoot.'

'Ah,' says William, lowering his voice to a whisper, his face close to mine. 'A Lightfoot. Rex *was* right to pick you out. You *are* the reason I find myself suddenly drawn back. Here we go again! Are you strong?' he asks me.

I jerk my head back from him. 'Who are you?' I say. 'And who do you think *I* am?'

'In there.' It's like William can't see the fear he's put inside me, and he points to my heart. 'You'll need to be strong there, for what's coming . . . for all our sakes.'

Then he suddenly changes his tone completely, and I'm so shocked I'm unsure if maybe I imagined what he'd said. Now he's all big smiles again as he asks, 'What's that in your basket?'

This time he's pointing to the box.

'A miniature theatre,' I say slowly, to buy me some time to try and work him out. 'It's a sort of protest.'

'Excellent! Another one for the collection. You can pop it with the others. Wood or paper?'

'Wood,' I reply.

I lean forward as William opens the box and peers inside.

'It's, well, it's a model of the old Arts Centre,' I find myself sputtering out as I try to figure out what I really want to say.

'That's top work,' he says. 'Harcus would be very impressed. All by your own hand?'

'No,' I say. 'I did the wobbly bits. It's my grandad's really. Edward Redwood. And who's Harcus?'

William stares at me and whistles as he breathes out. 'You're a Lightfoot and a Redwood? We could be in trouble here.'

He's totally ignoring my question about this mysterious Harcus.

'Sorry,' I say. 'What do you mean? You're not making any sense, and you're scaring me a bit. Hold on, did you say *another one for the collection*? There are more models here?'

Gift yells over to me from the doorway. 'Come on, Hettie, we'll miss our audition!'

'You're not serious about actually going through with it?' I yell back.

'Well, obviously,' she says in a hard voice that I don't recognize.

'But, Gift, they're mean!'

'All the better to stand up to them, and show 'em what we're made of!'

'Or we could just go home?' I shout across the room.

This place is creepy; there'll be spiders next. I expect her to do a double take, realize what she's doing, and come over to join me. But without a second glance she turns and skips into the audition room.

I look back at William, as I try to brush off what Gift has just done, even though I feel sick and as if I might burst into tears.

'What collection?' I ask.

Chapter Thirteen

Way Back When

As soon as little Harcus realized the ghosts were gone, he started screaming and writhing and would not shush. The carriage driver rushed to open the door and get them out, and then drove away in haste.

'What are we going to do?' cried Lucie. 'We don't have enough money to get back home, and now our mam's gone forever!'

Araine felt sick to her stomach at the thought that she'd lost Nora again.

'Have you still got the diamond?' asked Lucie.

Araine felt in her pocket and its smooth, cold surface was still there under her fingers, crackling with the same dark energy as before, making her arm tingle, firing thoughts into her brain. Suddenly she understood everything.

'Stop crying, Lucie. The ghosts are fine; they just can't travel beyond the web under our village. They'll be right there waiting for us once we get back to the church.'

'You promise?' Lucie asked, sucking in her chest to control a sob.

'Yes,' said Araine, and her composure made Lucie believe her. 'We just need to stick to the plan and steal Lord Machiavelli's money.'

'How do we do that without the ghosts?' said Lucie as she picked Harcus up and comforted him, bouncing him on her hip.

'We know all his secrets – Nora told us. And he has no idea the ghosts aren't here. We can just pretend they are!'

'To scare him? Will that work?' asked Lucie.

'Only one way to find out,' said Araine with a grin as she opened the gate and marched up the driveway. Lucie hurried along behind with Harcus.

The butler showed them into Lord Machiavelli's study. He had not wanted to let them in, until Lucie offered him their last coin, and then he swiftly changed his mind and became ever so polite. 'Long-lost relatives, you say? I'm sure he'll see you after all.'

They could see him polishing the coin as he left the room.

Lord Machiavelli's study smelled of cigar smoke and he had a big wooden desk the size of a bed. Hundreds of books filled the cases on the walls.

Araine was tracing her fingers along the spines of the books when the door was flung open and Lord Machiavelli strode in.

'I have no clue how you got in here, who you are, nor how you managed to bamboozle my butler, but I demand you leave immediately!'

'Really,' said Araine with a cold smile. 'We may have had to tell a little lie to get in here, but that's because we have something to offer you, something that you will not believe!'

Lord Machiavelli scoffed, but there was something about Araine that intrigued him, and he stopped pointing at the doorway for them to leave.

Araine gestured to the chair behind his desk, and his legs took him there, even though he wasn't sure whether he wanted to sit down.

Harcus went over to him and held his hand, just as they'd practised.

Lucie and Araine stood in front of them and spoke at the same time. 'Ghosts of the underworld, the other world, come to us now. We call you to speak through us, to channel us. Send us a message for Lord Machiavelli!'

Araine held up her arms and Lucie wobbled around, her eyes shut tight.

Suddenly Lucie's eyes flew open and she made her voice sound like an old lady. '*Mac, this is your Nanny Ethel speaking from the other side. Have you stopped weeing in the flowerpots yet?*'

Lord Machiavelli gasped and sat bolt upright. 'How did you know –' He went bright red and started to sweat.

'*Remember you said I was the only one who was kind to you? You didn't show me that kindness when you made me take the blame when you flooded the bathroom, and you had me dismissed!*'

Lord Machiavelli was transfixed. 'I never told anyone that. Nanny Ethel, is that really you?'

'Of course it is,' said Araine as she snapped her fingers and Lucie pretended to come out of her trance.

'We know everything about you!' Harcus was bouncing from foot to foot in excitement.

'How is this possible?' said Lord Machiavelli.

'We can talk to the dead!' cried Araine. 'And if you want to hear more you had better pay us!'

Lucie, Araine and Harcus all huddled together in the corner of the parlour, trying to keep warm. Mansions might be huge and worth lots of money, but they were very, very cold.

Araine listened for sounds of Lord Machiavelli returning. The butler had put them in here after Lord Machiavelli had demanded they talk to the dead for what seemed like hours. He wasn't as frightened as she'd thought he would be. Luckily, Lucie could remember everything Nora had told them, and afterwards he'd backed out of the room, muttering to himself, closing the door behind him and shouting for the butler to keep them in the parlour under lock and key.

'So what do we do now?' asked Lucie. 'How do we get any money out of him? We're stuck if we can't talk to the ghosts. I don't remember anything else!'

The door banged open and made the three of them jump.

'You cannot wear those rags if I'm to take you out into society,' said Lord Machiavelli in a booming voice.

'Where are we going?' asked Harcus.

'You, boy, are going to the nursery. Jane will take care of you. As for you two,' Lord Machiavelli said, pointing at Araine and Lucie, 'I need to show you off to some investors of mine. You're coming with me.'

Araine looked at Lucie who shrugged; she didn't understand what was going on either.

'Where did you say you came from?' asked Lord Machiavelli.

'Atter–' started Lucie but was interrupted by Araine,

who said, 'Here, there and everywhere!' in a sing-song voice.

Lucie could see that Araine was clutching the diamond through her pocket. She'd never heard Araine speak like that before. Lucie's stomach began to churn; she suddenly felt completely out of control.

Lord Machiavelli chuckled. 'What you said about me, you won't –'

'Your secrets are safe with us,' said Araine and winked. 'For a price.' She strode over to him and took his arm. 'Now, where are we off to?'

Lucie couldn't stop stroking the skirts of her plum-coloured silk dress that she'd chosen from a pile that had swiftly been delivered to the mansion. As they'd travelled from the outskirts of York into the city, Araine was amazed by the amount of people, the smells, the noise. How did anyone live here? She missed the rolling hills.

There was a red carpet down the steps of a tall building and their carriage drew to a stop beside it. A man at the front of the building opened the carriage door, helping Lord Machiavelli down and then the two girls, one by one. Having done that, the man bowed deeply, stood back and directed the three of them up the carpet towards the huge open wooden doors.

Araine gazed at the sign above the porch, which was supported by columns on either side of the intimidating doors. *Machiavelli Theatre*, she mouthed to herself.

'This belongs to you?' she asked Lord Machiavelli as he held out both his arms for the girls to take.

'Of course, my child. Bath has the first theatre outside London with a royal warrant; we are expecting our warrant imminently!' He looked over his shoulder to check that no one was listening. 'I don't know how you did it, found out that information about me, but I admire your gumption, knowing to come to me with a business proposal.' He paused, then said, 'Ghosts indeed! I was furious that you knew my secrets, but where there's a will to make money, anything can be spun in its direction. There's a place for you here. In my theatre. You can work for me. With your kind of talent, you'll be wearing even prettier dresses soon enough!'

Lucie grinned, and Araine faked a big smile, but underneath it her anger burned white-hot. She would bluff and lie for as long as it took, until she had him in the perfect spot to bring him down. Her parents and sister would get their revenge for what this man had done to them.

They walked up the red carpet and into his theatre, Lord Machiavelli delighting in showing off the plush seats, the gold leaf and chandeliers, the thick carpet.

Then they took their seats in his box and watched as the lights dimmed.

After the show, Lucie could barely contain herself and excused herself and Araine from Lord Machiavelli to go to the powder room.

There were gold taps and marble counters. She'd never seen anything like it before!

'Did you see that –'

'How did they –'

'The bit where the ghost appeared –'

'Do you think it was real –'

'Of course not –'

'But ours are –'

Both girls gabbled over each other at the same time, not able to finish their sentences.

Lucie took a deep breath and held on to Araine's hands. 'We could do that, couldn't we?' she said, her eyes sparkling.

Araine nodded, her mind quickly pulling together a plan. 'You must stay here and learn the tricks we're going to need.'

'Me?' said Lucie, raising her eyebrows.

'Yes, Lucie – you! You won't see me getting onstage in a million years. I could never be convincing. It's no good you just telling them secret stuff, you have to make it eerie. They come for the information, but they really want a spectacle! Look what they did tonight! You need to learn all that, and then make it even better. You have to become a leading light, more famous than the ones we saw on the stage.'

Lucie puffed herself up at the thought. 'And what will you be doing?'

'I'll return to Attercop, to the church where the ghosts are waiting for us. I'll take a list of the richest people in York and I'll get Nora and your mam to find out everything they can about them, then I'll bring it back here for you to use.'

'What about Harcus?' asked Lucie. 'And my mam – I want to see her!'

'He can stay with you, be your stagehand. And you'll see her soon,' said Araine. 'But not just yet. I'll keep an eye on her, tell her everything, make sure she's all right. Harcus can come back with me every now and then! You too, once everything is in place. Just think how much money we can steal from these people! We can bleed not just Lord Machiavelli dry but every rich person who's ever wronged someone with less than them.'

Lucie nodded and smiled. They could make this work if the three of them stuck together.

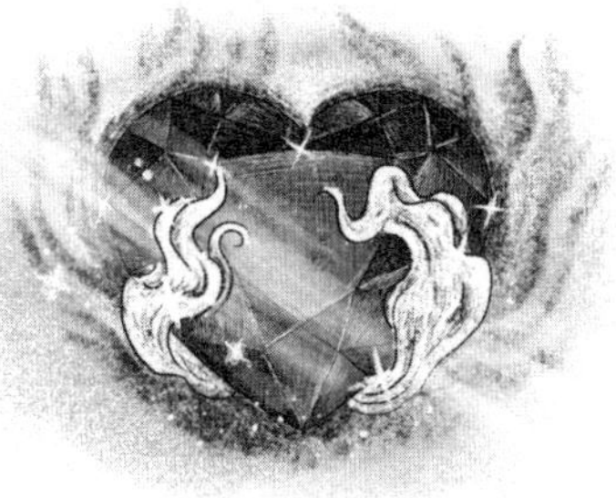

Chapter Fourteen

Then

Jack sat slumped in his chair. The spiders stayed on his wrists and ankles, but they were no longer necessary. Jack's grief pinned him down.

Araine said something, but he couldn't make sense of it as the block he'd placed in his memory now crumbled and fell away.

He shivered and wished somebody would light a fire in the hearth.

'Drink up!' said Araine, her voice floating in and out. 'This'll warm you.' And she handed him a cup and saucer.

'It will help,' said Harcus, and he urged Jack to drink.

Jack took a sip.

He looked down. Even more spiders, hundreds of them, were heading towards him. Spiders from behind the unlit fireplace, on the rug-lined floor, tumbling over each other. Jack's body and brain were frozen. He didn't move a muscle as he was covered in a mass of armour of legs and eyes that scrabbled over him.

Run! Matthew's voice was loud in his head. *Get out of here!*

Everything foggy, Jack looked up and saw Tattie shaking in fear next to him.

Araine clutched the diamond to her chest, and chanted in a language that Jack didn't know, an old language. Jack feared it was dark magic.

She clicked her fingers, and Jack sat up straight. He was not in charge of his body any more: somehow Araine had used her power through her army of spiders to manipulate him like a puppet.

'You need to remember what happened,' said Harcus.

Jack shook his head and a tear rolled down his cheek.

'No,' he whispered. 'Then it will be real.'

He cried out as the memory of his brother's death flooded into his mind. Tattie took his hand, but all of a sudden the room disappeared and Jack could smell the tang of the briny water from the river by the pumping station, the waterworks that supplied Cawlington: an amazing feat of engineering that Jack did not understand in the slightest, but his big brother was in awe of it. He wanted to design something as impressive when he was older.

He was back with Matthew. They were sitting on the bank of the river, eating hunks of bread and cheese, when a kingfisher darted across.

'Look at that!' cried Jack, pointing excitedly as the blue streak shot above the foam on the weir and dived towards the trees on the opposite bank.

'I'll catch it for you,' said Matthew, stripping off his top and winking at Jack. The sun beating down caused Jack to squint up into his brother's face, just about seeing his grin and freckles.

'Don't be daft!' Jack laughed as Matthew ran down the bank and dived in, his body slicing through the air, fingertips touching the surface of the water, then the rest of his body sliding gracefully in. Jack could only jump into the river; Matthew hadn't taught him to dive yet, but he said he would this summer.

Jack waited for Matthew to reappear, knowing his brother could hold his breath for ages. He counted to ten, twenty, and then stood up and scanned the river, anxious now, waiting for him to explode out of the water, laughing at him.

Nothing.

'Not funny, Matthew!' he called.

The sun continued to beat down and the water over the weir frothed brown. Jack saw a little stream of bubbles to its left and then Matthew bobbed to the surface.

'You fooled me!' called Jack, waving to him. 'Best one yet!'

But Matthew didn't blow water out of his mouth like a spout nor yell at Jack to join him. He floated face down, gently swirling in the current.

Jack couldn't believe what he was seeing and then plunged into the river, shouting for help.

He opened his eyes as a gruff man slapped him on the cheek. Jack was coughing and spluttering on the riverbank, limbs flailing as he gasped for breath, freezing cold, his fingers blue and numb. He glanced to his right as he saw movement out of the corner of his eye. Another man he didn't recognize was crouched over the still body of his brother, trying to breathe life back into him.

'Matthew!' yelled Jack. He scrambled up and half-ran, half-stumbled towards his brother, throwing himself down on the ground next to him.

Matthew was white, his lips blue. Not breathing.

Jack looked at the man beside Matthew who slowly shook his head.

'No!' screamed Jack, tears streaming down his face. 'No! You've got to save him!'

Jack wailed, but the sound coming out of him didn't feel like his. He embraced his big brother, held his lifeless body to his chest and slowly rocked him.

The kingfisher flitted back over the river, causing a shadow to streak over Jack, black like the colour flooding his heart.

The riverbank dissolved and Jack found himself back in the present, in a room filled with spiders. He screamed.

Tattie still held his hand. Jack's skin was clammy and he felt as though he was going to be sick.

Harcus stared at him. 'You remember now?'

Jack nodded.

Tattie handed him his handkerchief and Jack blew his nose, wiped his tear-stained cheeks.

'But it doesn't have to be like this,' said Harcus. 'You don't have to lose him. Does he?' he asked Araine.

Araine smiled – another expression that didn't reach her eyes – and held out the heart-shaped diamond to the two boys. 'Jack, it does not have to end like this. You want a chance to see Matthew again, don't you? Tattie wishes to see Priss too.'

Tattie reached out and touched the diamond and Jack felt the energy pulsate through the room. 'Don't you want to see Matthew again?' he asked Jack.

'Complete the triangle, Jack,' said Araine.

Jack stared at them. He knew this was evil, that Araine was not to be trusted; he could still feel the fear from being paralysed by the spiders, and Araine clawing through his mind.

But Matthew.

All the grief that Jack had needed to keep locked up came pouring out. If there was a chance to see his brother again, surely he should take it?

'All you have to do is touch the diamond, Jack. The three of us are all half-lives with one foot in this world and the other in the next. Then my power will return, and you will have your brother back.'

Tattie and Araine held the diamond out to him, their hands leaving a gap for his.

He looked at Harcus, who gave him a wavering smile. He could see the terror in Harcus's eyes but also the longing. If Jack touched the diamond, they'd all get their loved ones back.

Jack had one moment of hesitation when he thought he heard Matthew telling him to stop, to run, but that was just his fear talking. Jack desperately wanted to hear Matthew's true voice. He grabbed the diamond, and Araine moaned as the room exploded into bright white light.

Jack blinked and blinked and, when he could see once more, he had to blink again, to make sure his eyes weren't playing tricks on him. 'Matthew, is that you?'

Standing before him was his brother, tall, strong, exactly the same as he had been the last time Jack saw him, just fainter now.

He ran into his brother's arms as Tattie cried out excitedly for his pigtailed sister, Priss, and dashed to her.

As he was hugging Matthew, Jack opened his eyes and saw a girl in an old-fashioned dress, so faint he could barely make her out. Her voice was quiet and rasping.

'Araine, what have you done?' she whispered.

Then Harcus erupted into pure rage, wrenching over the table, smashing lamps.

'Where's my sister? Where's Lucie? You promised me she'd come back!'

Chapter Fifteen

Now

The lift clanks as it heads down, deep into the bowels of the theatre.

'You sure this is safe?' I ask William, and he shrugs but gives a wide grin at the same time. I don't know whether I can trust him, but I do know I need to find out more from him.

'Can't believe Gift wouldn't come with us,' says Nikesh who I can't see and can only hear as they're shoved under William's armpit and crammed behind me at the back of the lift. Even though it's big enough to transport scenery, two Free Spirits, a Mean Machine and William make the lift feel very small.

I can't believe it either. Even with Nikesh asking Gift to come with us, she wasn't having any of it. It wasn't like I was going to plead. If that's her choice, so be it. My voice in my head is stronger than I feel. Gift has never chosen to do something I haven't done since we were tiny and became friends when our mams met at toddler group at the Arts Centre. She's been by my side constantly since Grandad died. Even if she doesn't always completely understand how I feel, she's there and she tries.

Now she's not.

The lift dings and comes to a halt. Its doors, as large as those on a truck, split open in the middle and pull apart. The smell of damp immediately hits my nostrils. It's cold, no heating down here. We all hang back.

'Does anyone believe in ghosts?' whispers Nikesh.

I think of the dog, the note from Jack, and I don't answer.

William steps out and clicks a switch on the wall. Ahead, a string of bare bulbs trails along the curved brick ceiling, a bit too far apart, leaving shadowy spaces in between – spaces where nothing is quite as it seems and it feels as if something could be lurking. The ground is silty, damp enough for my Mean Machine to leave tracks when I pull out of the lift.

'Where are we?' I ask.

'The whole of Cawlington is built on underground tunnels,' says William, waving us out of the lift and stomping ahead. 'We call them the catacombs. It was once the place where people buried their dead. The bones are long gone now. Imagine it like a cobweb with us in the centre.'

'A cobweb?' I brush my arms and face repeatedly. 'A cobweb with spiders in it?'

'You're fixated on *spiders* not bones? Spooky!' cries Nikesh at the same time as the lift closes behind us with a clunk, and we both scream.

William walks on down the tunnel.

Catacombs. That's a horror-story word.

The lift clanks its way back up, and I realize there's no escape, nowhere to go but to follow William. We didn't tell anyone where we were going. My mam would have a massive go at us if she knew. Must remember to tell Nikesh not to accidentally grass when she picks us up.

I scoot on, speeding up in the dark parts where the bulbs don't reach and shadows loom, and catch up with Nikesh. William plods onwards, his shadow lengthening and shortening as he passes the bulbs.

'Did you have any idea this existed?' I ask Nikesh when I reach them.

'Nope,' they say, looking absolutely furious that they're having to admit to not knowing something. 'How was this beneath us all those years without any of us knowing?'

'They were blocked off!' calls William over his shoulder. 'Too dangerous. You know, after, well . . .' He trails off.

'After what?' asks Nikesh. 'Is it something to do with the fire?'

William just grunts. He stops being his open self and refuses to answer any of their questions. I can see the sadness in his slumped shoulders as Nikesh interrogates him, and suddenly I recognize myself in him. William has lost someone he loved too.

I think of the pain losing Grandad caused me, and I wonder if I look like that too, if other people can tell. I try not to think about it and stare at the roof of the tunnel instead. It's green and mossy in parts, tiny little yellow flowers growing on it.

I tune back in to find Nikesh in full lecture mode with William: they've obviously failed to get any information out of him, and they're showing off instead.

'Lots of the crews were out-of-work sailors, hence the no-whistling rule backstage.'

'Is there such a rule?' I ask.

'Don't you remember Gift constantly getting told off for it?'

'Oh, yeah,' I say. 'But I thought that was just because it was annoying.'

'True,' says Nikesh, 'but also a superstition, with good cause. Most superstitions and ghost stories come from facts, and sailors used whistling as a cue to raise or lower ropes. So hearing a whistle in the theatre might mean the entire rig was about to be unknotted and drop on your head.'

'Ouch,' I say.

I have a sudden feeling, like a sparkle shining inside, of Grandad being beside me and his heart beating in time with mine, and I whip my head round, sure he'll be standing there.

My heart breaks all over again when he's not. When will it stop hurting? Why did Jack send me that horrible invitation? Even though it's obviously a bad joke that I don't understand, it's given me the tiniest glimmer of hope. And that's unbearable.

When I turn back round, William is staring at me. 'You OK? You've gone very pale. You miss him terribly, don't you?'

I nod my head.

William returns my nod, then moves quickly down the tunnel.

Hold on a second – how did he know about Grandad?

'Seen these?' asks Nikesh, squatting on the floor.

'Budge your big head out the road so I can actually see,' I say to Nikesh, and they shuffle out of the way. I do a big sniff to suck in my tears. 'Is that –?'

Nikesh interrupts me. 'The logo on Jack's T-shirt.'

Not just Jack's T-shirt. My *invitation too!*

Carved into every other stone slab is a triangle with a heart in the centre and blobs on each of the corners. I'm about to tell Nikesh everything when they yell 'Spiders!' and wiggle their fingers in my face and then dash after William. They both disappear out of sight as the tunnel bends.

I take a moment to compose myself, then hurry after them.

'Hello?' I call at the huge closed double doors that I reach on the left-hand side. The tunnel runs straight as far as the eye can see, so they must have gone in there.

I notice the door handle in the shape of a little brass fist, and I do the only thing you can do in a situation like this. I give it a fist bump, and the door slowly opens in front of me.

My mouth drops open.

The room inside is like a box with shiny white walls, really modern and angular, apart from the floor, which is still the smooth stone with just three of those triangle symbols.

This space can't exist here, in these old tunnels, can it?

I can feel my throat dry up as creepiness crawls all over me. Something else to add to the big stash of 'what on earth is happening here?' clues that I can't understand or piece together.

William and Nikesh are inside, looking at the theatre models encased in glass domes that sit on top of white plinths of differing heights, one on each.

Who made them all? The mysterious Harcus who William was talking about before, when I showed him mine?

I go over to them, making sure that I turn the dial for my speed right down slow. I don't want to ram into anything.

There are beautiful theatres, some made of cardboard. I feel a bit embarrassed about mine with the wonky bits I did.

I head to one in pale greens and yellows. When I peer over the top of its dome, I can see the way it's been put together and that you can slide backdrops for different scenes into hidden slots at the sides. The one currently in place is for *Cinderella*, the kitchen where the prince gets them all to try on the glass slipper, and then lying next to it is the backdrop for the royal ball. The characters are two-dimensional, made of card too and on strips so you can push them along channels from the side. Grandad told me they were really popular toys in the Victorian era, and this looks like an original!

I wonder if this place is some sort of museum. But why would it be all the way down here? And how is it so neat when the theatre has just opened and there's bits still cordoned off upstairs? Why would this be a priority to build and finish?

I glide past a simple tent with acrobats outside. Then there are architectural models, which I'm guessing were used for the theatre we're now underneath, the building that stole the precious spot of my beloved Arts Centre.

Each model is dated. I find the oldest one, then look at them in chronological order, the design becoming more refined with each model until it's an exact miniature version of what we saw outside.

There's an empty space in the roof just to the side of the water tower on one of the earlier models, as if whoever made it wasn't sure what it was to be used for. Then in the later models that space is missing, well, not missing: it's just that the walls are no longer there and it's simply an empty roof. I wonder what it was supposed to be? The lowest level shown on the models is the space under the stage; the tunnels we're in and this room don't appear.

Then finally there's a model way bigger than all the rest and it's not finished yet. It's like a palace rather than a theatre.

Nikesh runs from dome to dome, *ooh*ing and *aah*ing. They're a nightmare in a museum when I want to stop and admire the detail on something and they want to take in everything in one go.

I get to William who is standing by an empty plinth. The only one in the whole room.

'Look,' he says. 'I think your theatre must be made for this space, the final piece of the puzzle!'

Something happens when he says that and I get that feeling, the one that Mam describes wrong and says someone's opened her coffin, like when I thought Grandad was behind me, and when I saw the dog from the minibus.

'Someone walk over your grave?' asks Nikesh, startling me and making me jump.

I laugh them off, and when they look away I peer over my shoulder, just in case.

'You feel it too?' asks William.

'Don't know what you mean,' I say abruptly, and he turns away, disappointed. I didn't mean to lie, I think to myself, and wish William hadn't looked so hurt.

My breathing comes faster and I can't hold all my thoughts together. My head is whirling and the walls are too bright. I can't focus.

'Who made these?' I ask William as a peace offering. I want to know, and him talking will give me a chance to calm myself down.

William carefully takes my box out of the basket and places it on the floor so that he can take the model out of it safely.

'We don't know who made the original models – that's a mystery all of its own. But the later ones? My dear friends – Harcus, his sister Lucie, Jack and Snod.'

I move round to the other side of the plinth so that I can lift up the glass dome.

Hold on a sec, I think to myself. *Did William just say Snod, as in Snod's Edge, my wooden man?* My mind races as I try to hold everything in my head all at once.

'Watch where you're going!' William shouts at Nikesh who is walking backwards rapidly towards me. William grabs the dome out of my hands before I drop it, as Nikesh flips over my handlebars and sprawls on the floor.

I check that Nikesh is OK, but they ignore me, their gaze caught by my theatre on the other side of the plinth.

'I thought you'd made our Arts Centre,' they say to me. 'That's what Ed Red was building.'

'Well, yes, it is!' I say. 'Obviously. Did you just squash it?'

I gasp too when William lifts the model up and places it on the plinth so that I can see it as well.

'That's not my theatre,' I say. 'I didn't make that.'

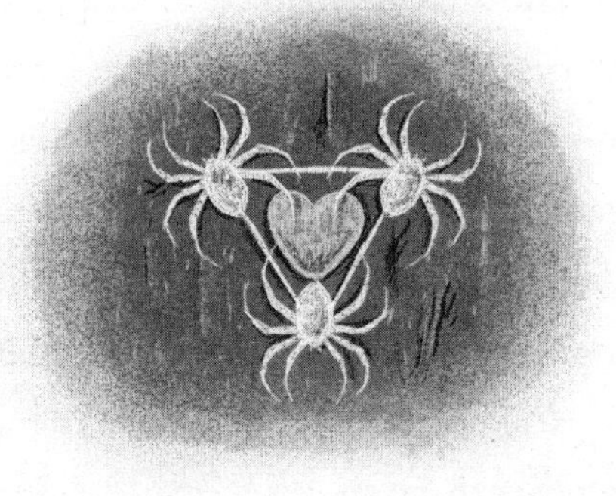

Chapter Sixteen

Way Back When

Araine and Harcus watched from the wings of the Machiavelli Theatre in York as the now-sensational and world-famous clairvoyant Lucie Lightfoot took her final bow and walked towards them with a bouquet of roses. Ten years had passed since they first came to York as wide-eyed children. Harcus now towered over both women.

'Lord MacVillain says there were people from *America* here to see you tonight, and that's *really* far away,' said Harcus as Lucie came over to them.

'It *is* really far!' said Lucie, giving him a squeeze on the cheek. 'And don't let Lord Machiavelli catch you calling him that!'

'Everyone does,' said Harcus, scowling.

'Well, we don't – he's good to us!' said Lucie.

'Not as good as he could be,' muttered Araine as she trailed after Lucie and Harcus towards her dressing room. There was a playbill of Lucie on the wall, an enormous black-and-white sketched image of her, a tight hat covering her forehead, beads dripping down from it, and her big soulful eyes looking out.

COME AND SEE MADAM LUCIE LIGHTFOOT AND HER INCREDIBLE CHANNELLING ABILITIES. WITNESS HER COMMUNE WITH THE SPIRIT WORLD!

Araine scratched her nail right through one of Lucie's eyes.

It was all well and good for Lucie, being wined and dined, taken out for champagne, people wanting her autograph, telling her their secrets. Araine was sure they were slipping Lucie jewels that she didn't tell Araine about.

Then there was Araine's humdrum life. Going back and forth to Attercop, always travelling in those uncomfortable stagecoaches filled with people coughing and burping and picking their noses. And chickens! Because Lucie insisted they didn't have enough money for a personal carriage. It was Araine doing the work!

Designing the shows, finding their next rich victim and collecting all the information about them.

And Nora was being grumpy with Araine for constantly summoning her for information and then leaving her again; she was no fun any more. Araine shook her head to try to rid herself of what Nora had said to her when she'd last made the journey home to get new information from her.

They'd sat in the cool quiet of the church and Araine could tell something was wrong. Nora always fell silent when something was troubling her.

'Out with it, Nora,' said Araine. 'I've come all this way to spend time with you and you're silent and moping.'

'To spend time with me? You do little else but pester me for facts about some new rich victim, and then you leave. I'm lonely!'

'How can you possibly be lonely with all those dead people to talk to? And you've got Lucie's mam!'

'It's not like having friends. You've trapped me half in this world and half in the next.'

'I've *trapped* you – that is what you think? I'm keeping you alive!'

'No, Araine. I'm a ghost who's imprisoned on earth. And you're living a half-life. Not fully in the real world. You're so set on revenge and money that you're not living properly, making the most of everything that your precious life has to offer you. How about travelling the world, or falling in love?'

Araine stared at the stone floor, at the symbols that had started it all.

'So you want me to leave you?' she asked. 'You cannot be saying that.'

Nora was quiet.

'Nora, you can't mean it!'

'Araine, you have to let us go.'

Araine hadn't told Lucie and Harcus that their mam wanted to leave too, to cross completely over to the other side. Nora was lonely? Well, Araine was too, so her sister had better get used to it! Araine was also jealous and angry. This had not been the plan. Lord Machiavelli was getting even richer as a result of Araine's hard work.

This wasn't revenge. Lucie was content to become one of them, cavorting with the rich folk and leaving Araine behind! How had Araine just stumbled blindly along with it? How had she not seen clearly the way she was being used by Lucie?

She held the diamond in her hand and it dug into her. Nora, Lucie, Harcus – all of them getting what they wanted, but who was thinking of Araine? Who was making sure that people like Lord Machiavelli paid for what they had done? No more playing along: it was time to bring these people to their knees.

Araine stormed into the dressing room, which was full of flowers from Lucie's admirers, and slammed the door behind her. 'Now see here, I have had enough!'

Lucie looked shocked and Harcus took a sidestep towards the door.

'You've been delaying matters long enough. We know where he keeps his riches, so we steal them and leave MacVillain destitute. Then we return to Attercop and open our own theatre!'

'But he's been so kind to us!" exclaimed Lucie. "It's a good life here, is it not? Harcus, you like it, don't you?'

'Lucie!' yelled Araine, frustration bubbling up in her. 'He's kind to *you* because you earn him money. How much do you think he's getting every night while he just pays us a meagre wage? We'll never afford to leave at this rate! And have you forgotten what he did to us? He left our families to die!'

Lucie's voice was small. 'Of course not.' Then she became bolder. 'You're just jealous that you're not the famous one.'

Araine's face burned. 'You have forgotten where you came from and why we're here! You don't go back to

Attercop any more. People have tried desperately to rebuild their lives, people you worked in the fields with!'

Araine saw Lucie shudder at the memory. 'It's no use pretending you don't come from there: it's our place, our home. We owe it to the people in Attercop to make life better!' she shouted, a new plan forming in her mind, tinged with the jealousy she was embarrassed that Lucie had seen.

'Did you know that MacVillain has refused them any aid to ease their suffering *and* he's put the rents up? They can barely afford what it is now. Just because you can't see it, doesn't mean it's not happening. Lucie, people are starving!' Then Araine's voice became softer, sly. 'And your mam misses you. When was the last time you saw her? She's growing so faint I can barely see her.'

'You didn't tell me that!' replied Lucie. 'Harcus, did you know?'

'No!' said Harcus. 'Of course not. I would have gone back immediately. She's all right, though, isn't she?'

Araine shook her head at him in disgust.

Lucie stared at her with pleading eyes. 'But Lord Machiavelli is good to us, and we're safe here. Araine, I don't want to go back to that life.'

'I'm not asking you to. We can take this life with us and make things better for everyone!'

Lucie looked unsure.

This was Araine's moment. 'With every private seance you do, he pockets the cash. Not us. He killed Nora and your mam!'

'Well, not personally –'

'Lucie! Have you heard your own voice? That's it – come with me.' Araine grabbed Lucie's arm and started dragging her to the door. 'It's about time you listened to what your so-called friends say about you when you're not there.'

'Is there really any need for this?' asked Lucie. She was squeezed behind an ornate table with a potted plant on top, in the corner of the theatre bar, with Harcus and Araine crammed in beside her.

'Here they come,' said Araine quietly.

'Oh, Lady Maplethorpe!' whispered Lucie. 'She says we can spend the summer in her –'

'Shhh, just listen!'

The three of them kept hidden as York's finest made their way into the bar after the show, Lord Machiavelli clicking his fingers for champagne to be brought to him and his fawning cronies.

'Did you see the way she held her head tonight?' said Lady Maplethorpe. 'I've noticed her watching me, trying to copy my posture. You're either born with it or you're not!'

The ladies around her laughed and fanned their faces while they reached for the champagne that the butler had discreetly placed on their table.

Araine watched Lucie's face begin to crumple.

'She's not talking about me. She can't be!' Lucie whispered.

'Heard the news of more sickness sweeping the land, old boy?' said one of the men in evening attire to Lord Machiavelli.

'It won't reach here,' Lord Machiavelli replied. 'Too much money. It's a poor person's disease!' He guffawed and everyone laughed.

'Leave them all to die, I say. Good riddance!' said Lady Maplethorpe.

Araine could see Lucie mouthing the words, as though she was trying to work out if they could possibly have another meaning.

'What worth do they have anyway?' Lady Maplethorpe continued.

'Less than the price of my new cow!' said Lord Machiavelli.

'Or my new earrings,' she added, playing with the huge sapphires in her ears and letting out a tinkling laugh.

Lucie burst into sobs and ran from the bar.

In the dressing room, she grabbed the flowers from the table, tore down the prints of her face. 'I've been such an idiot!'

'No!' Harcus said, and ran to hug his sister.

'I thought they –'

Araine rushed to hug her too, feeling Lucie's tears soak into her dress as she held her tight against her. 'They're just very good at what they do best.'

'What's that?' said Lucie in a muffled sob.

'Using people while pretending to be their friends.'

Lucie stood up straight and wiped her eyes. 'Never again!' she cried, grasping Araine's and Harcus's hands in hers. Harcus and Araine joined hands and they formed their triangle once more.

'Free Spirits,' Lucie announced. 'We're going home.'

Two years later, the villagers gathered for the opening of Attercop's very first theatre. Lucie had painstakingly built the miniature that they modelled their theatre on, taking all the best bits from theatres they had visited, to create their masterpiece.

Araine, Lucie and Harcus had blackmailed Lord Machiavelli and Lady Maplethorpe, threatening to reveal their darkest secrets to the world, leaving them penniless. Araine had been surprised and delighted at how much pleasure Lucie took from it. They used the ill-gotten money to convert the spiders' church into a theatre, with the villagers' blessing. Based in Attercop, there would be no more need for carriage rides to see the ghosts: they could be right here with the three of them.

They emblazoned the triangle symbol on the front of the theatre, knowing they owed their new-found wealth to the ghosts to whom the spiders had connected them, even though the spiders had never intended for it to last this long, nor go so far.

'Who will come *here*?' asked Lucie.

'Once they see the theatre's name, we'll be inundated with audiences from far and wide.'

'What do you mean?' asked Lucie.

Araine nodded at the farmhand next to her, who untied a ribbon with a flourish, and the velvet banner that covered the theatre's name dropped to the ground, revealing gold and red paint on a huge board declaring the building the Lightfoot Theatre.

Lucie gasped. 'You named it after me and Harcus!'

'And our mam,' said Harcus, smiling.

'We're going to be so happy here,' said Araine as she touched the diamond in her pocket.

She had never told Lucie and Harcus that when she'd been coming back to Attercop for all those years, she'd refused the spiders every time they'd pleaded with her to return the diamond. Eventually she grew more powerful and had them under her control. They were hers to command now.

No one would ever again tell her what to do, or when or how to do it. Never.

Araine took the diamond out of her pocket and attached it to the long chain that hung around her neck. It was time to step completely into the dark.

Chapter Seventeen

Then

The dining hall was crowded and noisy. A man wearing a donkey's head was ladling out soup from a giant pot as he attempted to prevent an entire ravenous theatre troupe from going hungry. Snod was trying to keep everyone in an orderly queue and failing.

Jack was sitting at the longest table with Tattie, and Rex was underneath, his cold, wet nose nudging Jack's knee in the hope of a morsel or two. The rest of the room was packed with performers, all huddled up at their tables. Even though Jack and Tattie had lots of room on theirs, no one else sat with them. It was as if the troupe were keeping their distance on purpose. It had been three weeks since they'd been reunited with their ghostly siblings and had met Araine's ghost sister, Nora. That was the last time they'd seen Harcus.

Jack screwed up his face: he couldn't get the sound of Harcus's roar out of his ears when Harcus realized Araine had tricked him and Lucie wasn't coming back.

'Do you think they're scared of us?' Jack asked Tattie as he looked at the rest of the troupe and shoved his bowl to one side.

'You not eating that?' said Tattie.

You could never get him to answer anything when food was around. When Jack shook his head, Tattie grabbed the bowl and shovelled the soup into his mouth. He dropped Jack's bread on the floor for Rex.

Once Jack saw Tattie had finished eating and would be able to concentrate, he said, 'Don't you think it's strange that we're only allowed to see Priss and Matthew when Araine is around? Surely we could have time with them without her. I always feel that she's listening in to everything we say.'

Tattie shrugged. 'I'm just happy I get to see Priss at all. I mean, she is dead!'

'Shhh,' said Jack as he clapped his hand over Tattie's mouth. 'No one is allowed to know! That's one of the rules.'

'There are lots of rules,' said Tattie. 'I thought talking to ghosts would be more fun. And rehearsals are hard work.'

Jack had thought it would be wonderful seeing his brother again, and it was! But not the way Araine only gave them ten minutes together after each rehearsal as a reward if they did everything right, especially with her keeping watch with her beady eyes and battalion of spiders.

The voice in his head that had told him to run hadn't quietened. If anything, it was louder than ever, and he was sure his brother was trying to tell him something . . . if only Araine would turn her back for one moment.

Tattie put the bowl on the floor for Rex to lick. In less than two seconds, it was clean and Rex had soup on his ear that was just out of reach of his tongue. He kept leaping round and round to try to get at it. Jack laughed at him and wiped the gloopy smear off the dog's ear and held out his fingers for Rex to lick.

'Tattie,' said Jack quietly. 'Do you think this is all right?'

'Priss and Matthew being dead?' asked Tattie, looking him directly in the eye. 'Or what Araine did to Harcus? No, I do not think it's all right. You shut it out somehow, but I had to live with that pain for months all alone, with no hope, before Araine found me. And then years of waiting until we rebuilt the theatre and found you.'

'Years?'

'She knew you would come. I had to watch her wither and fade. She used all her power to keep me the same age.' Tattie bows his head in shame. 'She said you'd trust me more that way. She can't stay alive long any more without the power of the diamond: she has to hibernate. That's why she needed the two of us half-lives, a Lightfoot and a Redwood, to activate it again. And now she has . . .' Tattie trailed off and Jack could see how scared he was.

'What do you think she's going to do?' whispered Jack.

'Well, it's none of our business, is it?' said Tattie, his happy face painted back on. 'I've got Priss, and that's all I care about. And you've got Matthew!'

Jack nodded and smiled. Rex wiggled on his back for a belly rub. Tattie was right: he was living in this wonderful theatre, he had a new best friend and a dog – and his brother was back from the dead. What more could anyone ask for?

But it didn't stop the feeling lurking inside him that touching the diamond had been the very worst thing he had ever done.

Chapter Eighteen

Now

Nikesh, William and I all peer very closely at Grandad's theatre that William has placed on the plinth, which is not the theatre he'd made.

Not any more.

The only thing that's remotely the same is the weathervane on top, and Grandad didn't even make that. This time there's no denying, thanks to the red-and-gold ruff and the little white eyebrow, that it's the same dog that came leaping out of the stage door earlier.

'And you've never seen that dog before today?' asks William for the second time, as he places the model on the plinth. Then he pulls a packet of butter mints out of his green beard and offers them to me and Nikesh.

'Never mind the dog,' I say as I unwrap a sweet and pop it into my mouth. 'I've never seen it before today. And I've *never* seen this theatre! Everyone has the same name, and you know what's going on and you're not telling us!'

William just shrugs.

'A shrug is not an answer!'

'Maybe the box was swapped?' says Nikesh.

'But why would someone do that?' I ask, and throw up my arms.

The theatre is beautiful and far more intricate than anything I could ever make. It's so good it would have stumped Grandad too. I wish he could have seen it. I wish so hard I think my heart is going to burst open, and I feel William place his big hand on my shoulder. The thing that grabs your attention is right in the centre of the model. Growing through the stage is the most stunning cherry tree in full bloom.

'How did anyone come up with the idea for this?' I ask, shaking my head. 'It can't be real, can it?'

'Let me have a closer look,' says Nikesh. They budge William out of the way and stick their head right up close to the tiny tree.

I wish Gift was with us. It feels really important for her to be here: the Free Spirits together. I shudder as I think about our name on that poster of Araine. All these names interconnecting. Gift would have some good ideas, and hugs.

'Ah, there! Look here,' Nikesh says to me. 'Just there.' They haven't been focused on the tree but on the box that's stage right, where there is elaborate scrollwork with tiny writing. 'You see it too?'

I read out loud. '*Designed by Jack Redwood, William Tattie Lightfoot, Snod's Edge, Harcus and Rex – Our Escape*.' Just below the phrase is a blurry number. 'Eighteen eighty-something?'

'Eighty-three, I think,' says Nikesh. 'The year it was made?'

I say their names out loud again. 'Jack Redwood, William Tattie Lightfoot, Snod's Edge, Harcus and Rex.' I slowly look up at William. Nikesh stares at him too.

'You related?' Nikesh asks, crossing their arms.

'Sort of,' says William. He coughs on his sweet and turns away.

'Sort of – that's all you can say? My head is going to explode. You need to give me answers, now!'

'Hettie, you OK?' says Nikesh. 'It's just a name – maybe it's a coincidence.'

I wish I'd told Nikesh everything. 'It's not just a name . . . It's *all* the names! The mixed-up theatres. I didn't make the weathervane that's exactly the same as the dog we saw. William is hiding something, and everyone's called Free Spirits, and –'

'And what?'

And I got an invitation telling me I can see my dead grandad again.

My throat cracks and I can't say that bit out loud.

'Hold on!' I shout.

'What is it?' asks Nikesh.

'There's more writing on the weathervane.'

'There's a message!' Nikesh cries out.

'Well, don't keep us in suspenders,' I say, and William laughs and it makes me smile even though I don't want to.

'That's a Shirl special,' says Nikesh.

I'm about to explain when a gust of wind blows through the door we came in and slams it shut.

'We're trapped!' shrieks Nikesh.

The glass domes covering the other theatres all shake and begin to sing, high-pitched and ghostly. I know I should be scared, but something about this feels familiar, like it's echoing through time, and I want to know what's going to happen next. We stand still and silent. Barely breathing.

Suddenly the lights in the room go out. I scream. It's pitch-black.

'Are you two OK?' we hear William ask, his voice shaky.

I nod, then realize it's pointless because he can't see me. There's a loud click from the opposite side of the room from the door, but no light comes on.

'Did you hear that?' says Nikesh. No one replies.

Next comes a creaking noise, slow at first, like the ratchet sound you can make in your throat, then it gathers speed and gets louder.

'Who's there?' wails Nikesh, and grabs my arm, poking me in the ear first.

'Look,' I say, and point towards the sound. There's a glow in the wall, three sides of a tall rectangle, like light is seeping round the edges of a door. It creaks and opens a little more, and then the noise stops.

'Can you see what's there?' I whisper.

'Nope,' says Nikesh. 'And I really bloomin' don't want to.'

'I thought you weren't afraid of ghosts?' I say.

'I'm not,' they say. 'Because ghosts aren't real.'

But in the shadowy light from the open door they can see my hand and they reach for it. Nikesh's hands are clammy, and mine are too. I make a shaky move towards the door, but Nikesh holds me back.

'You want to go in there, where the ghosts are sending us?' they squeak in a high-pitched voice.

'No!' I say, nearly crying. 'I don't want to be brave!'

'You have to,' says William from behind us, and he steps towards the door before I've got a chance to shout at him to stop.

He pushes it open.

The sudden light makes me blink rapidly, and when I can see again William has vanished through it.

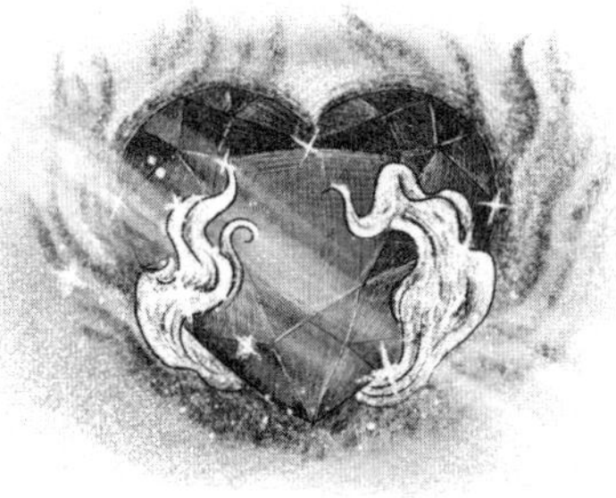

Chapter Nineteen

Way Back When

'We need to talk,' said Araine, closing the door to Lucie's workshop behind her. Over the past months, Lucie had been spending more and more time in there when she wasn't onstage, building her intricate miniatures.

Araine could hear the stagecoaches outside filling with passengers travelling back to York and Newcastle, those who couldn't find lodgings in the village. Not village any more but town: Attercop had grown, merging with Cawlington, and was full of hotels, and pubs, and shops selling trinkets for tourists. The Lightfoot Theatre had ensured its growth.

'Can we talk later?' answered Lucie. 'This is a really intricate bit, and I need this to calm me down. You never understand just how trying it is, performing under those lights, with all those people watching –'

'Well, you never let me understand –'

'Oh, jealous again, are we, Araine?' Lucie snipped off a bit of metal. 'Go on then. You try your hand. Please do – you know I don't want to do this any more! Oh, I don't feel too well,' said Lucie suddenly, dropping her cutters to the floor. Harcus dashed to her side.

Araine looked at Lucie. She did appear pale. So did Harcus, for that matter.

'Why can't we just cancel tomorrow's performance?' asked Lucie as he mopped her brow.

Three little fluffy jumping spiders with huge eyes crawled on to Lucie's outstretched arm and snuggled into her. The spiders gave Araine a wide berth: they were too scared of who she'd become, their lost diamond glittering round her neck. If it wasn't for the promise they'd made to her mother, they would have finished all this long ago. But spider promises are as strong as silk.

'What kind of attitude is that?' shouted Araine. 'You're always complaining and whining!'

'Araine, Lucie has got a point,' said Harcus. 'She's exhausted. It's not as if we need the money. I can't remember the last time we had a day off, did something together. It'll be like the good old days. We could go to the river, take bread and feed the ducks, just as we used to.'

'The good old days? What was good about them? When Nora was alive! When your mam was! When we were scratching around for enough food to eat while Lord Machiavelli ruled over us all! How many times do I have to tell you?' said Araine as she stabbed one of Lucie's paintbrushes at Harcus, emphasizing each word. 'It's not about money!'

'Well, what is it about then?' said Harcus. 'You finished him off – the game is up and you won!'

Araine growled. 'It's about making them pay, making them *all* pay. As long as there are people ruling over others, starving them, I will not rest, and neither should you,' she said.

'But look at what we're wearing, how we live. Aren't we the same as them now?' asked Lucie.

Araine screeched and Harcus clapped his hands over his ears.

'How dare you say that? We have brought fame and glory to this town. Our little village! The place you didn't want to come home to.' As Araine stormed out of the workshop in a flurry of black satin and lace covered in golden thread spiders, she snarled, 'Hurry up, Lucie. You've got a private seance to perform.'

'I think it is us who are paying,' whispered Lucie, gently placing the spiders on the table and then rubbing her temples as Harcus helped her up and out of the door.

Another year passed. The arguments grew less as Lucie's strength faded and Araine's power increased and she stalked round the town, people scattering before her, scared of the look in her eye and the way cobwebs fell to dust as she passed. Yes, she'd brought riches to Attercop, but a darkness had come with her too; they could feel it, even if they couldn't name it.

Nora and Mrs Lightfoot became paper-thin, mere wafts of ghosts that were nearly invisible. Araine was scared. What if her power was failing? What if the spiders had been right and the diamond wasn't meant to be used like this? She blustered through so that no one could know what she was thinking. It couldn't come crashing down, not the wealth she'd amassed, not the power. She stroked the diamond at her neck, rallying herself before she went into the dressing room. She *would not* lose this power.

Or her sister, of course. She couldn't lose Nora – it's what all this was about after all: keeping her sister close. Yes, she told herself, she was doing it all for Nora.

But what was Nora doing for her?

Sometimes flashes of Araine's old self appeared in her mind, and then the diamond sparkled and she'd touch it – and the old Araine would be smothered by pure rage and the lust for power.

She took a deep breath and opened the door.

'That was an excellent session!' she said, making her way through yet another mountain of flowers that had arrived in Lucie's dressing room.

Araine read the note on a huge vase of lilies and said, 'Lucie, Lord Foster requests another appointment with you. Make sure you ask your mam to find out all she can first. I'm sure you'll be written into his will!'

'No,' said Lucie quietly.

Araine whirled round to face her. '*No?*'

'No. I'm not doing it any more. I'm tired. Have you seen the way the villagers look at us? At you? They're scared of us.'

'Of us! Idiots, peasants – we're the ones bringing them their good fortune!'

'Have you listened to yourself, Araine? Who have you become? We should never have pulled down the church and built this theatre. It's evil. Like you! That diamond has consumed you. No, that's wrong: *you've* consumed *it*! This quest for revenge, for power – it's not the person you really are!'

Araine pretended to look hurt. 'Not this *poor me* story again. Look at everything you have. Look around you. We built this from nothing!'

'Not nothing though, was it? Everything comes at a cost – you just can't see it. Not any more. Your heart is clouded. My mam is so faint I can barely hear her. Look, Araine, look!' Lucie held up her hands.

As she twisted them in the candlelight, Araine could almost see through them.

'I feel like I'm living a half-life,' said Lucie, pleading with her old friend. 'I want to leave the dead behind. Live fully here and now. We have everything we ever wanted, could ever need, more in fact! We must put the diamond back, Araine. It is time. Harcus wants that too.'

Araine jerked her head up to stare at Harcus who didn't quite have the courage to speak, but simply nodded.

'We were only ever meant to be given a chance to say goodbye,' said Lucie. 'Not use it like this! Something bad is happening to me. I can feel it. My skin is all but transparent!'

Araine picked up the vase of lilies and dashed it against the wall, splinters of glass flying across the dressing room. One caught her cheek, but she felt no pain.

Harcus cowered and took a step backwards.

'Stay where you are! You were all happy to join with me to exact revenge.'

'I know, I know!' said Lucie. 'And don't you think we have that now? Lord Machiavelli is dead – he died with his name sullied – we have the theatre, and the town is thriving. We could be happy!'

'*Happy?*' spat Araine.

'We could finally say goodbye,' said Harcus. 'That's what they want.'

'*Who* wants?' said Araine in a cold voice, turning sharply to Harcus.

'The ghosts. Our mam,' said Harcus, and then he dropped his head and spoke just above a whisper. 'Nora.'

'What?' Araine snarled. 'Just because you are unhappy you're using my own sister against me?'

'Ask her,' said Lucie.

'I will!' cried Araine.

'She's just there.' Lucie pointed to a velvet chair in the corner of the dressing room.

A flash of shock and fear shot through the little bit left of the old Araine as she finally saw Nora the way Harcus and Lucie did. Their mam was standing behind Nora and was even more faint.

Araine could see that Harcus and Lucie were pale and worn, that holding on to the ghosts for all these years had faded them without the aid of the diamond that she wore.

The diamond that had cracked and snuffed out the last sliver of her own heart and replaced it with darkness.

There was always a price to pay.

'Hello, Nora,' she said, hugging her sister as Harcus and Lucie left with their mam.

'Ask her,' said Lucie at the door.

'Get out!' screamed Araine as the lamps' flames grew to the size of furnaces. 'Get out, get out, *get out*!'

Harcus and Lucie ran, spiders scuttling to get out of the way as the door slammed behind them, no one having touched it.

'Oh, Araine, what have you done?' asked Nora, still a little ghost girl with messy pigtails. 'Come and sit with me. Mam's really worried about you.'

It was hard to tell where Nora's edges were, she was so faded now. When Araine blinked, her sister almost disappeared.

'Why?' she snapped.

'It's heartbreaking watching you turn into someone else, some creature that scuttles and delights in causing pain. The diamond is eating you up. You have to put it back. I'm terrified of what will happen to you if you don't. I'm scared of you! My own big sister. Dad said you were meant to keep me safe, remember?'

Some far echo tugged at Araine's heart, but black swirls grew out of the diamond and swathed her like silk scarves. The theatre echoed and rumbled around them, doors slamming everywhere.

'It's time to let us go,' whispered Nora.

'Did Harcus persuade you to do this? He and Lucie have been –'

'You don't laugh any more, Araine. I loved the sound of your laugh! You need to find that again, and the only way you can do that . . .' said Nora without wavering, even as a tear ran down her cheek. 'The only way is by saying goodbye.'

Araine turned her head and refused to look at her little sister.

'It's killing Lucie and Harcus. Can't you see? They're disappearing in front of you! You're killing me!' pleaded Nora.

'You can't die. You're already dead,' said Araine with the faint hint of a smile.

'See,' said Nora, wriggling so Araine had to look at her. 'That smile. That smile needs to become a laugh, and it can't while you're so set on revenge. It's not even revenge any more – you're not doing this for me, for the village. It's all for you! You've got to let me go! I'm tired, Araine. I'm so very, very tired.'

'No!' cried Araine. 'Never!'

They were all working against her, trying to take control; they wanted the diamond for themselves – they weren't going to put it back! That was not going to happen: it was hers. Araine stormed out of the dressing room, leaving Nora calling after her, and marched out on to the stage.

She had a plan.

Chapter Twenty

Then

Jack headed for the undercroft, the area under the stage that was named after the old church that had once stood on this ground. He hoped that Harcus might finally be back, working on the traps and mechanisms for their show that evening. Surely he wouldn't miss that?

Jack turned a corner to find himself face to face with a cage full of wolves, and he couldn't contain his delight at seeing these magnificent creatures close up. All the wonders he got to marvel at, every single day, and he could share it all with Matthew. Wasn't that worth it? But when the rest of the troupe kept their distance, and he thought about Harcus . . .

Jack blamed such worries on being nervous. Even

though they'd rehearsed it, the show was going to feel so different with an actual audience.

He walked past one of the giant playbills advertising Araine Machiavelli's seances, but this time to be joined by her Free Spirits, her fellow ghostly half-lives. The triangle symbol with the heart and the spiders was emblazoned on Araine's forehead. SOLD OUT banners were stuck on the bills.

Jack had been fretting that he might have done something wrong in choosing to bring Matthew back, and that was why he really wanted to see Harcus, because the worry had grown from more than a prickle into something that was weighing him down.

The corridor opened up above Jack. He was standing beneath the area where the acrobats rehearsed. Tightropes criss-crossed the wooden vaulted ceiling. Platforms stuck out at various heights around the room with ladders reaching up to them. Jack couldn't fathom how on earth everything fitted into the theatre building.

All of a sudden a trapeze artist whooshed past so close that Jack could feel the breeze by his ear. The performer gracefully unfurled himself to thrust a note into Jack's hand, before swinging back up to the rafters.

Meet me in the catacombs. Harcus

‘Excellent!’ He was back!

Soon, Jack was making his way along the silted-up tunnel. He’d heard about the catacombs, walked past the entrance in one of the cellars many times, but had never been down here before. Not that he was scared. The lamp in his hand swayed as he walked, and it felt as though something could leap out at him just beyond the safety of its light. That ghosts were hidden in the shadows.

Ghosts? He barked out a laugh but its echo frightened him. He knew ghosts weren’t something to be scared of.

So why are my hands shaking?

He looked down. The triangle symbols were etched all over the smooth stone floor.

Jack wished he was back up in the warmth. It was cold down here and lately he’d been really struggling to feel anything close to a comfortable temperature. Maybe he was sickening with a fever? He found it difficult to hold on to time too. How long had he been here now? A few weeks? Six months?

Just when Jack thought he’d gone the wrong way and should turn back, the shadows got longer towards the left-hand side of the tunnel and then disappeared entirely as light came flooding out of a door with a brass fist for a handle.

Jack stepped inside a bright white room with lights of a sort that he had never seen before. A constant flame, no flickering.

He peered back outside to check, but the tunnel and room didn't seem to match: it was as if they'd been brought together from different places. From different times. The room was filled with plinths, each one of them holding a miniature theatre in a glass dome. Jack stood on his tiptoes, moving from plinth to plinth, until he stopped at the model of the theatre he was in now. A click and a creak made him look over to the opposite wall where a door had opened.

'In here!' called a familiar voice.

Jack went over and peered round the door.

'Don't look too disappointed,' Tattie said. 'I'm sure Harcus will be here soon.'

'Did you get an invitation too?' Jack was surprised to find that he was jealous.

Rex leaped over and licked Jack's leg, then thrust his giant head into his hand for a fuss. Jack took the moment to compose himself.

Tattie passed Jack a cup and dragged Rex off him, pointing the dog to his bed in the corner. 'Freshly brewed and strong. Looks like you need it!'

Jack stared at the walls. Tools hung from nails, and each tool had a painted outline to show where it belonged.

‘Everything neatly in its place,’ said Harcus in his booming voice as he entered the room. ‘I am sorry I’ve been absent, young ’uns. Is Araine treating you well?’

Jack didn’t know the polite answer to that because he couldn’t work out whose side Harcus was on. How could he pretend that they hadn’t seen him lose his temper in Araine’s room, and that he then vanished and left them behind?

‘Welcome to the catacombs. Araine has her velvet spider lair, but this workshop is mine. Actually, hopefully,’ said Harcus, putting his arm round Tattie’s and Jack’s shoulders, ‘*ours*.’

Jack smiled shyly at Harcus, and Tattie couldn’t hide the big smile that rushed all the way up from his feet to settle on his face. But Jack knew he should be wary. He couldn’t forget the scene in Araine’s room and the fact that Harcus had abandoned them.

‘What do you do here?’ asked Jack.

‘This,’ said Harcus, as he held out his arms, ‘is where both the magic *and* the miniatures are created.’ He laughed as though nothing had happened, and took a pair of round-nosed pliers off the wall, leaving their empty outline behind. ‘Here, every man needs a tool of his own. These used to belong to my sister. Keep them safe.’

Jack took the pliers. ‘Araine makes miniatures?’

A scowl crossed Harcus’s face. ‘My sister is not Araine.’

The pure venom in his voice frightened Jack. He'd never seen him like that before. Maybe he wasn't on Araine's side, but how could Jack be sure?

'I thought your name was Harcus Machiavelli?'

'Theatre is all smoke and illusion, Jack. Brother-and-sister acts are fashionable, so Araine needed a brother, and we stole our names from someone who had once wronged us to become just that. Without you two to power the diamond and be able to communicate with the ghosts, we had to hold seances the old-fashioned way – by lying! And Araine had to conserve her energy and mine, so she needed to hibernate for long stretches until we found you two.'

Tattie bumbled in as if he hadn't understood anything Harcus had said, and Jack was glad of it. He didn't like the look in Harcus's eyes.

'I'm glad you're back before the show,' said Tattie. 'It wouldn't have been right to use your ghost-glide without you. You make them, don't you? All the traps and tricks and mechanisms, like lights-up and all the others. That's my favourite, that is. The way the theatre is all dark and everyone is waiting, then the lights rise up out of the stage and everyone gasps. It's the signal for the magic to begin!'

'You made the ghost-glides we'll use tonight? When we pretend to be ghosts in the seance?' asked Jack, his blood running cold and his fingers turning to ice. When he held out his hand, he thought he could see the workbench through it, then he blinked and the illusion was gone.

Jack, he muttered to himself silently, *focus! You're doing this for Matthew, and you'll get to see him by yourself at the show, finally – Araine will be too busy performing to spy on us!*

Harcus brought over a working replica of the stage. The cut-out model showed the mechanisms underneath the stage. The trap for lights-up was there in miniature, with all the lamps on the wooden plinth that got hauled up on the pulley system to start every show.

'This is the section for the ghost-glide,' said Harcus, pointing to barrels, ropes and pulleys, and two ramps going in opposite directions. 'Sailors will be under there with you, heaving up.' He tugged a string to demonstrate how the pulleys worked.

'Not very scary,' said Jack.

'Imagine lights-up is extinguished except for one lamp so the stage is all gloomy and full of shadows. Then we fill the auditorium with smoke; the audience are already apprehensive and excited before they come in, they do half the job for us.' Harcus pulled the string a little more. 'As the rope is heaved, you and Tattie rise as ghosts from beneath the stage and the trapdoors open, looking like you're being raised up from the depths –'

'– of hell!' shrieked Tattie, then made a ghostly noise.

Jack jumped. 'Why do we have to do all this?' He waved his hand at the model. 'Surely the fact that we *can* talk to ghosts is enough. In fact, why doesn't Araine just use our ghosts?'

Harcus smiled. 'Smoke and mirrors, remember? The audience can't see or hear the ghosts. They need you. But most of all they want to be entertained. Give them the real story and it becomes too terrifying. Take away the illusion and no one would come. You, with your ghostly painted faces passing on what the ghosts tell you, are somewhere in between. The audience know it must be an illusion, but they can just about believe it to be real.'

Jack was going to ask Harcus about Lucie, and all the jumbled thoughts in his head about Matthew and Araine, but there were footsteps by the door. Snod burst through, carrying a basket of apples and cheese.

'Sustenance has arrived!' cried Harcus. 'Eat up, boys. I've much to teach you.'

Later that afternoon, Araine, Jack and Tattie – all wearing black costumes covered in stitched gold spiders – were sitting in the dressing room. Jack couldn't stop his leg bouncing and Tattie was unusually quiet.

They'd had their faces painted so that they glowed white.

'It's time!' she said. 'Aren't you excited by your first performance with an audience? To see your ghosts once more? I know I am!'

'Araine,' said Jack quietly, 'why can't we see them all the time? Why do you keep Priss and Matthew away from us?'

She whirled round to face him. 'Can't have too much of a good thing, can we, boy? Can't have you getting spoiled. Be a good lad and perform just how you've rehearsed, and you'll get ten minutes with them afterwards.'

'With you watch–'

Tattie kicked Jack in the shin and shook his head at him, desperately trying to make him shut up.

'I've given you a home, brought you back your brother, Tattie's sister. Everything I do for you and you want –' Araine stopped herself as the spiders carefully wound round her wrists and neck. 'It's just first-night nerves. I'll let you off for that. But you must learn how to be grateful to me, Jack. I could take all this away in a second.'

Could you? thought Jack, but kept his doubts inside. *The way I see it, you need us just as much as we need you.*

Araine marched them out of the room, prodding them along until they got backstage.

Jack could hear the audience behind the curtain and he felt sick as he thought of performing in front of them all. But he'd get a precious few moments with Matthew without Araine being right beside them, for the first time since Matthew came back. Jack had so much he wanted to ask his brother and so little time. He concentrated on working out which questions took priority.

Araine walked to the centre of the stage and took a seat at her square card table.

Harcus led Jack and Tattie into the undercroft below the stage.

To hell, thought Jack.

Tattie and Jack didn't speak to each other; they were too nervous. They'd rehearsed hard, laughing and joking, but with an audience above them their stomachs were tangled in knots. They were placed in position on opposite sides by the sailors who didn't look them in the eye and then retreated to manage the pulleys and winches. The smell of damp wood caught in Jack's throat. It was too warm and he struggled to breathe. His heart felt like it would leap out of his chest.

Suddenly Matthew was beside him: the show was about to start. Jack was filled with love for his brother and forgot all the questions he wanted to ask. He went to hug him, but Matthew stopped him.

'Listen, Jack! We don't have much time. You and Tattie are in terrible danger. The spiders' heart keeps Araine safe while we ghosts are here, but it doesn't protect you two. The longer we stay here, the more you two will become ill. She's holding you both at the same age as it's good for her show, but she can't prevent you fading. You'll die! That's what happened to Lucie!'

'You're not making any sense,' said Jack. 'I don't understand!'

The sailor standing nearest to him looked scared to see him talking to himself.

'Nora says –' Matthew began.

'You've spoken to Nora?'

'Hush, Jack – listen to me! Nora says Lucie made a recording; it will explain everything you need to do to stop Araine. It's somewhere in the theatre. Find it!'

'What's a recording?' asked Jack.

'I don't know – some sort of message. Lucie was a genius; she invented something that she didn't get a chance to patent before she died – she's still really grumpy about it,' said Matthew.

'You've spoken to Lucie? Can I trust Harcus?' But

before Matthew could answer his brother disappeared up through the stage floor, summoned by Araine.

Jack could barely contain himself. He lurched to one side and steadied himself as his ramp rose to take him towards the trapdoor on to the stage.

'I call you!'

Jack could hear Araine warbling from above him at the card table at the centre of the stage.

'I call you to me now! My Free Spirits, rise up and show yourselves. RISE UP! RISE!' Ghostly creaks and moans wailed through the theatre from the orchestra pit. 'They draw near! I hear them! Can you?'

'Yes!' cried out some braver members of the audience.

'I can *feel* their ghostly presence coming through the boundary twixt life and death. The veil is getting thinner!' shouted Araine.

Jack's white painted face and head popped out of the trapdoor on to the stage. He tried not to cough as the smoke hit him. A part of him wished he was in the auditorium watching this, an absolute triumph of make-believe weaving its magic over the audience in the plush red-and-gold seats. Only one of the lights-up gas lamps was lit, its long shadow painting the stage. Jack couldn't see the theatregoers but could hear their gasps. As he had been taught, Jack kept his head still, his body responding automatically as he'd rehearsed so often, while his brain frantically whirred.

He and Tattie might die!

He noticed Tattie and Araine out of the corner of his eye. No wonder the audience were scared: Araine had the appearance of death herself, and Tattie looked like a floating head the way he'd been lit, so Jack guessed he must too.

'These are my Free Spirits,' said Araine quietly, using the audience's desire to hear her, to get them to quieten down. 'Conduits to the other side: half in this world, half in the next. Our very own half-lives! Tattie, Jack, are you connected to what lies beyond the veil?'

Jack nodded just as he'd practised in rehearsals.

'Any questions for the spirits?' called Araine to the audience.

She already knew who the audience members with the most money were. She'd make sure they got the chance to ask a question, and Matthew and Priss would find out the answer before reporting it back to Jack and Tattie. That would encourage them to book a private seance with Araine.

'You there.' Araine placed her fingers on her temples as if she was channelling spirits. 'Lady Appleford, is it not?'

A woman in the audience gasped and clutched the

pearls around her neck. Her voice cracked as she spoke. 'My husband, God rest his soul, hid the key to our safe before he died. Could you ask him where it is?'

Araine bluffed and spouted mystical nonsense to fill in time while Matthew went and asked some other ghosts to find the answer. Then Jack heard Matthew whispering in his ear.

'Tell her it's in the old watering can on the bottom shelf in the shed at the end of the meadow. And not to let the foolish old dear spend all my hard-earned guineas betting on the horses! I probably wouldn't say that last bit out loud,' said Matthew.

Jack repeated the answers in the eerie monotone voice Araine had taught him. As he looked down, he realized his hands were now completely transparent.

'Find Lucie's message,' Matthew whispered. 'Before we all run out of time.'

Chapter Twenty-one

Now

I whizz forward on my Mean Machine to go after William, who has disappeared through the glowing door, abandoning us both.

'Oi!' calls Nikesh. 'Don't leave me here!'

'I'm not staying if there are spiders!' I yell.

'And I'm not staying alone in the dark!' they yell back, running after me as I push through the door.

My mouth actually drops open as I blink in the light of the hidden room, my eyes getting accustomed to it after the darkness, and find a workshop that Grandad would have killed for. And, as someone who has being organized high on her list of priorities, it works well for me too.

There's a long wooden workbench with half-finished models. On the walls hang small tools with their outlines drawn round them, with an empty spot where a pair of pliers should go. I clutch Grandad's in my pocket.

Shelves and shelves full of boxes catch my eye. I go nearer so that I can see the handwritten labels on them: *Assorted wood offcuts under three inches*; *Lace*; *Half-inch nails*; *Piping*; *Salvaged fabric* and *Fat quarters* . . . and my firm favourite: *Bits*. Excellent labelling, and they're all square and neat.

But even they can't stop the unease growing in me. Not unease . . . fear! And anger that William isn't telling me everything. I desperately try to piece the puzzle together, but I can't make it fit.

At the centre of the room is a giant wooden box and inside are lots of gold tubes that have little indentations or missing pieces. There's a huge brass trumpet sticking out of the side of the box, like the trumpet on an old-fashioned gramophone.

I'm about to yell at William to tell me what's going on when the wooden box begins to shake, and we hear cogs turning, then whirring, clicking and clacking, and the gold tube on the top slowly begins to revolve. As it does, a ghostly voice starts to speak:

'*My name is Jack Redwood, the year is 1883 and I hope someone listens to this and rescues us. Do not fall under Araine's spell. Do not become a half-life and form a triangle with her, even though she will offer you the chance to get your loved ones back from the dead. We are the Free Spirits. My friends are William 'Tattie' Lightfoot, Harcus, Snod's Edge and Rex. You must find our theatre; you need to find Our Escape.'*

Those are the names from the model theatre with the cherry tree in the centre! And Our Escape is its name – where do we find it? And Araine from the poster? She'll be long dead by now.

The voice begins to speak again, to tell us more, but suddenly the box and the gold tubes jerk and hiss, then make a huge rattling noise. I clamp my hands over my ears and duck as it explodes in front of us and pieces go careering round the room.

When I lift my head, I see William picking a bit of wood out of his beard.

'Everyone OK?' he asks.

We nod. Then I shake my head. 'Those names,' I say with a calm in my voice I don't feel, 'are the same ones that are on the model of that theatre. Jack Redwood was speaking in 1883 and he's also upstairs, right now!' My voice gets louder as my anger and fear rise. '*Your name* is on that theatre!' I say, pointing at William. 'How is that possible?'

My mind is racing, my heart hammering in my chest. That's what Jack has offered me – what he's just said on the recording: a chance to see my grandad once more!

'You believe all this claptrap? You believe in ghosts?' William shouts back at me.

'Yes!' I say, louder than I intended, suddenly realizing that I do believe, feeling Grandad's presence close at hand, wishing he could be here beside me.

Can wishing and wanting this hard make ghosts real?

'And you do too!' I say, pointing at William, remembering when we were in the outer white room and he asked me if I could 'feel it too', and I'd brushed him off.

I *can* feel it. Something lurking in the shadows.

My skin crawls as if there are spiders on me and I itch to get them off, to desperately try to claw away all this scary stuff. I wish I was back in my bedroom and that I'd never come here.

'Good,' William says, and he smiles. 'Sorry about all this. I needed to make sure that you were on our side: we've been tricked before. Please call me Tattie, just like my friends do. We desperately need your help.'

William – er, Tattie – walks over to me and crouches down so that his gentle eyes are level with mine.

'Hettie Lightfoot-Redwood, I'm not the only one who will ask you for help. When the time comes, you'll have to decide which side you're on.'

I don't know whether to laugh or cry and a sort of giggle pops out of me. This makes no sense and yet at the same time all the sense in the world. How can that be true?

'What do you mean? Choose sides?' I ask.

Tattie stands up and gives a little whistle, and from under the wooden bench comes the dog from earlier, the one that definitely matches the weathervane. He comes sleepily over to me and holds his paw out, like he wants to shake my hand. He smells of warm biscuits. I waggle his paw and he leaps on to my lap, nuzzling his cold, wet nose into my neck.

'Of course! You must be Rex,' I whisper to him, and he gives a gruff little bark, as if he's saying yes, and licks my ear.

Nikesh comes over to pat and fuss him. 'You're the little guy we first saw from the minibus!'

Rex squeaks with glee and wriggles with all the attention, thrusting his big head into each of our outstretched hands in turn.

'So what next? How do we help?' Nikesh asks Tattie.

But Tattie has vanished.

Chapter Twenty-two

Way Back When

'So you do agree to it?' said Lucie, a frown on her face as she sat up in bed, holding Harcus's hand.

Harcus and Lucie were so pale that Araine could see the floral pillow behind Lucie through her face; they were almost like ghosts themselves. Whatever was happening to them, the diamond had protected Araine from it.

'We're just going to let the ghosts leave?' asked Lucie warily.

'Even though that means saying goodbye?' said Harcus, his big eyes staring at Araine.

'Yes,' said Araine, forcing out a tear and wiping it quickly away. 'I've had time to think since I got so angry with all of you yesterday. You're right. It's time.'

'And you'll return the diamond?' Lucie's voice betrayed her disbelief.

'We'll seal the drawer shut,' said Araine, 'so that it can never be opened again.'

'What if people want to say goodbye to their loved ones?' asked Harcus.

'It's too dangerous – we know that now,' said Araine. 'The spiders can't control the diamond's power. If I can take it, anyone could. It's time to finish this once and for all.'

'When we've said goodbye,' said Lucie, giving her old friend's hand a squeeze.

The spiders lined the sides of the tunnel as Lucie, Harcus and Araine walked through the catacombs, then they stood solemnly at the edge of the doorway as the two Lightfoots and one Redwood entered the white room where it had all begun.

Lucie and Harcus went to kneel down to trace the triangles in the stone to open the drawer, but Araine called them over.

'It has been an adventure, hasn't it?' Araine said, and she walked over to the very first theatre model she'd seen when this all began, when Lucie had had to tell her how to pronounce the word.

Theatre, Araine mouthed to herself. She stole a glance at Lucie and Harcus; she could see the walls through them now. Araine examined her own solid hands. They could have taken the diamond, but they hadn't. Lucie and Harcus had chosen this.

Weak. Unworthy.

'I think we should put the diamond back now,' said Harcus.

'Never!' hissed Araine, her face now full of fury. 'You want me to leave my sister? Leave all this behind? You've betrayed me! I won't ever stop! Not until I bleed dry every one of those people who could have saved her! Until I am the most powerful person in the world!'

'You lied to us!' cried Lucie. 'That's what this is all about – *power*. You don't care about us or your sister. You were just using us all along because you couldn't do it alone.'

'Oh, I can,' said Araine. 'You're both too weak. I can do this by myself. Watch me. No one will tell me what to do ever again!'

'Please!' cried Harcus. 'Let us all go!'

'No!' Araine drew every ounce of her rage into her lungs: the death of Nora; these people she'd thought were her friends wanting her to leave it all behind; the power trickling down the back of her throat from the jewel she would never, ever give up. As she focused on the heart-shaped diamond around her neck, it burst into black fire and smoke, and Araine screamed.

The spiders at the door's edge screamed too, flailing their legs in horror as they hurtled towards her, pulled through the air by the black flames in the diamond.

'No!' cried Nora faintly as she appeared through the smoke. 'Araine, stop while you still have the chance!'

But Araine couldn't hear her sister any more, not above the rage and greed that was consuming her. She opened her mouth to scream and as she took a breath all the spiders were sucked inside her in a huge bubbling whirlpool. She coughed and choked, bent double, then slowly rose to her full height. She was transformed.

Araine grinned at Lucie and Harcus, filled with power and the spiders inside her. She grew until she towered over them, limbs twitching like spider legs.

Lucie, Harcus and the ghosts huddled together in fear and disgust at the transformation happening right in front of their eyes.

'The ultimate penalty for the ultimate betrayal!' Araine's voice boomed round the white room, cobwebs flying out of her mouth. She laughed. 'I'll split you up! You two can feel what it's like to lose your other half. That's what you wanted me to do, to give up Nora. Well, you can lose each other!'

'No!' shrieked Lucie, desperately clinging on to her little brother.

'You, dear friend –' Araine's spider-leg fingers traced along Lucie's cheek – 'you, Lucie Lightfoot, you ungrateful brat, can join Nora and your mam as ghosts, to do my bidding when I summon you. I shall keep Harcus here with me.'

Araine clicked her fingers and the last bit of life drained from Lucie, who was now completely transparent just like the other two ghosts. Araine opened her arms wide and then clapped her hands together. Harcus leaped as he heard the sound of the theatre above them exploding.

'Time for a new beginning!' screamed Araine over the noise of the fireball up above them. 'Time for me to take centre stage at last!'

When the sound of the flames and the theatre crashing and burning finally stopped, Araine opened her eyes.

Lucie had vanished with the ghosts. Harcus stood in the corner by the mirror, touching his face.

He looked over at Araine. 'What have you done?'

Harcus's face was a decade or two older, a pointy moustache beneath his nose.

Araine chuckled. 'I needed you to appear older, more in keeping for the show I have in mind. Brother and sister, that's the way forward, with me onstage.'

The spiders were wriggling inside Araine, fully under her control now.

Araine called the ghosts to her. They would all realize how powerful she now was, what had happened to Harcus! She couldn't wait to see the look on Lucie's ghostly face.

She called again. They still didn't come.

She touched the heart-shaped diamond around her neck. It was cold. She could feel her limbs weakening.

'What's happening to me?' Araine screamed.

'You broke the triangle when you killed my sister,' said Harcus quietly, tears rolling down his face. 'The ghosts are gone forever.'

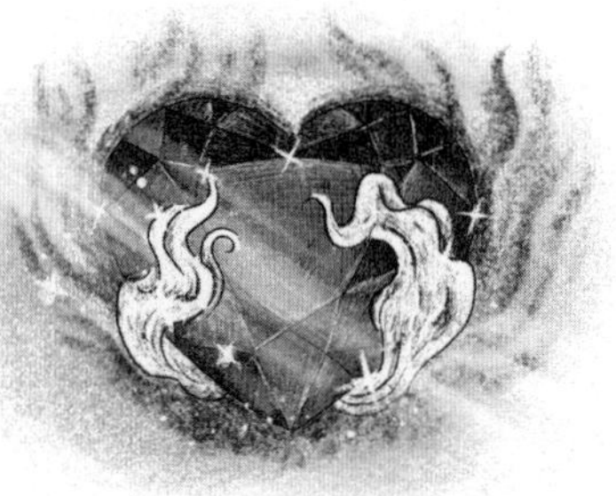

Chapter Twenty-three

Then

Straight after the seance, when Araine was lost to her adoring audience, Jack drew Tattie to one side, looking around in case anyone was listening, then whispered in his ear.

'Matthew told me that we'll die if we don't find the message Lucie left.'

'But Araine's the one letting us see Priss and Matthew.' Tattie wiggled his arm to try to shake off Jack. Rex gave a little growl.

'Haven't you noticed how well Araine is looking?' whispered Jack. 'It's as if she's getting younger as we stay the same age and fade away. Have you noticed your hands? Mine are sometimes translucent.' He held one up for Tattie to see, but it was solid.

'Jack, your hand is fine! It's just grief catching up with you, playing tricks. You hid it for so long, and now Matthew is back and you haven't had time to deal with it all. But I have. And I'm not going back to how life was without Priss.'

Jack tried a different tack. 'What about everyone here? They completely ignore us, flinch when we go near. They're scared of us.'

'So they should be,' said Tattie, trying to lighten the mood by pulling a scary face. Jack ignored him.

'I'm being serious, Tattie. Matthew said there was a recording from Lucie hidden somewhere in the theatre and we need to find it. Nora said so.'

'And I'm being serious too, Jack. You must forget all this nonsense. You're not spoiling this for me! And what even is a recording?'

In three short strides, he had turned the corner, Rex chasing at his heels, and Jack was left alone.

* * *

The next day, Jack clambered down the tight spiral staircase to the undercroft beneath the theatre to find Tattie. He hoped that Tattie had had enough time to cool his heels; Jack had to make him understand.

Yesterday, when Tattie stormed off, Jack had told Snod he'd lost his slippers and needed to find them, knowing full well that the giant wooden man couldn't bear to have anything out of place. Together they searched the entire theatre, from the water tower to the props store; the dressing rooms to the costume store; the acrobats' nets to the laundry. Nothing. No recording. It didn't help that Jack had no clue what a recording was and so no idea what he was looking for.

The only place they didn't check was Araine's lair, which was locked up tight. And anyway that would be the last place Lucie would hide anything.

Bless Snod. That morning there had been a new pair of slippers outside Jack's door. Jack guiltily gave away his old pair to one of the sailors so that Snod wouldn't find out he'd lied to him.

When Jack got to the final spiral, he almost tripped over Rex, who'd leaped up to greet him.

'Hello, you! I've no food on me.' He held his hands up to show he wasn't hiding anything, but Rex jumped up anyway and nuzzled at Jack's pocket.

'I've got nothing! Are you down here, Tattie?' he called out.

Tattie's head popped out from behind one of the huge handles that operated the ghost-glide.

'Boo!' he yelled, making Jack jump. 'Welcome to hell.'

'I wish you wouldn't call it that,' said Jack. 'Every

time you do, it makes me shudder and grow colder. We need to talk –'

'Well, he's technically correct!' said Harcus as he clambered out from underneath lights-up, the mechanism that allowed the gas lamps to rise up at the front of the stage. 'This hellmouth of a trap is baffling me. Can't see what's wrong and why it won't rise, and we need it working before the next performance, and –'

'Cup of tea?' asked Tattie.

Jack wished Harcus would leave so he could persuade Tattie to help him find Lucie's recording. He looked at his fading hands: they didn't have much time!

'Yes please,' said Harcus, and wiped his brow with his sleeve, smearing dust and grime across his face. 'I could do with some refreshment.'

Tattie went over to the little table in the corner where they kept a stove, ducking under the beams to avoid the dangling ropes.

Harcus stretched and groaned and sat on one of the little folding chairs. Rex kept pawing at Jack.

Jack followed Tattie, making sure Harcus wasn't listening and they were out of earshot, and tried to talk to him, but Tattie shushed him by holding up his hand. Jack could see Tattie's face through his almost completely transparent fingers.

'I'm not believing you yet,' Tattie whispered. 'You

understand, don't you? I don't want to because –' he was close to tears – 'if I do, I have to say goodbye to my sister and I can't do that again.'

Jack put his arm round him. 'I understand, Tattie, I really do.' Jack could feel him nod against his chest.

Then Tattie straightened up and held out his hand to examine it. 'Last night, before I went to sleep, I nearly screamed the place down when I could see my pillow through my hand. I'm starting to disappear too. I really think we need to find that . . . what was it?'

'Recording. Snod and I searched the theatre looking for my slippers –'

Tattie cocked his head at Jack.

'Best not ask – I don't know where else this recording, whatever it is, could be!'

'So what are we going to do?' Tattie straightened up and wiped his nose on his sleeve.

'I have no idea. Keep looking? Ask Harcus? But Matthew disappeared before I could ask if we can trust him. Get off me, Rex! What's the matter with him today, Tattie?'

'He was asleep in his bed until you got here, nee bother,' said Tattie, pouring boiling water into the cups. He walked back over and sat down next to Harcus, handing him one.

'Well, you're a bother now!' said Jack to Rex.

'Stop fussing him and just sit down. He'll stop if you do.'

Jack reached for his cup just as Rex launched himself at Jack's pocket. Jack just about managed to keep his tea from sloshing out and burning him.

'Rex!' they all yelled at once, including Harcus on the other side of the room, and Rex sat up in front of Jack on his hind legs, begging.

'Are you sure you haven't got any scraps hidden in your pocket?' asked Harcus.

'For goodness' sake,' said Jack, standing up. Tattie laughed as Rex leaned his head against Jack's leg and drooled.

Jack turned out his right pocket and left it dangling so that it looked like a rabbit ear. 'See? Nowt!' He turned out the other pocket and Rex dropped to the floor and immediately began to snaffle something that had fallen out.

'No!' yelled Harcus, and grabbed Rex. 'Tattie, quick, open his mouth!'

Tattie got on his knees and prised open Rex's jaws as Harcus held him still.

Jack reached in and took something wooden and shiny from Rex's mouth.

'What on earth? That's not food,' he said as he peered at the tiny object that glistened with dog drool. 'That –'

'– is a miniature lights-up mechanism,' finished Harcus.

Indeed, in Jack's palm was a small replica of the contraption Harcus has been trying to fix.

'You don't remember putting this in your pocket?' asked Tattie.

'I think I'd recall that, don't you? I've never seen it before in my life!'

'Look, there!' said Tattie as he snatched it out of Jack's hand.

Rex trotted off in a huff to his bed after the indignity of having his mouth forced open and his prize stolen from him.

Tattie walked over to one of the lamps, and Jack and Harcus followed. Jack noticed out of the corner of his eye that Harcus's hands were shaking. That scared him.

Tattie turned the miniature in his hands under the lamp. A tiny, barely visible golden tube shone in the light.

'It can't be,' said Harcus. 'That looks like one of Lucie's recording tubes –' He ran towards the broken mechanism he'd been working on.

'One of Lucie's what? Harcus, what do you know about a recording?' asked Jack, too unnerved to wonder any longer if they could trust him.

'Maybe . . .' Harcus replied. 'Jack, bring that lamp!'

Jack did so, and the three of them crouched behind the wooden cogs and the ropes. Harcus studied the miniature, turned it in his hand until it was in exactly the same position as the mechanism in front of them.

'That's why it wasn't working,' muttered Harcus as he wriggled underneath the lights-up trap. 'How did I not spot that?'

As Jack and Tattie watched, Harcus reached through a small gap and pulled out a gold tube from exactly the same place that its tiny replica was on the model. He wiped muck and dust from his moustache.

'Is *that* a recording?' asked Jack.

Harcus dashed to his workshop, Tattie, Jack and Rex struggling to keep up. He wouldn't answer any of their questions. He was pale as he dragged a large wooden box, hidden under a pile of cloths, into the centre of the room.

Jack peered inside and saw lots of gold tubes, like the one Harcus was holding.

'Who made this?' asked Jack.

'Lucie,' said Harcus, his voice wobbling. 'Lucie Lightfoot, my sister. She made all the miniatures after finding the first ones in the white room, taught herself how. She invented so many things, a complete genius. Not that a woman was allowed to do anything like that, so she had to keep it all hidden. She invented a way to store voices.'

Jack and Tattie looked confused.

'Keep up, young 'uns – this is a recording!'

Jack and Tattie turned to each other, open-mouthed.

'How does it work?' asked Tattie.

Harcus fiddled with the gold tube and managed to open it, revealing a wax cylinder that, after a bit of trial and error and one or two fancy oaths, he managed to slot into the top of the wooden box.

'The grooves on the cylinder record sound,' he told them as he adjusted the giant brass trumpet. 'You turn the handle and you can listen back to what's been recorded.'

'Not sure about that,' said Tattie, stepping back a pace and making Rex yelp when he stood on his foot. 'Sorry, boy.' Tattie picked Rex up in his arms and rubbed his face on his ears. 'That's a bit too much like capturing ghosts.'

Jack shook his head and scowled at Tattie, then turned in excitement to Harcus. 'This is what Matthew told us to find!'

'Sure you want to hear it?' Harcus readied himself to turn the handle.

'No,' said Tattie as Jack said, 'Yes . . . No . . . I don't know!'

Jack was confused. Matthew hadn't said whether they could trust Harcus, but then again he hadn't said he could trust Tattie either. He hadn't really said much at all! But if Lucie was Harcus's sister, surely they could trust him?

'There's no coming back from this, Jack,' Harcus said. 'Once you know, you can't undo it.'

Jack nodded.

Harcus turned the handle and stepped back as the tube began to turn and a scratchy voice came booming out of the trumpet. '*My name is Lucie Lightfoot, older sister of Harcus Lightfoot, and I was once the best friend of Araine Machiavelli.*'

Jack looked at Harcus and could see he was struggling to control his emotions as he heard his sister's voice.

'Oh no, I do not like this!' yelled Tattie as he squeezed Rex so tightly that he yelped and wriggled out of Tattie's arms. Rex dashed over to Harcus, who crouched to stroke him, burying his face in Rex's fur.

'That's eerie,' Tattie said, talking over the recorded voice. Jack shushed him.

'*I'm recording this in secret as I know my days on this earth are numbered, and in the hope that someone finds this and rescues us, or that it can at least stop the cycle from happening again. My brother Harcus and I once took the spiders' diamond with our friend Araine. We should have given it straight back once they'd allowed us to say goodbye to our mam and Araine had bidden farewell to her sister, but we kept it, thinking we could use it to seek revenge. Araine was overtaken by the dark within the diamond, which made her greedy and hungry for power. It has consumed her: it was never meant to be worn this long nor be fed by emotions as strong as hers. I'm fading fast, Harcus too. I am scared about what will happen to us, but even more I fear what Araine will do without us trying to keep her in check. And if you're now part of the triangle, if you're a half-life too, you need to escape, like I never could, before you fade forever! You must destroy Araine – there is nothing of my old friend left inside her – by setting the sweet spiders free and giving them back their diamond heart so it can never, ever be used again.'*

The recording hissed and clanked to a stop.

They all sat in silence; even Rex stopped scratching.

'*Sweet* spiders?' said Tattie, finally breaking the silence.

'Is that all you have to say?' asked Jack, getting up from his seat.

'*Sweet?* Have you not met them?' said Tattie, shuddering.

'I'm not sure that was the main point she was trying to get across,' said Jack. 'Hold on a second. I think that miniature was put in my pocket on purpose . . . Someone wanted us to find this.'

'And who would do something like that?' asked Snod as he came jerkily into the room, carrying Jack's old pair of slippers.

Harcus, looking ashamed and as though his heart had broken, stared at Snod. '*You* gave the recording to them?'

Snod nodded as Jack's and Tattie's heads turned towards him. 'It's useful being a lumbering piece of wood – you hear and see all sorts of things that no one thinks you're clever enough to bother about. It's time to break Araine's spell.'

Chapter Twenty-four

Now

'Tattie can't just vanish like that!' says Nikesh.

'Well, he has,' I say. 'Left us, and this little fella.' Rex whines and burrows into me.

'Do you think any of this is real?' I lean forward and look at Nikesh. 'Or just some elaborate sort of hoax.'

I need to know if I can trust them, to tell them everything so they can help me figure it all out. I need to tell Gift too. We must get her back!

Nikesh stares off into the distance and doesn't answer.

'Nikesh?'

I expect them to tell me not to be silly, that there's a perfectly rational explanation for a model theatre that magically transformed in my box, and a bunch of people from well over a hundred years ago having the same group name as us, and asking for help by leaving a recorded message that blows up before a man with a green beard vanishes.

Nikesh surprises me when they look me right in the eye and say, 'They're real. They're ghosts. And we have to help.'

I groan. That's not what I want to hear. And I didn't even want to come in the first place! If they hadn't made me, we wouldn't be in this mess.

Nikesh yanks a chair over to me and sits so that we're side by side. They grin at me from under their fringe, shyly in case I shout at them.

'Hettie, I know you're not going to want to hear this, but I'm going to say it anyway. We loved Ed Red. Not as much as you, we never could, but don't you think he'd want you to solve this mystery? Think how much he would have loved it!'

I nod at Nikesh. They're right: he would have done. But if I leap into things without Grandad, then I'm leaving him behind. Why can no one understand how much that hurts? How much I want him here beside me! The pain is physical, like I'm being wrenched apart, pulled in two.

'I thought you were going to be a world-famous producer and work all over the world, and we were going to come to Las Vegas when you were in charge of all the shows there,' says Nikesh. 'How will you manage that, and make Ed Red so proud, if you won't do what you love?'

I choke out a laugh. 'Did I actually say that? My head is *big*.'

'Oh, we know!' They squeeze my arm. 'You could though. You have no idea how clever you actually are.'

I blush and give a tiny smile, finally knowing Nikesh is right. I want to make Grandad proud of me, more than anything.

'Right, this is what I need to do. Still not being big-headed, but it is all linked to me. I mean to my name. There's Jack Redwood; he has the same name as Grandad, and he's upstairs as a nasty artistic director, and he's also on a recording from a hundred and forty years ago. When he was nice. Apparently.'

'Ghost?' yells Nikesh.

'You don't say! They had the same name as us, the Free Spirits – that's another connection – and I'm a Lightfoot, just like Lucie. We need to find the theatre they called Our Escape. I'm guessing there's a real actual one, not just the model.' Nikesh looks dazed.

'And this dog –' I scratch Rex under the chin.

'Is a ghost dog!' gasps Nikesh.

I nod. 'One last thing. Erm.' I take a deep breath and garble out, 'Jack the ghost sent me an invitation telling me I could see my dead grandad.'

I hang my head, absolutely exhausted from keeping that bit inside and finally saying it out loud.

Nikesh shakes their head, then explodes. '*And you didn't think to tell us that?!*'

'I didn't want you to tell me that it wasn't real,' I say, wiping away a tear. 'I really want to see him again.'

'Oh, Hets,' says Nikesh, and gives me a huge hug. 'I know. Do you think Araine is behind all this?'

'She has to be. That's who Jack was afraid of in the recording – all the ghosts were. Something must have happened to bring her back. Wake her up. And to change Jack . . . I don't know. Why is all this happening now?'

'Because of you,' says Nikesh. 'Because of you and your grandad. It has to be. We just need to work out why.'

Then I get worried, and my voice comes out high and panicked. 'Tattie said about choosing sides; that means something evil is out there. Why would I not take theirs? What if I pick the wrong one? What if Araine's got Gift! She's following Jack around like a puppy up there. The Jack who sent me the invitation! And we left her all by herself!'

I think Nikesh's eyeballs are going to pop out of their face. 'What are we waiting for? Let's go!'

With that, they run out, through the white room and into the tunnel.

Rex licks my cheek with his sandpaper tongue and we zoom after Nikesh, but then I jerk to a sudden halt next to the Our Escape model theatre that should have been the Arts Centre model I finished for Grandad.

Rex nuzzles my hand and I think he's trying to comfort me, but then I realize that he's nudging it towards the model.

'What are you trying to show me? That's what we have to find in real life, so are you trying to tell me the model is important?'

He looks at me with those big eyes of his, then startles me by leaping off the scooter and running in tight circles, like he's trying to catch his tail.

As he does, the dog weathervane on top of the model of Our Escape whirls in the breeze he's creating and begins to spin. The petals on the blossoms of the little cherry tree begin to fall. They swoop in the breeze created by the weathervane and then slowly float upwards.

'Rex, are you doing that?' I ask in a shaky voice. 'It's beautiful!'

The blossom swirls and glides – I'm mesmerized – then it slowly separates into clumps until there is a message in petals hovering before my eyes.

Rex keeps spinning and spinning as I read it out loud: '*Free Spirits, now we know you're on our side, you have to save us. Follow Rex. He'll lead you to us at Our Escape.*'

As soon as I've finished speaking, Rex stops spinning and the petals drop back down to the miniature theatre and land in piles on the stage. I can't believe Nikesh has missed this!

Dizzy Rex goes one way and then the other, and finally flops on to the floor with his head on my foot and his big eyes staring at me.

'They're your friends, aren't they?'

Rex whines, then gives a low, soulful howl.

'Hop on,' I say, and he leaps on to my Mean Machine's footplate and looks very chuffed with himself.

'We need to help your friends, don't we? *Your* Free Spirits,' I say, and Rex gives such a massive woof that I jump in my seat.

'Grandad would never forgive me if I didn't try to help someone in need.'

As I say that out loud, I realize it's actually true. We zoom out to the mouldy tunnel and catch up with Nikesh at the lift.

'Haven't you pressed the button yet?' I ask.

'Where have you been? We don't have Tattie's pass to get back up,' says Nikesh. 'We're stuck!'

Rex nudges my hand and then scrabbles to get into the basket at the front of my Mean Machine.

Nikesh reaches in and pulls out the pass. 'Ta-dah! Tattie must have left it for us.' They press the button.

'Nikesh, you go and try to get into the archive, see if you can find anything useful. Rex and I will find Gift and tell her what's going on. And then we'll all meet in the foyer in thirty minutes. Got it? We need to follow Rex; he'll show us where the ghosts' theatre is.'

'Someone get her a clipboard – our Hettie is back,' says Nikesh, grinning as they step through the open doors of the lift. 'You really think there are ghosts trapped in here?' They peer into the darkness as the lift doors grind shut.

'Yes,' I say, thinking what Grandad would have said. 'And we're going to save them.'

Chapter Twenty-five

Way Back When

Araine crawled out of the cocoon the spiders had built for her. It was the only way she could stay alive, hibernating for long periods of time while Harcus went out and looked for half-lives. Why weren't the half-lives successful though? No matter how many times they tried, they couldn't form the triangle and get to the ghosts. The half-lives he found were certainly grieving, desperate to see their loved ones again, just like they had been. What was she not doing right?

She looked in the mirror before her and licked her finger, stroking her long curly hair, to make sure that the escaping wisps were slicked back. No strands of blonde remained, just a shock of white.

Lucie wouldn't recognize Araine now, in this shabby

theatre, with such a poor crowd. And a new name. She'd stolen one final thing from Lord Machiavelli. No longer little Araine Redwood – Araine Machiavelli carried much more weight!

Araine shook her head to rid herself of the old memories of the golden times with her best friend Lucie Lightfoot and little Harcus all those years ago. She needed to focus, but that was becoming harder as the dregs of her power grew weaker and her body faded. She could spend very little time outside her cocoon now.

The heart around her neck seemed dead, and she could feel her skin becoming brittle. Harcus was becoming more translucent. Each day there were piles of dead spiders beside her, their shining cobwebs quickly breaking and dulling.

They were finding people with fire and anger woven through their grief. Why wasn't that enough?

Araine carefully traced the sign of the triangle in the air: power comes in threes.

'What's in a name?' she said quietly to herself, thinking about how she'd stolen hers from Lord Machiavelli.

Something lit up in her brain. The name! Their names! Lightfoots and Redwoods had always been in Attercop. They were the ones who'd first stolen the diamond. Maybe the half-lives had to be related? People who were grieving but who also shared their bloodlines, a web leading back to the spiders!

'Harcus!' she cried. 'I know who we need to find!'

The diamond heart crackled just once, telling her she was right.

'Just got to keep going until I find them. That's all I need do,' Araine muttered to herself as she pulled on her robe with the gold-stitched spiders.

'Call time!' came the voice outside Araine's dressing-room door, summoning her to the stage.

The remaining spiders in the corner shuddered and rustled as Araine commanded them to her. She gobbled them up, feeding on their strength, hoping they would sustain her just long enough.

Nora's voice sang in her head. Araine was too tired and weak to make it quieten down. *The spiders just brought me to you so that I could say goodbye, and you could move on, and I could too. This was never meant to last like this! Lucie knew that. You know it too!*

'Do not mention Lucie's name in here!' Araine yelled at herself. 'I know now what we need to survive: our names! Bloodlines of half-lives! To complete the triangle. New Free Spirits connected to the old. I will be all-powerful once more! And, Nora, I will bring you back to me!'

Araine walked to the stage and peered out from behind the curtain in the wings, taking deep breaths, calming herself before it was time to step out. She now relied on the stagecraft and trickery of those fraudulent seance artists. Audience numbers were already starting to fall, nowhere near the heights of Lucie's fame, and she couldn't have that, not the great Araine Machiavelli!

Harcus leaped off the stage with his acrobats tumbling after him, and landed next to Araine, twirling his moustache. He had been working on his routine for years, to supplement their paltry income. She made the sign of the triangle at him, placing the tips of her forefingers together, and then her thumbs. He shuddered and went to wait in the darkness of the wings.

She peered back through the curtain. There weren't many jewels round the necks in the audience tonight.

Araine paused and the spiders' heart began to throb.

She looked down at her hand and saw the lines, the papery skin, the age leaking out of her. Then she felt it, the sadness floating up like a breath to the wings of the stage where she was hidden. She sniffed; grief always smelled of lemons, Nora's favourite cake. And this was so strong it almost overpowered her.

Her eyes followed the lemon scent until they stopped on the first row of the balcony. Araine spotted the bright green beard first. Sadness and loss oozed out of him.

'A half-life! I knew it!' she whispered to herself with glee. 'And this one feels different! Box Office! Come here!'

A man with pencil smudges on his fingers stumbled towards Araine as she barked her question at him. 'Row A, seat seventeen in the balcony – who bought the ticket?'

It was Box Office's job to know all the names of those in the audience and to dig up any information he could to help Araine with her seances, now that she couldn't contact the ghosts.

'Well?' she spat. 'With speed, man!'

'William,' said Box Office, frantically shuffling reams of paper. 'William Lightfoot. Nickname Tattie. Wasn't Lightfoot the name of –?'

'Silence!' snarled Araine. 'Make sure you bring him to my dressing room during the interval. We will have a lot to discuss.'

Box Office nodded and scuttled away.

Araine did a giddy little dance to herself. She would endure. If she could find this William Lightfoot so easily, she would discover another related half-life. This was what she had needed to do all along! She squealed with delight and sniffed the air.

'We will beg, steal and borrow, burn down this old shell and rebuild a theatre in my new name! I shall be rightfully restored!'

When the stage was in darkness, Araine took her place at the card table, the small audience whispering with excitement. Araine was excited too, for the first time in a long while. Soon she would meet William Lightfoot, get back to her peak and reclaim the stage!

Chapter Twenty-six

Then

Jack looked over at Tattie who was frozen in his chair, his face fixed in a grimace. Rex leaped up at Tattie, trying to get on to his knee, but Tattie didn't seem to notice. Jack realized he was shaking with – fear? No, rage.

'What have you done, Harcus?' Tattie asked quietly. 'Why did you let Araine take us? We trusted you. You knew what would happen to us.'

A single tear ran down Harcus's face. Snod passed Harcus a handkerchief, but he didn't wipe the tear away.

'Araine said it was the only way to see Lucie again and I believed her. No, maybe I didn't. But I wanted to. And that meant I'd do anything, including bringing you two here.'

Jack wrestled with the emotions warring inside him. Harcus had brought him and Tattie into such danger! But it did mean he'd found Matthew. Jack knew how much he'd longed for his brother, how he missed him so hard his brain managed to think that Matthew was still alive. Jack knew that grief could make you do awful things. Could he have said he wouldn't have done the same as Harcus?

'Harcus, how long have you been here?' he asked.

'It feels like forever. Too many forevers. Everything Lucie said is true. Come on, Tattie. You need to move.' Harcus pulled at Tattie's arm, and Rex tugged at his sock.

'Why can't you see Lucie any more like we can see Matthew and Priss?' said Jack.

'Let's get this lump some sugar.' Harcus gestured to Snod to help him haul Tattie to his feet. 'Then I'll give you answers.'

They found some sugared fruit cubes in the dining hall and then headed along the corridor to Araine's lair, Harcus in front, Snod guarding the rear.

Harcus caught a woven spider star from the wall hanging, and when he wiggled his fingers its thread turned into a key.

'Should we be going in here without Araine?' asked Jack.

Harcus shook his head, opened the door and stepped inside.

Jack and Tattie followed, while Snod waited in the corridor. Harcus moved one of the wall hangings to the side, and traced his finger round the edges of an exposed brick. With a clunk, it sprang outwards, and the fireplace slid open with a long creaking noise, as if it needed oiling. Without saying a word, Harcus got down on his knees and crawled through the hole. Tattie followed and so did Rex, his tail wagging.

Jack couldn't decide what to do! Then he thought of being here alone if Araine came in and he scrambled after them.

At first Jack couldn't see much, just some faintly glowing shapes, maybe on shelves? As his eyes grew accustomed to the dark, however, he began to make out shadows that formed into objects.

He stood up. 'Oh goodness!'

They were in a vault, a giant treasure chest. Gold bars were stacked in one corner, a mound of brilliant yellow. The shelves contained piles of jewellery, emerald earrings, necklaces of rubies and sapphires, a mountain of diamond bracelets.

'How much is this worth?' whispered Tattie. 'And who does it belong to?'

'Who knows?' said Harcus. 'A lot! Many lives' worth. It's stolen, or blackmailed, or gifted for knowledge of loved ones. All from what Araine learns from the ghosts.

This –' Harcus waved his arms – 'is what Araine took for herself when she killed my sister. Lucie could no longer stand by and watch Araine change into something so wicked. So Araine punished us both – killing Lucie and keeping me here. And that is why I can't see Lucie any more. When she died, something in me died too. I was used up, left here in limbo with Araine. I thought if she formed the triangle once more I'd see my sister again. That's what Araine swore would happen. But she lied. I understand that now. She'll do anything to increase her power. Anything. Including getting rid of you when she's used you up.'

'You knew the dangers all along and you didn't tell us!' cried Tattie.

Harcus hung his head in shame. 'I couldn't! But I'm telling you now so we can work out a plan. To save you. We need to take the heart from Araine and return it to the spiders, just like Lucie said in her message.'

'Or Araine will leave our empty husks somewhere for spiders to nest in,' said Jack.

Tattie shuddered at the thought. 'We could just leave!'

'You could,' replied Harcus. 'But your brother and sister will be trapped in limbo, just like my mam. Not in this world nor the next. Permanently lost and alone.'

'So we can't leave – we're trapped here,' said Jack. 'Priss and Matthew are our responsibility – we brought them back! But how do we take the diamond from Araine?'

Harcus kicked over a pile of gold sovereigns. 'If I knew that, don't you think I would have done it by now? But if we all work together –'

'What a pleasant surprise,' said Araine, right in Jack's ear. He jumped and she laughed, throwing her head back and holding her hand to her belly, a deep noise that made Jack shudder.

'Your guard is terrible. I threatened to toss him on a bonfire and he gave you up immediately. Have you told them all about the spiders and the heart yet, Harcus?' Araine asked, caressing the diamond around her neck.

Harcus shook his head.

'Oh, no need to lie, my darling. I know you better than you know yourself! Couldn't resist wanting to help. You get that from your sister.'

Jack shrank back as the spiders poured into the vault at the sound of their mistress's voice.

'Lucie thought she could stop me, take away my Nora, but I soon put a stop to that idea. Kept you for myself, didn't I, dear Harcus, while she faded to nothing!'

She held out the heart to Jack. 'You want this? Think you can control it, or give it back to the dear little spiders?' She pouted. 'Then who do you lose in return?'

Jack's face fell and Tattie cried out.

'That's right. Your precious brother. And your precious sister. Trapped for all eternity in the in-between.'

Araine smiled and spiders crawled out of her ears and formed a chain at her neck, a living, crawling necklace spiralling over the diamond heart.

'I think this will help you make up your mind.' She clicked her fingers and Matthew appeared in front of him, so faint he could barely see or hear his brother.

'Jack, are you there?' Matthew's voice was little more than a whisper. 'I don't know where she's put me! I can't see you any more. I can scarcely hear, Jack. It's so cold! I'm scared!'

'You two are entwined,' said Araine. 'You're not the only one who is trapped. Matthew is as well. You leave and he'll be caught in nothingness and cold forever. Priss too. You wouldn't do that to Tattie, would you? Stay, Jack, and I'll let your brother out.'

Jack lunged forward to grab the diamond from Araine's neck, but she easily stepped out of reach and he tumbled to the floor.

'Now, now, think before you act in haste.'

Jack looked pleadingly at Harcus, but he wouldn't meet Jack's eyes.

Chapter Twenty-seven

Now

When the lift pops us back out at the ground floor next to the box office, Nikesh is about to go straight over to ask where the archive is and blag their way in. Nikesh will bore them until the staff give up; they're good at that.

'Hettie, look at this!' They're standing to the side, in front of a blown-up old black-and-white photo on the wall that's been framed.

'Is it just me –' I say.

'– or is that Tattie?' finishes Nikesh.

You can't tell the colour, but Tattie and his beard are definitely in it. I read out the year that's stuck on the frame: 1878!

'That's the year the theatre opened under Araine

Machiavelli,' says Nikesh. 'Hettie, there really are ghosts here!'

'So Tattie's definitely one,' I mutter because, although I'm sort of believing everything that's happening, I'm also having a very hard time convincing the sceptical side of my brain. Rex licks my hand, and I look again at the photo and spot a dog by Tattie's feet. 'And so are you!'

'And who do you think Tattie has his arm round?'

I look at the two boys; they're blurred, but you can tell they're beaming at the camera. We have photos of us like that. Best friends.

'That's Jack Redwood,' I say, and Rex grumbles low and long to tell me I'm right. 'And there's Araine Machiavelli, right in the centre. That must be Harcus with the moustache.'

'Look there – it's your automaton. That's Snod's Edge!'

'Snod's Edge is part of this too? Of course he is! That's why he felt so familiar when we found him. It's all linked together.'

'Yup,' says Nikesh, their eyes wide. 'We really do need to save ghosts, don't we?'

'Yes,' I say, snapping back to attention. 'We're on a mission! Meet here in thirty minutes!'

Nikesh wiggles the wrist with their calculator watch on it. 'Then, with Gift, we can find Our Escape and save the ghosts!'

'Right,' I say to Rex as Nikesh runs off. 'We've just got to rescue Gift first.' I pat him on the head and he nuzzles into my hand and whines. 'I know the message says we need to follow you, but I have to save my friend too. Do you understand?'

Rex cocks his head at me as if he's trying to follow what I'm saying. Then he leaps off my scooter and uses his giant thick head to nudge open a door for me.

'Good boy!'

We go down a short corridor, then Rex pushes wide the door that leads to the back of the auditorium and holds it open for me as I go through to find Gift and prise her from Jack's clutches.

The carpet is thick, bright silver pile. I wheel slowly down the centre aisle, past chairs in the folded-up position with silver swirls round the tops and black upholstery. The front of the stage is unlike anything I've seen before – none of the usual gold and reds with carved cherubs and fancy chandeliers. It is all glass and metal, black paint and silver highlights, sharp angles and slick technology, with the lighting rig way up high.

In the front row of the auditorium sits Artistic Director Jack Redwood, the ghost who's working with Araine.

'Next dancer!' shouts Jack. 'Gift Ambrosia! Rice pudding as well as a present?'

I want to ram straight into him and scream at him for mocking my best friend, but I keep calm and bide my time. Hopefully, I can just call her over when she finishes and we can sneak out.

Gift walks on to the stage from the wings. She looks tiny and really nervous. Jack wouldn't know that, but she's fidgeting with her sleeves and that's her giveaway. She nods and music begins to play through the speakers; the surround sound fills the auditorium.

The trumpets in the jazz piece she's chosen go off on an electrifying riff and I can see Gift fill with the music. Her fidgeting stops and she's focused. She leaps across the stage, twisting and soaring, falling to the floor, somersaulting and springing back up.

Even Jack looks up from his tablet and is transfixed.

Rex bounces in time on the footplate and I sway along with him.

The music comes to a stop and I accidentally cheer.

Jack turns round and glares. If looks could kill . . . Then, when he realizes it's me, he gives a little wave. Fear races up and down my spine and I want to be sick. There's something dark inside him; I couldn't see it before. He spots Rex who gurgles in his throat and bares his teeth.

'Not bad, not bad at all,' he says about Gift, but keeps staring at me.

Rex's growl becomes louder and his hackles rise, the hair standing straight up. He tenses as though he's going to spring off the scooter and attack.

'Steady, boy,' I whisper to him. 'Steady.'

Jack continues to stare and scratches his arm. When he rolls up his sleeve, I feel sick and want to reverse straight out of here, screaming, because I can see thousands of tiny spiders racing up and down his arm.

Jack holds it out to make sure I've seen, then changes his tone and turns back to Gift. 'Excellent. Unexpectedly so. You're in. Dismissed.'

She races down the steps at the side of the stage, then bounds over to me. 'Hettie, did you hear what he said? Did you?'

I nod at her and try to smile. 'Gift, it's important you listen to me. So much has happened since we left you earlier. We need to leave now. It's too dangerous to stay here.'

I'm slowly reversing up the aisle and I can't stop thinking about the spiders on Jack's arm. I can feel imaginary spiders crawling all over me and I have to check to make sure they're not real.

'What's up with you?' she asks. 'And where's Nikesh? Is that the dog from this morning?'

'I don't have time to explain.' I look at my watch. 'We have to go and meet Nikesh. There's so much we need to tell you, but it's not safe here. You have to trust me. We've got to go. *Now.*'

She rolls her eyes at me. 'Hettie, you are full of it. Just because you don't want to be here doesn't mean you can spoil it for those of us who do.'

'You what? I'm not! It's not about that!'

'The Arts Centre was a mess,' says Gift, who is not following me.

Jack gets up and begins to walk towards us. Rex's growl is getting louder.

'You're right, Gift,' I say – anything to make her move, leave with us. 'Come with me,' I say to her. 'I can explain.'

'Hettie Lightfoot!' shouts Jack.

'Come *on*, Gift!'

I see one of the little spiders sneak out from Jack's cuff and wander down to the back of his hand. He watches it and turns his hand gently over so that it can creep on to his palm. He holds out a finger for it to walk along, then pops the spider into his mouth and grins at me.

'Did you see him do that?' I say to Gift. 'We need to go – come on!'

Rex's hackles rise again and this time it's as though his whole dumpy little body is vibrating.

'See what?' says Gift.

'Gift,' says Jack, 'come back over here and sit with me. Bring your friend.'

'Gift!' I say. 'Don't. He's dangerous.'

'Don't be silly,' says Gift. 'You're just too scared and too stubborn to audition, and jealous that I'm moving on and you're not. That someone like Jack can see how talented I am.'

'Hey!' I say to Gift. 'It's not like that at all.' I take her hand to pull her away, but she wrenches it free and goes slowly back to Jack like a zombie.

That's not my Gift; my best friend would never say that. I stare as she walks away from me, and it's as though her hair is rippling on her scalp. I squint my eyes . . . There are hundreds of little spiders running through it, churning the roots and making it move by itself!

Jack's captured her – I'm too late! What am I going to tell Nikesh? What will Jack do to her?

'Gift!' I scream, but she doesn't stop until she's standing by his side.

Jack sneers at me. 'I had a feeling the ghosts were up to something, that they'd try to tempt you to them. When Araine hibernated this time, they found a way to come back by themselves without us. But once you join us, they'll be back under our control. So, to help you choose the right side, I thought I'd offer you a little present. A gift, one might say!'

Jack throws back his head and laughs, and spiders flood out of his mouth as Gift stands frozen beside him.

I scream and Rex barks, then darts between my legs, cowering away from him. 'But your new friends have nothing to offer you,' said Jack, 'while we can give you everything your heart desires.'

'Can you hear this, Gift?' I ask her, but she stares at me with blank eyes. The spiders are crawling all over her, climbing up her nostrils, dangling from her braids. I want to retch and be sick, or make for the door, but I'm rooted to the spot.

'You belong here with us, Hettie Lightfoot-Redwood,' Jack says to me. He points to Gift. 'She can't hear us.'

He reaches into the top of his T-shirt and pulls out a heart-shaped diamond that he's wearing round his neck. It's full of shadows and mist.

It looks like the one from the poster. The one Araine the clairvoyant was wearing.

I can see spiders crawling out from Jack's sleeves, flowing down his jeans and on to the carpet.

'You're the ghost story I used to scare myself with,' I say, barely able to get the words out of my mouth. 'The reason I had to put my notebook in the airing cupboard. Magic spiders and a diamond heart.'

'I don't know what you mean,' he says, and smiles. Then laughs hysterically. 'Who am I kidding? I'll take the tiniest bit of fame. We both will. Araine is dormant for now. We're waiting for you, and then together we will form the triangle and be powerful once more! You came. You accepted my invitation.'

'Jack, if you think I'm ever going to help you, or this place, you've got the wrong idea about who I am. Look what you've done to my friend!'

'Oh, I know exactly who you are. I can feel you. You're what woke us up – the smell of lemons! I understand those feelings. I have them too. The rage that no one else gets, the grief that twists you in two.'

He cocks his head and stares at my shocked face, the single tear that courses down my cheek.

'I know what you want and I'm the only one who can give it to you.'

'I don't want it!' I scream at him.

Jack closes his eyes and tightens his jaw. The spiders come flowing out from under his clothes and I suck in my breath with disgust. As the spiders move, they slowly begin to tower on top of each other until they're the same size as him.

'I'm going to use the last dregs of power to show you what we can do!' he snarls.

I gasp as Jack changes in front of my eyes, his skin becoming transparent with the effort. I can see through him to the stage behind. Rex begins to howl.

When I look back at the spiders, I start to shake my head repeatedly. My whole body is goosebumps and wobble.

The spiders are in a shape I recognize.

My heart aches as I see my grandad standing before me. How is this possible? He's there. If I just reached out, I could touch him, hold his hand.

Grandad's voice comes out of his spider mouth. 'Whatever he says, pet, don't listen to him. Don't be tempted by anything he has to offer. Let me go!'

The spiders fall to the floor and scurry back to Jack.

'Not quite what I hoped he would say,' says Jack, wheezing with the exertion, some of his form coming back to him, but I can still see through him in parts. 'But you get the idea, don't you? What we can do for you. What the three of us could achieve together.'

'That was my grandad,' I say, not able to believe what I've just seen.

I hate Jack with every vibrating, painful bone in my body for what he's doing to Gift, but – No! What kind of friend am I to even be tempted? I scrub my sleeve across my face to wipe away the tears.

'That was just spider magic and hocus-pocus. When you join us, he'll be real, right next to you. For as long as you want. Even *forever*. Imagine that, Hettie. Your grandad back with you!'

I gasp. Then I think about what Grandad said. Not to be tempted.

'You were different once, Jack,' I say. 'Tattie told me so. What happened to you?'

'I got a better offer.'

I begin to reverse quickly up the aisle towards the doors. It's too much to process. 'You're evil!'

'I'm a half-life, and so are you. You will return, Hettie,' says Jack.

'Gift!' I scream. 'Come on!'

'I control her now.'

'Gift,' I whisper. She doesn't move, doesn't even seem to see me.

Jack smiles at me. 'You've got a decision to make. The biggest of your life. And not just your life!' He prods Gift. 'I will give you three days to decide which side you're on. Them or us. I'll just hold on to Gift in the meantime, to help you make the right choice. You can tell her mam she's staying at yours. You know your grandad will be here to welcome you with open arms.'

'I don't know what to do!' I cry out. I can still picture Grandad standing there; he was real!

'You know you'll come back here and you will choose us. Not just for her.' Jack nods at Gift who's now standing behind him. 'Then we will wake Araine and we'll be three once more, and the ghosts will follow.'

'No,' I say. Rex grabs my foot and shakes it.

'You will be back!' cries Jack. 'Tuesday by noon! Tick-tock, tick-tock!'

Spiders drop from the lighting rig, and I watch open-mouthed and frozen to the spot as they quickly bind Gift and Jack with their webs and haul them up into the ceiling space.

They're gone.

Rex shakes my foot again and I reverse all the way back to the door.

'I'll come back for you!' I call to Gift.

Out of nowhere, Jack's voice rings out.

'*Oh, I know you will, and we'll be waiting for you. Give my regards to Tattie and co!*'

Chapter Twenty-eight

Then

Jack stretched out in bed until his toes touched the board at the bottom and he felt himself untwisting and crunching back into place. Every morning he woke up bundled up in his bedcovers, pouring with sweat from his nightmares about losing Matthew. In the dreams, they're playing together at the river, and then suddenly Matthew's face is bloated and blue, and he's screaming for Jack to rescue him, but Jack can never get to him in time. He can't lose his brother again. There must be a way to save Matthew as well as himself.

In the dining hall, it was always quiet at this hour. Theatre is about late nights and even later mornings.

The chef stood sleepily in the corner and signalled for Jack to help himself.

Lots of actors and troupes travelled the country, and the world, moving from theatre to theatre, but the troupe here were embedded. They lived, slept and played under the same roof. The acts might change, with different characters and sets and stories, but the faces stayed the same. And the weekly seance was what kept them all in business.

Jack grabbed a plate of sausages and some bread to mop up the grease, then headed to one of the tables in the back corner. He was still in love with the theatre, loved his best friend Tattie – and Rex – and loved being in the workshop with Harcus and Snod. He still felt the magic of when he'd first come here. But it was now all wrapped up in fear and dread that he would fade to nothing and Matthew would be lost forever.

Jack cherished the moments he got to speak to Matthew when they were onstage. If Jack and Tattie gave good performances, then Araine would allow them a couple of minutes alone with Matthew and Priss – and that time was worth everything.

That's what Araine banked on, thought Jack to himself. *That as long as she has Matthew trapped I'll never leave him, and as long as Priss is under her spell Tattie won't either.*

But Jack had worked out a plan to save them all – if he could just find the courage to go through with it. He had decided to build a model theatre, one he could use the diamond to magic them all into so they could escape forever. He hadn't worked out all the finer details yet, such as how to snatch the diamond from Araine. Being connected to her, he knew what the diamond was capable of . . . If he could just get it, he knew the plan would work, then Araine would crumble without it, and the spiders could have it back. He wanted to share the plan with Tattie, but what if it didn't work and he let everyone down? Maybe he could just tell them part of it.

Rex trotted into the hall and hopped up beside him on the bench. Jack handed him a sausage.

'Eat up, boy. We need to find Tattie and the others.'

Jack turned a corner in the corridor and slammed against something solid. Tattie's chest. In a muffled voice, Jack said, 'Rex and I were just looking for you!'

Tattie laughed and pushed him away. 'What for?'

'I've had an idea and I need your help,' said Jack. 'And I'll tell you and Rex all about it if you help me find Harcus and Snod.'

In the workshop all together, Tattie sneezed as the sawdust caught in his nose.

Jack handed a puzzled Tattie, Harcus and Snod a stick of charcoal each, and laid down a large piece of paper on the table in front of them. On it was the outline of a building, but no details.

'Just imagine,' Jack said to them, 'if we made our own theatre. All of us together.'

'And Rex,' added Tattie.

'Of course! But no Araine,' said Jack, patting Rex's head as he barked at the sound of his name. 'What would it look like?'

'You know that's never going to happen: we'll never be free,' said Tattie. 'I can't abandon Priss.'

'But just imagine if we could. Pretend!'

Tattie smiled sadly at Jack. 'What the heck,' he said. 'We can always dream of our escape.'

The four of them began to fill in the design of the theatre, laughing and joking, scribbling bits out. They laughed when Snod wiped his face and accidentally gave himself a charcoal moustache.

They knew it would never really happen, that they were trapped, but sometimes you needed to make-believe. And that was exactly what Jack had them do until he could make it a reality for all of them.

Chapter Twenty-nine

Now

Rex and I zip out of the auditorium, along the short corridor to the box office, and I brake as I nearly collide with Nikesh.

'Watch it!' they shout, diving out of the way. Rex hops over to check they're all right and lick them better.

'Gerroff,' says Nikesh, pushing Rex away.

'Oi!' I say. 'Be nice to him!' Then I begin to cry, great big snotty sobs.

'What happened to you?' asks Nikesh, throwing their arms round me. 'Where's our Gift? Did you not find her?'

At the thought of Gift being taken up into the ceiling space with Jack, how he's spider-zombified her, I babble uncontrollably, trying to tell Nikesh everything that happened.

When I'm finished, they're speechless, which never happens.

'Nikesh, say something! What are we going to do?'

'Take a nice deep breath,' says Nikesh, handing me a tissue, then they fumble in my scooter basket and take out a packet of crisps. 'While I eat these.'

Rex sits in my eyeline and I watch him as I try to control my breathing. When I've calmed down enough, Nikesh gives me a weak crisp-crumb grin and plays with their fringe. I know they do that when they're trying to process so, even though I want to shout at them to hurry up, I stay quiet.

'So you have until midday on Tuesday to decide.' Nikesh checks their watch. 'That's less than three days. And Jack has Gift?'

'Yes,' I choke out. 'How am I going to explain this to her mam? Nikesh, it's all my fault. It's because I'm a half-life. That's what Jack and Araine are – what Harcus and Lucie and Tattie were – and they need *me*. That's what this is all about. The battle between the two sides. If I choose the ghosts, we can fight and maybe defeat Jack and Araine. But if I side with Jack and Araine, I get my grandad back and –'

'But you'd never choose those two! Did your grandad say anything when you saw him?'

This is the point in time when I should tell Nikesh

that Grandad basically told me not to trust anything that comes out of Jack's mouth, so I surprise myself when I say, 'No.'

I can't look at Rex. He knows I've missed out a very important bit of information.

'Did you get into the archive?' I ask, trying to change the topic.

'Not open until Monday. So what do we do now? How can we leave here without Gift? The theatre's closing soon.'

'This is where you've been hiding!' says my mam, coming through the doors as Rex springs in front of me, throws his head back and begins to howl. 'Is Gift staying for another round of auditions? Who does this dog belong to? And, um, what is it doing?'

'He's singing the song of his people,' says Nikesh. 'And who he belongs to is a very complicated story. Hi, Shirley.'

'You doing OK, pet? You look like you've seen a ghost.'

'Excellent time to finally get a saying right, Mam,' I say. 'What are you doing here?'

'Have you seen the time? We've been waiting for you round the corner in the only blue-badge spot for the last fifteen minutes! Did you know that the parking is abysmal now? That's all your dad is muttering about. Come on, chop-chop, time to go home!'

'We can't leave without G–' begins Nikesh, and I cut them off.

'Without hugging goodbye,' I say, holding my arms out to them.

When they hug me, I whisper in their ear, 'Gift's going nowhere: nothing will happen to her without me. We'll just have to cover for her. Can you do that? I'll pretend she's at yours and you can pretend she's at mine. I mean, she stays all the time to help her mam out – no one will question it. We can't do anything more without first getting into that archive. Meet here after school on Monday.'

'What about finding Our Escape?' says Nikesh.

'You think now Mam's here she's going to let me follow a random dog? Monday, after school. We'll solve it all then, in time to come back for Gift.' I make my voice sound more convincing than I feel.

Nikesh pulls away from our hug and nods at me.

'What about Rex?' I say to Mam. 'Can he come too?'

'No way, Hosannah! I'll be the one left doing the walking and the poop-picking-up after you get bored. Has he not got a home? Shall we ring the dog warden?'

Rex lets out a tiny little yap that sounds very like *nope*, drops his tail, gives my hand a quick lick and races off down a corridor.

'We'll be back!' I yell after him.

I'm lying in bed late that night, and I can't get the image of Grandad made up of spiders out of my head. It's there every time I close my eyes.

Though I know to my bones that there's something rotten inside Jack, I can't bear the thought of not seeing my grandad again.

That's a chance I can't give up. Just to see him once more. Just to say goodbye.

That's all I want. I won't need more than that.

And to get Gift back! I hope she's OK.

I'm exhausted and my body is in so much pain from sitting upright for so long. My eyes close, and I begin to drift off, when suddenly I realize what's different about my room and I sit bolt upright to check.

My waterproof and dressing gown are missing.

And so are my automatons, Snod's Edge and Wallish Walls, who were wearing them.

Chapter Thirty

Then

Jack was sitting in the workshop, waiting for the others to arrive: his Free Spirits. He shuddered because that's what Araine called them. But that's who they were now, outlaws – him and Tattie with Rex, and Harcus with Snod. And the ghosts. All Free Spirits. Or at least that's what they hoped to be if Jack's plan worked.

It was five whole years since they'd touched the diamond and become Araine's fellow half-lives. They'd lasted far longer than he ever expected.

He hadn't told Tattie, didn't want to frighten him more, but Jack could feel himself getting colder, and these last few days he'd struggled to get up.

Jack was scared that what Araine had said about using them up was finally happening. And what happened to

Tattie and Harcus if that came about before his plan was complete?

That's why he'd been working even harder than usual. Every minute he wasn't needed in the theatre, he'd been scurrying away to the workshop to spend more time on the model.

'Shall I pop the kettle on?'

'Thanks, Snod, good plan.'

The work had been painfully slow, taking far longer than Jack ever imagined. Since the incident in the vault, Araine was always watching or giving them jobs; they barely had any time to sneak off. The work had gone much faster, though, since Snod had been helping. And now it was finally finished. Harcus and Tattie probably believed it was just a simple expression of hope. He couldn't tell them of his plan to make the theatre real for them. What if Araine overheard? It would put them in far too much danger.

Jack peeped under the velvet cloth to make sure that everything was in its place, that nothing had come unglued or wobbled over. Snod tutted and smoothed out the creases that Jack had made in the fabric.

Jack heard them coming before he saw them, especially Tattie, his feet thudding along the ground.

'Door's open!' called Jack, and Tattie's face popped round it.

'What's all the mystery?' Tattie said, grinning at him.

Rex came in and snaffled a chunk of cake from Jack's plate.

'That has been there for months!' said Snod as he grabbed it from Rex.

Tattie laughed. 'Cast-iron constitution,' he said, patting Rex's tummy.

Harcus came in and pointed to the table in the centre of the workshop. 'I take it this is why we're here? A grand unveiling?'

Jack grinned shyly. Suddenly this felt very silly and he wished he hadn't made such a fuss about inviting them.

'Are you one hundred per cent sure that the surprise isn't cake?' asked Tattie.

'It's not cake!' yelled Snod and Jack at exactly the same time.

'Will you help me lift the cloth?' Jack asked Snod.

He bowed and creaked. 'It would be an honour.'

'You stand here,' said Jack as he took Tattie and Harcus by the hands and pulled them into position to stand directly in front of the model. Rex managed to sit on both their feet.

'Ready?' Jack said to Snod, and they each took two corners of the velvet cloth.

'Ready,' replied Snod.

'On three. One, two, three!' And they lifted the cloth so it flew up like a parachute, the air catching underneath to hold it up. Snod let go and Jack pulled the velvet towards him.

'Oh gosh,' said Harcus. 'I . . .' He walked towards the model, not able to take his eyes off it. 'That's –'

'Our Escape,' Jack finished for him as Tattie unlatched the panel on the front of the theatre and opened up its full frontage to see inside. 'It's based on the sketch we all did, on the day that –'

'– we said we can always dream of our escape,' said Tattie.

There was a sudden cough that sounded like a cuckoo clock getting tangled up.

'I helped,' added Snod.

'And aren't you wonderful?' said Harcus, who couldn't take his eyes off the wooden theatre.

He laughed and so did Tattie, then Snod joined in with the sound of rusty saws, and Jack smiled at them, his dearest friends. He knew that everything was going to be all right and his plan would work. He could rescue everyone.

Suddenly the cold came rushing up at Jack from his fingertips, straight into his heart, and he dropped to the floor like a stone.

Chapter Thirty-one

Now

Sunday is a write-off. I try to get up, but all the racing round the theatre, all the thinking, it wipes me out and I sleep pretty much all day. My parents take it in turns to make sure I'm OK, but this is a regular occurrence, so they're not overly concerned, thank flip.

This morning, before school, I check out the garage and the recycling. Nothing. Mam swears she hasn't binned Wallish Walls and Snod's Edge, and I know it must be Jack who's taken them, but I had to check, and Mam was the most likely suspect.

School drags. Nikesh and I talk at break and lunch, but until we can get into the archive we're no further forward, no matter how much we go round and round in circles. Nikesh phoned up school and did a brilliant impression of Gift's mam and said she'll be off for two days. That's all the time we have left. Less than twenty-four hours once we get to the archive later!

Dad dropped me off at the side entrance to the theatre, where I meet Nikesh, and as there's no Tattie to help me, Nikesh has to get the key for the lift. We're going to hit the archive. There has to be some information in there that we can use to help the ghosts beat Jack.

Once we're inside, Rex comes barging up to us, howling, then his tongue hangs out, and he shakes his big head, spraying saliva everywhere.

Jack walks past. I can see Nikesh shaking and I grab their hand. I turn and watch Jack head for the auditorium.

He winks at me. 'Keeping secrets, Hettie? Tick-tock, tick-tock, time is ticking!' He stalks off.

He knows the one bit I haven't told Nikesh is what Grandad said to me. Of course he does. He knows everything. But that bit's mine.

Where is he keeping Gift? I thought we might see her.

The archivist comes to find us as we agreed by email, and leads us up in the lift, along a corridor of offices, to the door to the archive.

'It's temperature-controlled,' she says, 'so I hope you brought some layers. It's always chilly in there. No liquids. Only pencil, and no writing anywhere near the documents. You can take photos, or I can do photocopies for you – within reason, of course. Nothing to go on social media without my approval. Understood?'

We nod.

'I do love it when people show an interest in our theatre – its history is my favourite thing!'

I bet you wish you knew why we're here, I think.

'We close at seven. I wouldn't normally leave you unsupervised, but, with such a glowing report from your headmaster, I think it should be OK.'

We nod again as she opens the door, shepherds us in and then hurries off. Rex leaps out from my basket where I hid him under my coat.

'Headmaster?' I say once she's gone.

'I have no idea what she's talking about,' says Nikesh in the spit of Mr Derringer's voice.

'You! Brilliant work.'

I look at the stacks of papers and programmes. It's overwhelming. Where do we start when we don't know exactly what we're looking for?

Nikesh rolls up their sleeves and gets stuck in.

Apart from wee breaks, and the archivist occasionally popping her head round the door to check we're OK, we stay hunched over in silence. After the first hour, Rex crawls under the desk, curls up and begins to snore.

Another hour later, I hate to admit defeat, but I've found nothing useful at all. I look longingly at Rex's sleeping body.

I place my head on my arms on the desk.

I wake up with a start when Nikesh calls me over. I sit up and can feel the lines in my face from my cardie, and I have to wipe drool from the corner of my mouth. I've transferred myself on to a wheelie chair to fit under the desk so I grab on to tables to zoom myself alongside them.

'Take a good look at me – I'm the boss of research! You have to read this,' says Nikesh, showing me a document they've found. My eyes can barely focus, and I'm not quite awake, so I ask for the highlights.

'It's a letter from the patent office,' says Nikesh. 'There are loads of them, all under the same name, for different types of theatre rigging, traps and tricks.'

'So what?' I say. I'm tired and grumpy, my neck hurts, and I don't want a Nikesh history lesson.

'All under the name of Harcus Lightfoot.'

I become lots more awake at the sound of his name. My name. The thing that links us all together.

Nikesh continues. 'This one is for a wooden automaton, name of Snod's Edge.'

'Harcus made Snod! And he's related to me too!'

'Yes!' says Nikesh. 'Once I found that out, everything started falling into place.' They pull out their notebook, which has pages and pages of their scrawly handwriting.

'How long have I been asleep, three years?' I ask, and Nikesh begins to speak.

'Big news first,' they say, and I do a drum roll with my fingers on the desk. 'It's no coincidence about your name being on Snod. You and Harcus are related, down Ed Red's side. But he's related to William Lightfoot too. No wonder you're important – you bring both bloodlines together.'

'I do?'

'And, get this, you're related to the evil Spider Queen herself, Araine Machiavelli, because she wasn't a Machiavelli after all but a Redwood! Something shady happened and she stole a lord's money and title somehow.

'Ready for the cherry on top? The site of this theatre wasn't always in Cawlington; where we are now used to be part of a tiny village called Attercop.'

'That's the name of my estate!'

Rex wakes up, yawns and stretches as I shout.

'That's not the exciting bit. What does *attercop* mean?' asks Nikesh.

I shake my head. How would I know?

'A spider in Old English. Or an ill-natured person. The clues were stacked up all along! In Middle English, *araine* means spider!'

My head is exploding. How does Nikesh do this stuff? They're a natural.

'I found ancient maps that show a church once stood on this very spot,' they explain, 'where all the previous theatres have been built, which always seemed odd. Why not build one in London? Or York? The church was marked with the same symbol that we saw in the catacombs and on Jack's shirt. The triangle, heart in the middle, spiders. That's why the theatres kept being built here: I'm sure that white room in the catacombs is the centre of the spiders' web and power.

'That's not even the best bit,' continues Nikesh. 'Harcus, your great-great-great-probably-times-a-billion-or-so uncle, was an absolute genius. That's where Ed Red must have got his skill at miniatures from. Harcus invented hundreds of things. But the incredible part is that these patents span way more than the length of even the longest life. By the way, it currently stands at a hundred and twenty-two years and a hundred and sixty-four days according to *Guinness World Records*, in case you were wondering.'

'You can't help yourself, can you?' I say, and Nikesh grins.

'And then guess who starts to pop up on the patents too?'

I shrug.

'Jack Redwood and William Lightfoot! The last one is registered in 1883 –'

'The year on the Our Escape theatre model,' I interrupt. 'Do you think that's where Tattie and the ghosts are hiding? The theatre can't just be a model – it *must* be real. We've got to follow Rex. I bet that's what he's been wanting us to do all along!'

'I wish we'd found some way to defeat Araine. I thought we'd find it here,' says a crestfallen Nikesh.

'It's not complicated,' I say, the research Nikesh has found giving me proof that this whole story is actually *really* real. 'We've got to get the heart off Araine and give it back to the spiders.' I shudder as I say that.

'So it's easy!' says Nikesh. 'You do something no one has managed to do over hundreds of years and defeat Araine, save the spiders that you're terrified of and hate, and give them back the heart. Oh, and then we save Gift too. Ta-dah!'

I groan. 'Do we really have to save spiders?'

'And, now we know all that, we have to do what the blossom message said and follow Rex!' shouts Nikesh as Rex's ears perk up at the sound of his name. 'Because he knows where Our Escape is!'

Rex gives a little sigh as if to say *finally*, and Nikesh nods and grins like the absolute ridiculous genius they are.

'And then do you think we *can* save Gift?' I ask quietly.

'That's how we can save *everyone*,' says Nikesh, giving me a hug.

I try to keep the smile on my face.

Not everyone, I think. *Not if we give the heart back to the spiders*.

Not my chance to see Grandad.

Chapter Thirty-two

Then

Snod carefully scooped Jack up from where he had collapsed on the ground, and they all ran to Araine's lair.

The hanging outside the door was no longer covered in spider stars to transform into the key; it was just plain black velvet.

'What?' Harcus muttered.

'Looking for this?' asked Araine as she waltzed down the corridor towards them, a magnificent creation on her head of feathers and tiny little mouse skulls with golden spiders crawling upon it.

'How do you like my new hat?' she asked Tattie who stared at her in horror. She pointed to Jack in Snod's arms. 'Having a little nap, is he?'

'Do something!' yelled Harcus.

'All your plotting and whispering and sneaking behind my back and now you want my help?'

'We don't want anything from you!' shouted Tattie.

'Oh, but you do. You want your precious Jack back!'

The golden spiders marched in procession from Araine's hat, down her arms and formed into a key that, once the velvet was pulled back to reveal the keyhole, she used to unlock and open the door.

'Let's discuss it all over a pleasant cup of tea. Won't that be nice? After you! Snod's Edge, place Jack there and leave. That will be all.'

'Don't speak to him like that! He's one of us!' said Tattie indignantly.

'As you wish.'

They laid Jack on the chaise longue in the corner. The rise and fall of his chest was barely visible. Harcus and Tattie sat in chairs opposite Araine as she sipped a cup of tea from fine bone china.

'We knew this time would come. All half-lives get to the end of their usefulness, and this one has just lasted longer than most! And you, Harcus, have become particularly attached to him.'

Harcus nodded. If he played along with her, maybe she would help Jack. 'You're right.'

'I beg your pardon,' said Araine, sitting up in her seat. 'Did I just hear that correctly?'

'I can't keep on losing people. You were right all along. Better to keep them at arm's length so when they . . .' Harcus's voice faltered as he looked at Jack lying there, shivering. 'So when they are used up it's, well, easier.'

'You can't mean that!' Tattie yelled at Harcus.

'Play things, that's what they are, just tools like the ones you use in your workshop.' Araine giggled. 'Much easier to see them that way.'

'But,' said Harcus, leaning forward, 'he has been a particularly useful one, hasn't he? You haven't had crowds like this before, and the vault has never been as full! It could take years to find another Redwood, especially one as powerful as him. Look how long he's lasted!'

'Things move on,' Araine replied airily. 'We shall move on.'

'We could, though, couldn't we, keep it going a little longer? I mean, wouldn't it be a waste to finish so soon?' said Harcus.

Araine screwed up her face so her eyes were like slits and she stared at him. She put her teacup down carefully on to its saucer. 'What are you suggesting?'

Tattie followed their conversation back and forth like a tennis match.

'Use me.' The words got tangled in Harcus's throat. 'Use me to extend Jack's usefulness. I've got some energy left – take it! He's worth more to you than I am. What else can I do for you now that I've lost Lucie?'

Araine bent her face to his, cocking it from one side to the other, trying to weigh up his offer.

'What is your plan?' she finally said. 'I assume you have one? I can't tell if you do, or if this is just you being *kind*,' she sneered.

'A swap. Take my remaining energy and give it to Jack. You can do that, can't you? It's not beyond your powers?'

'You'd lose your life for *him*? You have no plan other than that?'

Harcus held his head up high and let all the guilt for luring Jack and Tattie to this place and his grief for his lost sister weigh upon him. 'Yes.'

'No!' cried Tattie. 'You can't!'

Harcus gave him a soft smile. 'It's all right, Tattie. It's time. I'll see my Lucie again, I hope.'

'I wouldn't wager on that!' Araine laughed.

'Ask Jack to forgive me,' said Harcus to Tattie. 'I think it's best if you leave now. Snod, take him and Rex away.'

'I don't want to leave you,' said Tattie, and he began to cry. But he looked at Jack, lying cold and blue in the corner, his breath more shallow by the second.

'Thank you, Harcus,' whispered Tattie, and ran to hug him, his tears drenching Harcus's neck.

‘You, Jack and Snod have been the sons I wished I could have had.’ Harcus nodded at Snod, who drew himself up into a salute, and then wrenched the sobbing Tattie from Harcus and helped him from the room.

Rex waited for a moment, then held out his paw, which Harcus shook.

‘Take care of them for me, boy. That’s an order.’

Rex looked at Harcus for one final time, then turned tail and left the room, Araine shutting the door behind him.

Chapter Thirty-three

Now

'Do you think Gift will be OK?' Nikesh asks as we race out of the theatre right before closing time.

I nod. Then I shake my head. I don't know. 'I can't think about that now: it hurts too much. We need to focus. That's how we save her.'

Rex starts howling and doing zoomies up and down the pavement outside the theatre.

'We are go!' I shout to him.

He stops and stares at me and cocks his head. He doesn't move.

And then suddenly he's off, and we race to keep up.

We follow Rex helter-skelter, yelling at him to wait up. He can sneak between feet and dash round buggies, whereas I'm constantly held up by people heading out to the pub, dawdling as they check their phones or stop to look in shop windows.

I bang on the passenger door of someone who has pulled over the dropped kerb so I can't cross the road. They wind the window down.

'Need summat, pet?'

'Yes,' I say, pointing exaggeratedly at my scooter. 'You to move!'

'No need to be so rude. I was being safe, pulling over to check my phone. Mind a moment, this is important . . .'

Rex gives up waiting and makes a leap for it in front of the car.

'Rex!' Nikesh and I scream for what feels like the fiftieth time as a silver Fiesta gets within a whisker of him.

'Is he . . .?' I ask myself. 'I can't look!' And slam my hands over my eyes.

I peer through my fingers and frantically scan the other side of the road, hoping he'll pop out.

'There! He's there – he made it!' yells Nikesh. 'How is the ghost dog still alive with road-crossing skills like that? Actually, that may be the whole reason why he's a ghost dog.'

We have to wait until the man finally moves on with a cheery wave as I give him dagger eyes, and then we tear across all three lanes of the main ring road, and Rex howls again to tell us to hurry up.

I zoom past St Cuthbert's Church up the road where all the buses stop outside the shopping centre. Neighbour and security guard Alan is outside, having a skive.

'Oh no,' I say as Rex makes a right turn and dives at the automatic doors into the shopping centre. 'You've got to be kidding me.'

I turn the corner and see Rex bounce off the doors. They won't open for him.

'Automatic doors don't work for ghost dogs apparently!' Nikesh shouts as I race up to them.

I see Alan leap into action. 'Oi, dog – you're not allowed in there!'

This is going to get me in so much bother later, I think, as I zoom past Alan and scoop Rex up on to the footplate of my Mean Machine and yell to Nikesh to leap on the back as the doors open for me.

'The dog's with me!'

I turn the speed up on my scooter and we whizz through the ground floor of the shopping centre. Outside Greggs the bakers there's a massive end-of-the-day queue for the reduced stock, and I close my eyes and scream at people to get out of the way and pile on through.

I can smell people's perfume, we get that close.

I open my eyes and look back. Some shoppers are shouting, but no one's hurt. Thank goodness. I check

Rex is OK and burst out laughing. He's got a massive sausage roll in his mouth that he must have snaffled from someone.

'So ghost dogs can't open automatic doors, but they can steal food?' Nikesh says to him, leaning over to pat his head. 'Giz a bit!' But Rex raises that little white eyebrow at Nikesh and wolfs down the rest of his stolen treasure.

Rex woofs in my face like he's yelling at me to run, and I turn back to see a very sweaty, red-faced Alan legging it towards us.

I groan and press my throttle and zoom ahead, Rex giddy-dancing on the footplate, Nikesh clinging on, whooping and cheering.

I get to the automatic doors on the other side by the charity shop and they open for me. Rex leaps off and heads left up the hill by the mobile-phone shop.

We go tearing off as Alan stops and leans against the wall outside, trying to catch his breath.

'Wait until I tell your mam!' he yells after me.

'Not unless I tell her first!' Nikesh shouts back as I dodge a bin and we race away.

Nikesh leaps off the back and trips over the edge of the pavement, doing a spectacular somersault on to the new paving at the bottom of High Row.

I haul them up just as a bus whizzes by, centimetres away.

'You all right?' I ask Nikesh, and they just about nod as they get to their feet.

Rex hurtles up the ramp near the fancy water fountain and we race after him. I think he's going to head up the main yard in the centre of High Row, but instead he veers to the left and up one of the narrow ones, all of which lead to Skinnergate on the other side.

The yards are cobbled, so as we enter it I have to slow down or my scooter will have a conniption fit, as my mam would say.

Rex slows down too. So does Nikesh.

It's gloomier here, always in shade, even when it's bright sunshine. It feels damp and it smells musty. All the shops are boarded up, or shuttered, which is very odd; they're usually bustling with people getting coffee from Echo 3, or stinky cheese from the delicatessen.

I'm sure that's the yard we came down. Where has the coffee shop gone?

I look around and none of this is familiar. I've never been up here before.

It twinkles with fairy lights, and it would be beautiful if I . . . I realize I can no longer see Rex. Where is he?

'Rex!' I yell, but he doesn't come running and I can't hear him. 'Rex, are you OK? Did he definitely come up this yard?' I say to Nikesh and turn back to look the way we came.

My voice is too loud and warbly; it echoes and makes me feel very alone.

Nikesh doesn't answer. They've disappeared too.

I slowly creep forward on my scooter, speed on low for the cobbles, but also because the hairs on the back of my neck are prickling. I go to the corner where the yard does a little right-angle turn to the left before continuing on straight. Something does not feel right here. We haven't got enough time! Less than seventeen hours until we have to meet Jack with my decision. It's like I'm . . .

'Out of time!' yells a massive man made out of wood who is wearing my dressing gown.

Then it all goes dark as he drops a sack over my head and I'm too shocked to scream.

Chapter Thirty-four

Then

'Snod, Jack's coming round!' called Tattie.

Snod put down the bowl of warm water and the facecloth he was carrying and came jerkily over to the edge of Jack's bed where he had been keeping a careful watch over him with Tattie and Rex.

Jack blinked and tugged his hands out from under the covers to rub his eyes. The colour came back to his cheeks, rosy taking over from ice-blue.

'Steady on, lad,' said Snod, and helped him to wriggle up the pillows.

Rex stood on his hind legs to bite the blankets and tug them back round him and was rewarded with a pat on his head from Jack that was more like the flop of a hand, but Rex didn't seem to mind and squirmed until

Jack's fingers were over his favourite area, just behind the ears.

'What happened?' asked Jack. 'I remember showing you the theatre and then . . . nothing! Did you not like it?'

'Jack, we all loved it.'

'We did,' said Snod, giving Tattie a look that Jack couldn't work out.

'Why is there a tree in the corner of my room?' Jack asked as he saw the large tree in a pot.

'I couldn't find a plant or flowers, and the etiquette book tells me that foliage is a great comfort on recovering from illness,' said Snod. 'I thought that a cherry tree was appropriate.'

Jack laughed and stopped immediately as icy pains gripped him.

'Go gently,' said Tattie. 'It'll take a little while until the energy transfer is complete and you're up to full strength.'

Jack looked down and noticed that his hands weren't as translucent as before and Harcus wasn't in the room with them.

'Tattie, where's Harcus? What has he done?'

Jack looked at the grief-stricken faces staring at him, and his own face dissolved into sobs.

They sat round their table in the dining hall, Jack squeezed up against Tattie and Rex because Snod's Edge took up so much room.

Even though it was busy and crowded, no one dared come close enough to overhear them. Since Jack collapsed, the rumour mill had become frenzied, and people were more scared of the Free Spirits than ever before. Now, with Harcus's sudden disappearance, none of the theatre troupe even glanced at them.

Tattie crammed mashed potatoes and gravy into his mouth. 'When I'm sad, I eat! You've been unconscious for a week – we've been missing him longer than you.'

Jack couldn't bear to eat, couldn't bear to think that Harcus had sacrificed himself for him.

Snod coughed and a few splinters flew out on to the table that he casually brushed off on to the floor with a miniature broom that clicked out from his index finger.

Jack felt very alone.

'We're in this together,' said Tattie as if he had read Jack's mind.

Tattie handed his bowl to Rex for him to lick clean. 'They say the new magician can do all sorts with the elephant, even make it disappear! And properly, not just with a distraction technique. Let's go and watch the rehearsals. Maybe that will make you feel better?'

Jack didn't want to be distracted by an elephant; he wanted to feel this pain, to use it. 'Why don't you all go. You've been cooped up in my room for far too long. And I've been summoned to see Araine.'

'We could come with you. Maybe we should?' said Tattie.

'I just want to be alone for a little while first, if you don't mind.'

Sawdust puffed off the top of Snod's head in his excitement at seeing the elephant.

'If you're sure you'll be all right?'

Jack nodded.

'Well, I can't argue with Snod's eagerness,' said Tattie. He stood up and Rex followed him, jumping down from the bench.

Rex grabbed Tattie's sleeve in his mouth and tugged. 'It's the elephant dung – he's acquired a taste for it. Disgusting, I know. Come on, you two!'

Jack watched them leave the dining hall, one of the acrobats somersaulting out of the way. Once they'd gone, he wiped away the tears rolling down his face.

'Why did you do it?' he asked quietly.

But Jack knew why. He would have done the same. He'd do anything for his friends. Now there was one less to save and he didn't dare risk losing those that were left.

Jack had to protect them at all costs, just as Harcus had protected him.

Jack could see how pale and faded Tattie was, just like he looked before his collapse, and this time there was no Harcus to save Tattie if he fell.

It was time to put his plan into action.

Chapter Thirty-five

Now

I hear some snatched words, and I try to focus on them rather than on the fact that there's a sack over my head. But it's really loose so I can easily see a pair of wooden clogs below the bottom of my dressing gown, and metal feet and the hem of my raincoat.

Can it be . . . ?

'We're in so much bother . . .'

'Stop clanking . . .'

'I need oiling . . .!'

I've been kidnapped. By my own automatons. Who are alive and speaking. Which a few days ago would have been a big deal, but nah, I'm used to this sort of stuff now. Where's Rex? And Nikesh? Whose side are Snod and Walls on? It has to be the ghosts' side, doesn't it?

I feel the panic rise in my chest, my ears become all echoey as if I'm underwater and I keep trying to swallow, but my mouth's too dry.

I realize there are two distinct voices. One's a bit squeakier, sort of rusty? It grates and grinds. That must be Wallish Walls. The other is deep and resonant, like a cello. Snod's Edge.

'This gadget is beyond me. Where's the handle?' says Walls.

'Or the cogs?' asks Snod.

'Maybe it needs a magic word?'

'Just ask her.'

'Ask her?'

'Well, it's either that or tell Harcus what we've done.'

'Is Harcus here?' I ask. My great-times-a-billion-uncle! 'Take me to him!'

'Oh, she can hear us!' says Walls.

'Of course I can hear you. Did you think the sack would stop me?' I say.

'You did, didn't you? Oh, sawdust, they struck the jackpot when they made you!'

'Don't be mean,' says Walls's rusty voice.

'Oi!' I shout. 'I'm asking you a question! *Where is Harcus?*'

There's no reply.

'I can see your feet – I know you're still there!' I watch as the feet slowly and quietly shuffle backwards out of view. 'I know who you are!'

'This isn't going quite how I imagined it,' says Snod.

'Me neither,' says Walls. 'Shall we just leave her and pretend this didn't happen?'

'No!' I shout at the same time as Snod.

'You said that at the same time!' There's rusty laughter, then a big clang. 'Oops.'

'I've warned you about that,' says Snod. 'I haven't been able to fix it right since the incident with the bats.'

I see Walls's whisk hand on the floor as he bends to pick it up. 'Pardon me, beg your pardon, don't mind me, always happening! Blame my dad – shoddy workmanship.'

His dad: that's my grandad. I wish he could have been here for this! I realize my arms aren't tied up – none of me is. All they've done is put a sack over my head.

I swiftly move my right hand up to the edge of the sack and pull it up so it's resting on my forehead like a hat, and I see my two automatons in front of me, wearing my waterproof and my dressing gown, trying to reattach a giant metal arm.

'She's taken the hood off, hasn't she?' says Snod, who has his back to me. Little poofs of sawdust come off him.

'Yes,' squeaks Walls. 'She's staring right at us.' Then he closes his eyes, like Gift's little niece Bea does when she's playing hide-and-seek and thinks that means she can't be found.

I can feel my jaw dropping. Even though I should be scared, I'm in absolute awe.

Walls opens his eyes and sees me staring at him. 'Formal introduction time. I'm Wallish Walls. Pleased to properly meet you.' He clangs over to me and holds out the one arm that's still attached.

I stare at it.

'It's rude to stare.'

'You're right,' I say. 'Sorry.' I shake his outstretched hand that has thimbles for fingertips.

'You know my brother, Snod's Edge. He helped to make me when your grandad wasn't looking, and that's the reason my arm keeps falling off.'

'Nowt at all to do with the bats,' mutters Snod as he comes over and holds out his hand too.

His hand is cool and smooth to the touch, rosewood, each part perfectly articulating as he gently shakes my hand and then loosens his grip.

'You're both incredible!' I say, looking from one to the other. Snod, with his voice like a cello, smiles and I can see intricately carved teeth. He spots me looking.

'Got a full set!' I can hear the whirr of a motor as he opens his mouth much wider than a human possibly could to proudly display his teeth.

'Not at all terrifying and precisely what anyone would do in a situation like this,' I say quietly.

'Wood!' squeaks out Walls. 'She looked at you and she said wood, and that's funny because . . . you're made out of wood!' He begins to clank around, whirring and wheezing as he goes.

'How come you can speak?' I ask Snod as he brings his jaw back into a less terrifying position. 'And walk!'

'Because we are the automatons. And that's what we can do in Our Escape. This is what you were trying to find, yes? Follow us.'

I watch them clank and creak over to the side of the alley where there's a piece of material with a golden star on a dark velvet background, like a tapestry. Snod gently and slowly opens his hand and plucks the star from the hanging. When he wiggles his fingers, it unravels into gold thread and forms a key in his hand.

I gasp. 'How did you do . . .?'

'If she's impressed by that –' says Snod to his brother.

'– wait until she sees the rest,' completes Walls. 'Turn your steed on and follow me!'

Chapter Thirty-six

Then

'You honestly think this will work?' asked Tattie as he peered round the door to the dining hall where Snod had gathered the whole theatre troupe. Everyone except Araine who was off on one of her now-frequent hunting missions.

'It has to,' said Jack, Rex by his feet.

They'd been through this plan so many times that Jack was bored of talking about it. It was time for action. It wasn't the real plan, of course, just something to keep Tattie and Snod occupied while Jack carried out all the dangerous work. Tattie had said he would sneak in and take the heart himself, in honour of Harcus. Jack had to stop him trying to do that.

They watched as Snod clapped his hands. The sound

echoed round the hall and the noise of the theatre troupe died down to a mutter, and then silence, as the wooden man struggled up to stand on one of the tables. Rex gave him a helping nudge, but nearly knocked him over.

'You all know me as Snod's Edge. I was made by Harcus Machiavelli, Araine's brother. That is a lie.'

The crowd shuffled uneasily, glancing at one another. They had no idea what they'd been called together for, but it certainly wasn't that.

Snod cleared his throat, spat out some sawdust and continued. 'His name was Harcus Lightfoot. The world-renowned clairvoyant who also vanished, Lucie Lightfoot, was his sister.'

The crowd erupted. They all knew of Lucie Lightfoot – everyone in theatre did: she was legendary. But long before their time. How could she have possibly been Harcus's sister?

Snod shouted over the noise of the crowd and it soon died down again so that people could hear what else he had to say.

'I know you're scared of Tattie and Jack, even of Rex, of me. But it's Araine you should fear the most. She has the two boys trapped here under her power; you've all noticed that they do not age. You've cowered and pretended you can't see it, but you have not offered help. And she's obliterated Harcus. Murdered him!'

'We knew it!' cried one of the acrobats.

The magician called out, 'Something evil is afoot – we could sense it!'

'Yes!' shouted Snod. 'And what did you do? You ignored it, pretended it wasn't there as long as you had a roof over your head and food in your bellies.'

'That's not fair!' shouted one of the clowns, getting to his feet. 'How were we to know?'

'You never asked!' roared Snod. 'All these years watching those precious children fade away in front of your eyes. Not one of you asked if they were all right. Not one of you asked if they needed help.'

The crowd looked at one another, a different sort of energy bubbling through them now. Less righteous. More unsure.

'I've had a very large part to play in this, one that I will never forgive myself for. Not telling Jack and Tattie to run when I had the chance. I feared I'd be turned into chippings if I spoke out! But your part is worthy of guilt too. And I want you to use that guilt to help the two of them to make a stand with us. Will you do it?'

The crowd was uncertain. No one wanted to be the first to speak. Finally, the clown spoke up again.

'I will,' he said. 'I knew something was wrong, but I ignored it. I can't do that any longer.'

'Thank you,' said Snod. 'I'm terrified too, but imagine

how brave Jack and Tattie have been all this time and completely alone. It's time for us to stand side by side. Time for us to be as brave as them. Time for us to be a true company. Together!'

Snod beckoned for the boys to join him. Tattie looked to Jack for reassurance, and they walked out into the dining hall together.

The crowd of performers and backstage workers, curtain-painters and costume-makers, all the people who made the theatre run gasped as they realized how frail the children looked, that they could see right through Tattie. That they looked the same age as when they'd both arrived. It was so obvious now they could no longer turn away.

'I'll help!' cried one of the dressers.

'Me too!' shouted one of the ballet dancers.

'And us!' called the acrobats, and, as Jack and Tattie stepped up on to the table and Rex leaped up behind them, the theatre troupe stamped their feet and shouted that they were with them.

Snod draped his arm round Tattie and Jack. Rex leaped up into Tattie's arms.

Then they all stood together as the crowd surged forward to embrace them.

That night it took an age for the troupe to finally go to bed, far later than usual: they were so full of what they were going to do now they were united.

Tattie quickly started snoring, but Jack lay awake, waiting for the sound of Araine's carriage pulling up outside.

As soon as he heard her open the theatre doors, he sneaked out, turned the corner and headed along the corridor towards Araine's lair. Time to put the real plan into action.

Chapter Thirty-seven

Now

'Welcome to Our Escape,' says Tattie, with his green beard, who appears behind the velvet drape that Snod has pulled back to reveal a theatre foyer! 'It's grand to see you again. I'd usually be on the door, but these two buffoons wanted the honour.' He takes the sack off my head. 'Did a brilliant job of it, I see.'

'Hey, Tattie,' I say shyly, wondering whether it was polite to ask him more about being a ghost . . . or is he a half-life? I have so many questions. But first of all: 'Where's Nikesh and Rex?'

He winks at me. 'You'll see them shortly. They're safe in here with the ghosts. And I'll introduce you to Harcus. I'm betting that's who you're really excited to finally meet? I'm off back on door duty. Keep an eye on those two. Ruddy nightmares, they are.'

I whizz round the foyer in circles, trying to take it all in. How does this even actually exist? A theatre on the other side of a magical velvet curtain that's opened with a key made from golden thread? I can hardly believe it but here I am!

This place is exactly the same as the wooden miniature we saw in the white room. The walls are all wood and wonky, and you can see the nails that have been hammered in. There is a hatch for snacks and drinks with colourful bunting flapping above it, and hand-tied bags of sweets stacked on wobbly shelves. On the opposite side there's a booth that has the word TICKETS painted above it with a dribble coming down off the letter S.

'I told you she'd notice that!' says Snod, coming towards me. He has a bright red-and-gold tray strapped over his shoulders that's filled with tubs of ice cream.

'My arm seized up – can't be helped!' says Walls, who's now wearing a patchwork gold tuxedo jacket and a red bow tie. He clanks over towards me and bends down, creaking as he does so. He whispers, 'It doesn't spoil it? Does it?' And I can hear his chest go all jangly.

'No,' I say, smiling up at him. 'It's absolutely perfect!'

He grins and the colander on top of his head whistles and sprays out confetti.

'Get a broom!' yells Snod. 'Clean up all your excitement before it gets trampled into the carpet!'

Walls winks at me and clanks off.

I turn my scooter so I'm facing the door too.

'Don't just stop there – get in the booth!' Snod hands me a red-and-gold bow tie from the top of his tray. 'This will have to do. Hurry!'

'But I . . .'

Snod glares at me and I take the bow tie and pop it round my neck. It's elastic and twangs.

Snod tuts and makes sure it's straight and then shoos me off. I go towards the booth, wondering how I'm going to fit inside and get up the step. More ruddy steps! Then I notice there's a little handwritten TURN HERE sign pinned next to a wooden dial. I twist it and the door to the booth gently swings open at the same time as a wooden ramp at the perfect angle glides out. I zoom up it.

Inside there are tiny drawers full of different tickets, tiny pencils, and stampers and ink-pads. There's a punch that makes tiny mask shapes in paper, a till with giant plinky-plonky buttons. It's brilliant!

I wait, watching Snod, who rocks from foot to foot. Little bits of sawdust float off him.

I wait while he mimes pushing up a non-existent sleeve to check an imaginary watch on his wrist.

I wait as the poofs of sawdust become more frequent and violent.

I wait as Walls clanks over to join him.

I wait as Snod and Walls slowly turn to face me.

I wait as Snod slowly shakes his head and says to me, 'You did summon the rest of the Free Spirits, didn't you?'

Chapter Thirty-eight

Then

'Do you think this is actually going to work?' asked Tattie doubtfully as he looked down across the packed auditorium and up into the gods, from Harcus's box in the dress circle where he used to watch the shows and, more importantly, the audience's reactions.

'For the hundredth time, yes!' said Jack, poking Tattie in the ribs. 'Have some faith in me, would you?'

'It's odd seeing them there, as the audience, not on the stage or behind it.'

Sitting in the red-and-gold seats in the stalls were acrobats and magicians, cooks and stagehands, sailors usually up in the gantry working the rigging or in the undercroft operating the traps and mechanisms. They all looked uncomfortable in the posh seats that cost more than they earned in a year.

'It's all built on a lie,' said Jack. 'And our dead friends and relatives. It's time to bring it down. I'm going to check on the situation backstage. You lot keep an eye on things from up here.'

Snod looked at Jack and nodded his head. It creaked. 'I need waxing.' Rex yapped in approval.

Jack dashed along the corridor. Araine would be reaching the stage soon. He needed to be there to enter with her. Tattie and Snod thought that it would be the chants of the audience that would summon Araine, that working together as one was the magic needed to defeat her.

But Jack was the reason that Araine would come.

Because Jack had told her what they were about to do. He hadn't betrayed them, at least he didn't think he had. He just knew they would never agree to his plan, that it was far too dangerous. He had to do this alone.

The parrot – could it be the same one after all these years? – dived at him, plucked a clump out of his hair and screeched hello over and over again as he raced past it.

'Stop that, Albert!' Jack yelled as he batted him away.

'It's our only chance,' Jack muttered to himself over and over as he sped down the corridor, and jumped over some brooms and an open paint tin. 'It's the only way to keep them safe. It's what Harcus would have done.'

Jack ran down the black painted brick corridor, the one where Tattie had led and he'd followed the first time Jack ever came backstage and showed him the wonder of the theatre.

This time the hand that grabbed Jack by the shoulder and forced him to stop was cold and jagged, and he could feel the ripple of spiders underneath Araine's skin.

'Ready, half-life?' Araine whispered to him in the dark.

Jack gulped and struggled to get out the words. 'I'm ready.'

He could hear Snod and Tattie begin the chant in the auditorium from their box.

'I rather think that's our cue,' said Araine.

Jack's heart pounded as he saw the hole in the curtain he'd once peered through, so many years ago, and he remembered the pure delight and magic. Untainted by what was to come.

Araine stepped forward, and all of a sudden Jack could feel his chest tighten and it was hard to breathe, as though the elephant was sitting on it. He tried to pull out of Araine's grasp and run to his friends. What was he thinking? He was suddenly aware that this was a very bad idea.

Araine tightened her hold. 'Having second thoughts? Too late.'

He could feel the spiders crossing over her hand on to his. He tried to struggle free, but couldn't escape Araine's grasp. The spiders ran round and round his wrist and hers, forming moving golden handcuffs, locking them together.

Araine stepped out on to the stage and dragged Jack with her.

The audience of angry, chanting theatre performers, backstage and front-of-house workers, cleaners and cooks stopped shouting.

The sudden presence of their boss in all her magnificent, malevolent glory extinguished the fight in them and replaced it with fear, especially when they saw the gold spiders that were binding Jack and Araine together, cocooning them.

'Well done! Good work, darling Tattie, darling Snod – excellent work! All in it together, finally!' Araine laughed. 'It's been such a joy watching you all sneak about, thinking yourselves so very clever. What were you going to do, Tattie? Make me so distracted that you could take my heart? I didn't even need this one to come and confess all – I knew it already – but, Jack, it was such sport pretending I didn't know.'

Araine turned to Jack as she snapped her fingers to make the gas lamps of the lights-up trap slowly rise from beneath the front of the stage, thrusting their towering shadows up on to the bare back wall of the theatre.

'Nothing to say to that?' Araine asked Jack, and he tried to speak, but she placed her finger on his lips, and fear silenced him.

Jack felt the weight of the world crushing him as his plan shattered. How had he been so stupid as to think he could take her heart by himself when she thought he was on her side? She'd seen right through him. How would he rescue his friends now? What about Matthew? He had to try – he had to!

'Quiet, just the way I like it.' Araine pointed into the auditorium. 'I've had enough of all of you! You bore me. *Bore me!* And our audiences are dwindling. So I think it's time for a change, don't you?'

The theatre troupe looked about them in fear. One of them started to run towards the door.

'That's right, I won't stop you. Off you go – you're free to leave!'

'No!' yelled Tattie from the box. 'Don't go! We're stronger together. We can still –'

'Oh, darling, it's all about the individual. And the important individual here is me! Tattie, it will be magical starting all over again. Building an even better theatre right here on this sacred ground. I've already drained the water tower.'

Araine reached into her pocket and pulled out an ornate little silver box that she flicked open.

'It's time to burn and begin again, and this time –'

The audience began to scream and run to the door, bursting out and fleeing in panic.

'Oh, Jack.' She turned and looked him in the eye. 'We are going to be incredible together. I shall be more powerful than I ever imagined. Thank you for the idea, darling. I know it's not quite how you imagined this turning out.'

Araine struck the match and dropped it to the wooden floor as Tattie cried out and Rex howled and the last of the audience fled the building.

The cobweb tightened round Jack and Araine, and the heart about her neck began to glow. Out of it poured hundreds of thousands of sparkling black diamond spiders that wove round the gold web, binding Jack and Araine into separate cocoons, then joining them together.

'I knew this one had fire inside him, unlike you, insipid Tattie! I'll take him with me, teach him the ways of the spiders' heart. Another Lightfoot will come along, Tattie, to take your place. And, once they do, I shall be more magnificent than ever!'

The fire began to take hold, dripped over the edge of the stage, engulfed the curtains. The velvet on the chairs was set alight.

Rex cowered in Tattie's arms as Snod tried to drag them away.

'Tattie!' Jack shouted. 'Tattie, Snod, I'm so sorry. I failed. You need to escape. Our Escape.'

Tattie looked at what was left of Jack inside the cocoon. 'We'll come back for you somehow!' he shouted to him. 'We'll find a way! No matter what she does to you, know we'll come back.'

Araine laughed maniacally. 'Escape? There is no escape, you fools!'

'That's not what he said!' shouted Tattie. 'Jack said *Our Escape*.'

Tattie understood what Jack wanted him to do. He wiped his eyes and took one last look at his friend, now consumed by the gold-and-diamond cocoon, safe from the flames that ravaged the stage. 'We'll return for you, Jack!'

While Snod and Rex shouted and barked at Tattie to leave, Tattie pulled out the model theatre Jack had built for them, based on their dreams, from where they'd hidden it under Harcus's old seat in his box.

Tattie took a handful of stones from the ornamental cherries that he'd saved from the tree Snod had given to Jack, and he sprinkled them inside the model.

As the cherry stones hit the floor of the miniature theatre, they echoed, as if the space inside was cavernous, as all dreams are, built to contain whole worlds.

Tattie placed the model on the floor as the flames began to lick the sides of the balconies and stretched their fiery tendrils into their box. He hoped all the troupe had made it out in time.

He took hold of Snod's hand, who was cradling Rex. 'We'll be all right. Jack made sure of it.'

And then Tattie leaped on to the theatre, followed by Snod and Rex – and they were joined by all the ghosts who were released from Araine's power. Tattie had broken the triangle with his escape. Together, they floated into the miniature theatre like cherry blossom caught in the wind.

Chapter Thirty-nine

Now

'I, well, apart from Nikesh, and they're already here, and Jack has Gift and, well, I don't hang out with the old theatre lot any more, not since Grandad, so I guess it's just me . . .' My words dry up as Snod and Walls continue to stare at me.

My lower lip begins to tremble. I really don't want to cry right now.

'Oh,' says Snod. 'We thought there would be more of you. You miss him, don't you?'

I nod.

'Me too,' he says. 'Ed Red was a most excellent human being. Come with us.' He beckons me out of the booth and I trundle down the ramp.

Walls pulls back a curtain hand-stitched with sunset

patchwork, like the colours that light up the hill at the top of my street when twilight descends. Snod steps through and I follow on behind.

'If you thought the foyer was impressive, wait until you see this,' whispers Walls gently into my ear.

'Wow.'

I've come to a stop in the aisle running down the centre of the auditorium. It's lit by masses of twinkling lights. It's all wood and doesn't have a single thing that isn't wonky. I stare at the higgledy-piggledy balconies.

'When you magnify the size of a miniature, any slight imperfection grows larger and more noticeable,' Snod tells me.

This is the model we saw, made large. Made *real*. I roll forward a little more so I can see where the main light is coming from, up on the stage. It's a wrought-iron Victorian street light. It's illuminating a huge tree that is growing out of the stage, its trunk gnarly and twisted, covered in moss, the branches bare, reaching out towards the ceiling.

'What's that?' I ask, pointing to it.

'A cherry tree,' says Walls, smiling sadly.

'And –' Snod turns and grins at me, his face distorted in the shadow coming off it, and he whispers in a voice so deep it resonates in my tummy – 'the ghost light.'

'What's a ghost light?'

'Theatres always keep a lamp burning when everyone

has left and the place is in darkness. It's to guide an audience back and to keep the ghosts company. It –'

'Coming up to get a closer look?' asks Walls, interrupting Snod as he marches up the steps at the side of the stage.

I point to my scooter and say to Walls, 'Love to, but my trusty steed says no.'

'Why?' asks Walls. 'Is it hungry? I don't like moving when I'm hungry.'

I point at my wheels and then at the steps. Walls looks baffled and points back at my wheels and then to the middle of the stage.

I hadn't noticed it before, because it blends in so beautifully, camouflaged against the wood boards.

There's a gently sloping ramp that rises from the middle to the left, and then crosses back towards the centre of the stage, bringing you up to the very top.

I begin to cry. Walls looks horrified and leaps back down the steps towards me. Even Snod seems worried and forgets to be angry at me for not bringing anyone, and they both awkwardly hug me from either side.

'Is something wrong? Did we do it wrong?' Walls asks me.

'I told you you'd done it wrong,' says Snod, giving Walls's ankle a little kick so it dings like a bell.

'Don't kick him!' I say, and Snod looks a little bit

sorry, but not much. 'It's not wrong. These are happy tears – it's incredible!'

'It's just a ramp,' says Snod.

'It's not *just* a ramp,' I say, wiping my eyes with my bow tie. 'It's not a *just* at all. I have never, *never*, *ever* been able to get on the stage from the audience. At panto, they'd get some of the kids up to join in with this chorus bit, and Gift and Nikesh, they'd raise their hands and yell to be picked, but I never did. Not because I didn't want to. I wanted to be picked! But how would I get up the steps?'

'They should have used their noggins and built a ramp,' says Snod, knocking on his head.

'So it's really not a *just* at all, now is it?' I say, looking at them both in turn. 'Thank you.'

'I told you *my* ramp was beautiful,' says Snod to Walls. Walls kicks him. 'Hettie, did you see what he did!'

'Yes!' I say. 'And you deserve it. Now come on. I'm going up on the stage. Watch me!'

The automatons cheer as I move forward on my bright pink steed and ascend. I laugh as I get to the top and then stare in wonder at the tree. I see that it's even more detailed when I get up close.

'How did you get it to look so real?' I ask Snod as he makes his way over to me.

'Because it *is* real. This wasn't in Jack's original plans; he didn't know how to make this. It's from the tree I brought him on the day he woke up. It just got old and crooked. Like us.'

'Why doesn't it have leaves and blossom?' I ask as I stroke its spindly branches. They are soft to the touch, like they're covered in velvet.

'Because it's still linked to Jack. As he withered and turned rotten after all that time with Araine, something in the tree decayed too, and we're waiting for the petals to come back. That's how we'll know that we've finally defeated Araine and freed everyone.'

Snod walks over to the lamp on the stage and picks up where he left off. 'A ghost light shines a path for the ghosts to find their way home. We always hoped it would bring Jack back.'

There's a snuffle and a yelp, and then Rex comes bounding on to the stage towards me and leaps up into my lap.

'Hey, boy! Where have you been?' I scritch him behind the ears as he slobbers all over me. 'I've missed you!'

'He's missed you too,' says a voice from the wings at the side of the stage.

I can't see where it's coming from. There's just a slight stirring, like the wind has picked up, and then, very gradually, I can see him. See them all, transparent and barely visible as they step on to the stage in front of the ghost light.

I know Harcus Lightfoot, the inventor, from the photo in the theatre – I recognize his moustache. I feel shy. He's family! I spot Nikesh who waves. The boy ghost must be Matthew. I don't know the other two. The little girl has pigtails; the woman is barely visible at all, and wears an elegant gown, like she's a star of the stage, and has short tightly curled hair.

'Hettie, you are so welcome here,' says Harcus. 'Please allow me to introduce you to Tattie's sister, Priss, and this is Lucie Lightfoot.'

I'm in a theatre that was magicked out of a model, with walking, talking automatons and a stage full of ghosts. I feel like I've known them forever. This is wonderful! Tattie and Nikesh give me a huge hug. I feel like my heart might explode, for all the right reasons this time.

Rex is leaping all over me, and the ghosts and automatons are making me feel like theatre royalty, especially now Tattie has joined them.

They all begin to applaud so I sort of do this little bow thing that feels like a good idea in my head – the only idea in my head – but it just looks like I've sneezed, so I bow a bit lower and then feel ridiculous, and then it's been too long so I sort of pretend I'm looking at my shoe, and then I even say, 'Ah, my shoe.'

And now I just want to shrivel up and hide. There's a reason I prefer being backstage.

'Nice shoe,' says a low voice, and I look up and, although he's faint and I can see the tree through him and sort of in him, I can also see that Harcus is giving me an absolutely massive smile.

'Thanks,' I say shyly, and smile back. 'Nice moustache.'

Rex runs in a triangle, from me to Tattie to Harcus and back. He pounces at each of us and when we reach down to grab or pat him he careers off to the next person. He eventually lies on his back, paws waving in the air, tongue lolling.

'Good boy,' says Tattie. 'He really likes you – good judge of character.'

'Didn't he like Jack too?' I say. 'He got that wrong.'

Harcus says, 'I take it you've met Jack?'

'He's a nightmare. Literally! He's stolen my friend –' My voice tails off. I remember Gift under Jack's spell.

I've been so caught up in the excitement of this place and meeting the ghosts that I've barely thought about her, or Grandad. No, that's not true. I have been thinking about them because I love them; they just haven't been pulsating at the front of my brain so I can't think about anything else but them. Is that OK?

I yank the bow tie from around my neck because it's suddenly quite hard to breathe.

Rex springs up and nibbles at my hand.

'Hey there,' says Tattie. 'It's all going to be OK. Walls, would you mind before Hettie keels over?'

I can feel Walls gently take me in his arms, and I try to protest, but it's like my ears have gone underwater and I'm all floaty, and then everything just sort of drifts away.

I stretch out, and it's really comfy and warm, and I think I'm late for school and Mam will tell me off and why hasn't she come with a cuppa and toast, and then I absolutely scream my head off when a wooden face looms over mine.

'Charming. What a delightful reception,' mutters Snod. Then he cranks open his jaw and yells, 'SHE'S AWAKE!'

Harcus comes over immediately and smiles at me. 'Yes, thank you, Snod. We can see that.'

'Just doing my job. You said to yell! Can't do anything right around here . . .' He goes bumbling off into the corner and picks up a broom and begins to sweep his way out.

Walls clanks towards me and I sit upright. He brings me a cup of tea, most of which splooshes out over the blanket as he jerks it at me. 'Oops, sorry, need oiling!'

'No bother. My arms are like that too. Thank you – it's very kind of you.'

Rex leaps up on to me and laps at the spilled tea.

'See, nearly clean already,' I say, and point at Rex.

I gaze around me. My Mean Machine is in the corner of what feels like a cellar; it looks ridiculous, bright pink and shiny against all the wood, rope and brickwork.

'Where am I?' I ask. Then: 'What time is it?' as I frantically try to sit up.

'Hell,' says Tattie, stepping out from behind a pillar.

I scream. 'Am I dead too!'

'No!' says Tattie. 'You're not a ghost. This is what we call the undercroft, the space beneath the stage here. It's where all the magic happens. As for the time, Hettie – it is six a.m. You were out for the count and we couldn't wake you, but we need to get a wriggle on before time runs out. We've been working with Nikesh to get the Free Spirits here.'

'Six hours left,' I whisper. 'My mam! She's going to knack me for staying out all night!'

'Don't worry – Nikesh sorted it. But we need you now. You're the only one who can take the diamond from Araine and give it back to the spiders. Time is running out.'

I can feel the energy has changed in the building, the welcoming, light atmosphere replaced with charged electricity.

'I'm not sure I can. Didn't Jack try and fail?'

Harcus sits down on the edge of the bed next to me. I try not to stare, still getting used to the fact that I can see right through him.

'Jack was kind and funny and clever, and took far too much on his own shoulders, thought he had to solve everything by himself. That sound like anyone you know?'

I blush and don't answer.

'The difference here is that you won't be doing this alone: you'll have all of us beside you. Generations of Free Spirits. Now, Hettie,' says Harcus softly, 'I need to know: what has Jack offered you?'

I don't answer.

'Did he say he could bring your grandad back for you?'

I nod and squish my hands tight together.

'You can't do it,' says Tattie. 'You can't let him.'

Harcus takes my hand. 'You mustn't make the same mistake we did. Anger, that's what the diamond used against Araine, to corrupt her.'

I raise my eyebrows.

'It was exactly the same for her. It started with Araine wanting to see her sister, Nora. And then the same for Jack who wanted to see his brother, Matthew. But you have the chance to make it right, to stop the cycle. You need to learn from our mistakes and, no matter how much it hurts, let your grandad go.'

'Don't be tempted by anything he has to offer.' I whisper what Grandad said to me.

'What's that?' asks Tattie, and I shake my head.

'That pain you're feeling? It's love,' says Harcus.

I don't want to talk about this any more; it hurts too much so I change the subject. 'How come when we had our Arts Centre there was no Jack there, no Araine and her spiders?'

'After we escaped, it took a long, long time for Araine to gather her strength. All her power was invested in us, and we slipped from her grasp. She wasn't strong enough to come and get us, to do anything but lie in wait. All that anger and rage of hers bubbled into Jack. It wasn't his fault: anyone would break being that close to her for so long. Once Araine sensed your presence, the perfect half-life, someone who joined both bloodlines together and was in the depths of despair, willing to do anything for one last meeting, she woke Jack up to begin the cycle again.'

I'm shocked. Everything that I've done since Grandad died, what I thought I should do to keep his memory alive, pushing people away, not getting on with my life, the anger, not wanting to let him go, being willing to do anything to get him back – they are all the things that woke Araine.

I'm the one who caused all this.

'I'm the reason why Jack has Gift!' I cry out.

'We have to move quickly,' says Tattie, sitting on the other side of me and patting Rex. 'You need to take Araine's heart and free the spiders so they can have their diamond back, to end this once and for all. Just like we should have done.'

'And us before that,' says Harcus.

Snod peers round the door and nods at me. 'She understands.' He looks at the others. 'She's not as stupid as I first thought.' He smiles at me like it's a massive compliment.

'Thanks,' I say. 'And, once we do that, then –'

'Jack will be released and the cycle will finally be broken,' says Harcus, his moustache twitching.

'There's a room under the new theatre,' I say, thinking back, 'and it's full of miniature theatres. There's one that doesn't exist yet; it's huge and ornate, more like a palace, and at least ten times the size of any of the others. It isn't finished though.'

Harcus looks worriedly at Tattie. 'It's further on than we thought!'

'What is?'

'If Jack finishes building that model, just like we were able to step into our theatre, he'll be able to step into it and make it real. And if he can take you and Araine with him –'

'– then you'll be lost forever, and Araine will be able to control the whole world from her magical theatre, and nothing will be able to cut off her power,' adds Tattie. 'And Gift –'

He doesn't need to finish that sentence.

'So I have to stop Araine!' I say.

'*I?*' asks Tattie.

'Yes!'

He shakes his head at me.

'Groups of people equals committees and paperwork and votes and nothing changes!' I tell him. 'You come together and you lose!'

'And that's what you think happened with your Arts Centre?' asks Harcus gently.

'It's not what I *think*,' I spit out at him. 'It's what I *know*.'

'I can see why Araine chose you. You're wrong though. You didn't fail. Your theatre was old and dangerous and it had run its course.'

'Could you get onstage?' asks Snod quietly.

I don't have an answer for that, not one that helps me out anyway, so I stay quiet.

'What made your theatre special?' asks Tattie.

'Tell us!' says Walls and sits on the floor next to me with a massive clang, and he dings and clatters as he gets his legs crossed and rests his chin on his hands, staring at me. 'I love storytime. Go on.'

'Well . . .' I hesitate. 'You didn't have to audition for a start; anyone could join in.'

Snod nods encouragingly, so I carry on.

'We'd do these twenty-four-hour shows twice a year. Everything from scratch in one day, and not just the usual suspects: everyone would be invited, all the families, the people from the old folks' home, the bowling club, everyone! My friend Nusrat would record it for her podcast – she'd love all this! It was a way to get more audience, find the people who thought theatre wasn't for them. There'd be different rooms set up, and everyone would come and make costumes, and prepare food, do the props and the set; there'd be a massive chorus of singers. It was brilliant!'

Walls claps his hands so I go on. 'It's where Mam made friends when she had me and I was so tiny and she was scared. There was this playgroup thing, see, and that's where I met Gift. She's my best friend, and –' I stumble, thinking about her trapped with Jack. I take a deep breath to carry on. 'And it's where we all met, the Free Spirits, well *our* Free Spirits, not yours, and we'd argue a lot, but we just got each other.'

I pause and take a giant breath. 'It's where Grandad fell in love with theatre and I got to spend so much time with him – we all did. It's where I first had the courage to produce a show, and all my love of lists and organizing finally found a home. I'm really good at it!'

Tattie grins at me.

'That's incredible,' says Harcus. 'Do you know what though? You haven't once said anything about the building.'

I open my mouth to reply, and realize I don't have anything to say, so I shut it again.

'Theatres are houses and homes for people, for troupes, for community,' Harcus carries on tenderly. 'That's what they make – togetherness. For the people who make the shows, and the people who watch them. It's a place of coming together. Of making friends and working towards something – together. The building doesn't matter – they come and go; it's the friendships you forge, the community you create: that's what counts.'

'And you still have that, don't you?' asks Tattie.

I look at all the faces watching me, full of hope.

Chapter Forty

Now

'OH. MY. GOSH!' shrieks Mam, and she flaps her arms and spins round in the foyer of Our Escape. 'The note didn't tell us it was this beautiful. OH. MY. GAWD! Hettie, love, I don't know what's changed for you, but I could not be more proud of you for being here. Your grandad would be too!'

Snod shuffles over to me. 'Will she calm down? Should I fetch a bucket?'

I laugh and dry my eyes. 'Give her a moment.'

Dad is grilling Wallish Walls about how he works and dismantling his whisk and washing-machine arm and putting it back together without the squeaks; Lucie is huddled up with Priss, whispering in the corner, and I'm still weirded out that I can see through them both.

Alan walks in and gasps, the rest of the theatre crowd from the old Arts Centre following behind him.

Tattie and Nikesh come up to me. 'Excellent with the notes and Rex-powered delivery system. Let's get everyone in the theatre so you can explain the plan.'

Tattie goes to gather the troops and I roll down into the auditorium. The tree is in shadow from the ghost light. It looks sad and lonely.

'OH MY OH MY OH MY!' I hear as Mam comes in. 'IT'S SHAMAZING!'

I zigzag up the ramp until I'm on the stage and call everyone over. Nikesh stands next to me. People fill up the first half of the auditorium, Dad making Mam sit down and giving her a bag of my crisps to shut her up, as he speaks quietly to Tattie, Harcus and the rest of the ghosts.

'They can see the ghosts and walking, talking automatons,' I say to Nikesh, 'and they're not freaked out?'

'They've entered into the magic of this space with their whole hearts. They want to help!'

'Right!' I yell. 'Harcus will fill you in on all the twiddly bits. We haven't got much time and we've got spiders to save and their heart to give back to them.'

Dad and Mam and the rest of the audience are very quiet and look anxiously at each other. It's definitely not the response I was expecting.

'It's just that, well –' says Alan.

'Go on,' I say.

'It's just, Hettie, that last time we tried to save something, we lost and you were, well . . . We completely and utterly understand why, but you were awful!' He then really quickly and quietly says, 'So we don't want to do it again if you're in charge.'

Then he sits down with his arms crossed. Nikesh can't look at me.

'You're right.'

Nikesh stares at me now. 'He is?'

'Yes! I was horrible and selfish and I blamed all of you, but mostly I blamed myself for not trying hard enough. If I'd just done more, then maybe – It was all tangled up with how I felt about Grandad. I couldn't separate those two things out from each other. And I nearly lost all of you as a result. I promise I won't be awful again. No matter what happens.'

'But we can win, can't we?' asks Mam.

'With two lots of Free Spirits working together? Of course we can.'

Chapter Forty-one

Now

'This is not glamorous!' says Nikesh, whingeing.

'Do they always whine like this?' asks Tattie.

'Yes,' I say, and Rex joins in with a bark. 'We only have two hours left. Get a move on and quit whining!'

Tattie, Nikesh, Rex and I are churning through silt and mud in the tunnels underneath Our Escape, heading towards the new theatre.

The other ghosts are too weak to make the journey and the automatons are far too noisy. They're overseeing everyone else, getting ready to put up a fight for us.

'So is this how you vanished?' I ask Tattie who's leading the way.

'Exactly. The catacombs under old Attercop are like a cobweb. We're at the outer edges of it, and therefore at the limits of its power. This tunnel leads directly into our workshop below the Renaissance Machiavelli Empire at the centre of everything. Here we are!'

We all come to a halt in front of a solid wood door. Tattie goes up to it and presses his ear to it, then slowly turns the handle, pushes the door and pops his head back. 'All clear!'

We file into the workshop behind him, then move through into the white room.

'Does Araine, or Jack, know that this entrance to the tunnels is here?' asks Nikesh, blinking in the light.

'They didn't, but they will now,' says Tattie.

The massive miniature of the new-build theatre is on a plinth – it's nearly complete!

'Look, he's almost finished putting the glass in the windows and that's one of the last jobs,' I say. 'Grandad said it was much harder to move anything around and get access once they're all in place. We have to hurry. Jack will want this finished before our showdown. This is where he'll take me if we fail, and then Araine will be able to take over the world without anyone being able to challenge her.'

Tattie nods. I don't like to say anything, but he seems even more transparent than before.

Time is running out. For everyone.

We make a dash towards the lifts, and pop out at the level where the room in the roof should be. I desperately want to find Gift, but I can't help her if we don't head here first.

'It was on the first model, you see,' I say to Nikesh as Tattie and Rex scout out the way ahead. 'This empty space by the roof. But by the final one the room had disappeared. Which I thought was a bit odd; it was like someone didn't want anyone else to know it existed.'

'The perfect place to keep something hidden,' says Nikesh, grinning back at me.

'Or someone,' I say. 'That's where Araine will be.'

We turn into one final corridor and come to a complete dead end.

Tattie looks at me and shrugs his shoulders. 'What now?'

Rex goes over to a corner, gives it lots of sniffs and then begins to paw rapidly at it, as though he's trying to dig up a flower bed.

'Good boy!' says Tattie, getting down next to him. 'What can you smell?'

I go over to look. I stick my face right up against the wall so my cheek is flat against it and look along it. There's a little ripple in the wallpaper, like an edge. I glide my nail up and down next to it and the paper slices open. I give it a little tug.

'Oops!' I say as I rip, and a whole section comes off in my hand, revealing a hidden door behind it. 'Don't just watch – help me!'

Rex attacks one particularly large piece and pins it to the floor.

When we're done, there's a big pile of paper that Rex rounds up into a bed and plonks on top of with a sigh.

'I expected it to be harder than this,' says Tattie warily.

'Can't we at least be chuffed it wasn't!' I say, and try to pull the hidden door open. It won't budge. I give it a prod in frustration and it pops open with a little click, swinging back to reveal darkness and the smell of mould.

'After you?' I ask Tattie.

Rex gets off his bed and sits on Tattie's foot so he can't move.

Nikesh is shaking their head. 'This feels wrong,' they mutter.

I lead the way and they all follow. Inside, I find a pull light switch and give it a tug. A solitary light bulb flares into life and I close my eyes. When I open them, the image of it is lasered on to my retina and everywhere I look has a bright yellow flare in the middle.

Once that passes, I see the room is filled with two giant empty cobwebbed cocoons.

We're too late!

'Check everywhere, check the walls – the heart might be here even if Araine isn't,' says Tattie.

'Quick!' I yell. 'We don't have much time!'

'You're right,' says a voice I recognize.

'The clock is ticking, and your time is up!' Gift smiles at me with cold blue eyes, and I yell out to her to *please, no, stop*, as she laughs and slams the door shut.

We're trapped.

I look at my watch. It's been forty minutes – just over an hour left.

Nikesh goes over to try the door again, for the millionth time, just in case it finally opens. 'Erm, folks, I think you need to see this.'

I reverse and scream as I watch spiders come flooding under the door, racing through the crack and beginning to cover the walls. Little gold spiders creeping and crackling and sending out cobwebs behind them.

'Oh no,' Tattie says in a trembly voice I haven't heard from him before. 'Golden spiders. Araine is definitely awake.'

'I *hate* spiders,' I moan.

‘What do you think she’s sent them for?’ asks Nikesh, and they leap back and tread on Rex’s paw who yelps in protest. ‘Sorry, fella.’

Tattie picks Rex up and hugs him.

‘Hey,’ I say. ‘Look at that,’ and I point to the far wall where the spiders have congregated. They are wiggling about, but forming lines and curves and . . . ‘They’re spelling something out!’

Nikesh reads it out. ‘S-T-A-N-D-B-A-C-K.’

‘Stand back?’ I say. ‘What does that mean?’

Then the gold spiders wriggle and jiggle again and make a massive number five on the wall, then a four, then a three . . .

Tattie watches them, wide-eyed. ‘They’ve never done anything like this before. I don’t think they’re working for Araine. This is amazing, Hettie – we can win this, I know we can! Better do what they say,’ adds Tattie, and makes a run for it to the back of the room. Nikesh, Rex and I swiftly follow, and two seconds later there’s a massive boom and we all get lifted up and chucked against the wall.

I cough and splutter and wipe my eyes, and when I look at my fingers they’re all black and sooty.

‘Is everyone OK?’ I choke out.

‘Fine,’ says Tattie, appearing through the clouds of dust and smoke, still just as see-through and with not a fleck of muck on him. He checks it's OK with me to help, and then gently lifts me on to my trusty steed, giving the seat a quick wipe with his sleeve first.

'Am I the only one leaning into the sooty fashion trend?' I ask.

Nikesh nods at me, then laughs, then everyone laughs, but I stop abruptly as Gift reappears in the doorway.

Chapter Forty-two

Now

I pull Rex close and shout at the others to get behind me. I've been a rubbish friend for too long and they've all stuck by me. Now's my chance to repay them and do the same for them.

'Nikesh, move, quick – get over here!'

No one budges.

Gift takes a step towards me and I cower, but then I see her eyes; they're no longer blue and icy, but back to warm amber with flecks of sunshine.

'Gift?' I ask, barely above a whisper.

She launches herself at me and hugs me so tight with one of her strangleholds that I can barely breathe. I hug her with my floppy arms, then wrestle her off me.

I'm so happy to see her, back to her old self, that I can't let go of her hand. How could I have contemplated losing her? I nearly gave her up for the ghost of my grandad. He would never forgive me! And neither would I.

'It was like I was frozen in a block of ice,' says Gift. 'I locked you in here under Jack's command and then it was like something suddenly defrosted inside me and I was back to being me. The spiders were all giddy and scrambling over me, like I was their BFF.'

'The spiders?' I ask and shudder.

'They seem to be my friends now.'

On cue, spiders drop from the ceiling and whizz round, spinning a web together that spells out: WE ♡ GIFT.

'You've got a fan club. Rather you than me. And the explosion?'

'That was all me,' Gift says, looking impressed with herself. 'I couldn't undo my own ruddy lock! Jack had showed me where he keeps his stash of dynamite. They're planning to blow the place up! I knew me watching Channel Five adventure rubbish would come in handy at some point.'

Everyone begins talking over each other all at once, asking questions, exaggerating bits. Nikesh is re-enacting planting the explosives: they seem to be getting bigger with each bang.

'I'm so sorry I was such an idiot,' I tell Gift. 'I'll never leave you ever again.'

'And I'm really sorry I was won over by nice carpets.'

'Don't forget the heating,' I say with a grin, and pull her into another hug.

'I heard you,' whispers Gift in my ear. 'It was your voice that brought me back.'

She pushes me away and tells me: 'Araine has used all her power to wake up, so she had no choice but to let me go. Jack is putting the finishing touches to the model right now. As soon as you arrive, he plans to give you no way out; they're going to attack you and force your hand on to the diamond with theirs.' She gets hysterical. 'If they do that, you'll be lost forever and Araine will be free to do whatever she likes!'

'They'll never get me, I promise,' I tell her. 'Araine is at her weakest,' I say to everyone. 'It's time to make our move. Gift has managed to release the spiders.'

The spiders wiggle themselves on the wall and spell out 'YAY' and 'WOOHOO'.

'So we've just got a heart-shaped diamond to take and return,' I say.

'And the small matter of dealing with Araine and Jack on a rampage. They'll be desperate, furious about letting Gift go and losing the spiders. That makes them more dangerous than ever,' says Tattie.

'Action stations!' yells Nikesh, and we all go filing out of the door, Rex following behind.

We make it as far as the white room. If Araine has stashed the heart anywhere, it will be in there. Back where it all began.

I can feel the change in the air before I see them, but I don't have time to yell out before Jack and Araine hurtle towards us from the tunnel where they had been lying in wait.

'It's time!' calls the being that was once Araine. Once Lucie's best friend. Jack stands behind her.

She is undulating and oozing. Like a big larva or a slug. One minute all papery and haggard, the next squidgy and young and fresh. Changing before our eyes.

Around her neck is the heart.

'Hettie Lightfoot-Redwood!' she calls, and Jack sings along with her. 'Come and be mine! You can save all your little friends if you just come and join me!'

'Liar!' shrieks Nikesh. 'You said Hettie could decide!'

'Run!' yells Gift.

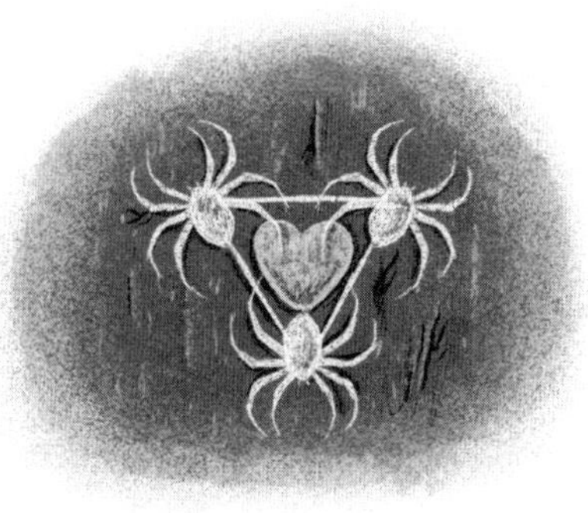

Chapter Forty-three

Now

We slam through the door into the workshop, and then through the hidden door to the tunnel leading to Our Escape. It's the only route available. We just have to hope our Free Spirits are ready.

'How can something that gross move so fast?' screams Gift.

Nikesh is hollering and shrieking.

I'm leading the way with my speed set at maximum and Rex on my footplate. My friends – old and new – are just managing to keep up.

I sneak a quick look behind them. Jack is now riding on Araine's gigantic larval form, like she's a horse, and they're just behind us.

I press one hand over my ear while I steer, trying to

block out her voice as we speed through the wet tunnels, slipping and sliding and holding each other up, hauling each other onwards, not letting anyone fall behind.

'Oh, Hettie!' Araine and Jack call in unison. 'You know what we can offer, *who* we can offer!'

'Don't listen!' Tattie shouts at me.

Gift takes my hand and I want to follow her, to hold on, I really do, but something in me makes me stop and take another look behind.

And that's all the time Jack needs to reach for me and grab me off my scooter.

'Well, well,' say Araine and Jack in unison. They slip and slide in her goo as they stalk round the bare cherry tree in the centre of the stage in Our Escape where I sit with my back to it. 'Isn't this homey? Not my taste at all, nor Jack's any more, but I can see why you would like it. It rather suits you scruffy folk.'

Everyone from the Arts Centre is in the auditorium, with Nikesh and Gift and the ghosts, looking up at the stage. They all grip and hold tightly to one another. Dad stops my mam from coming to get me, but I can see how much it's hurting them, wanting to be with me, but not being able to. It's as if the fear they didn't have when they met our ghosts is compounded and they suddenly realize what a nightmarish world they've stumbled into.

'Isn't it nice to have an audience one final time, before you join us and we rule this pitiful world together? I know you've got it in you,' Araine says to me, her sloppy mouth yawning open. I can smell the rot inside her. 'Why else would you have stopped? Oh, they may tell you thousands of reasons why you shouldn't listen to me. But there's only one that matters, isn't there? One thing you want more than anything in the universe, don't you, my dear? And I can give him to you. You just need to join us.'

Araine no longer has the spiders under her control – they are all sheltering and crowding round Gift – but she does have Jack.

'Here's something to tempt you.' Araine cackles and her whole body vibrates.

Jack starts to moan and writhe and change shape. I can't watch, but I can't bear to look away, as he morphs and wriggles and then he's there, standing in front of me.

My grandad. Ed Red.

The person who loves me the most in all the world.

It's like birthday and Christmas and everything rolled into one, and I open my arms and he crouches down and hugs me tight. It feels incredible. His whiskers tickle my forehead. This is all I've wanted. I can feel my arms relax as I sink into him.

I stiffen in his arms.

Something isn't right. I sniff.

He doesn't smell like Grandad, not of WD-40 and ready-salted crisps.

I put my hand in my pocket and hold out his pliers to him, but he doesn't seem to understand.

Araine snuffles and snorts with glee next to me. She distracts me and, as I look at her, I can see out into the audience, at all those faces staring at me.

Counting on me.

'This isn't him!' I scream at Araine.

'Of course it isn't,' she chuckles as Grandad fades away and rejiggles back into Jack's body. 'It's a promise of what can be, when you join us.'

Araine's clickety-clack claws reach into the oozing mess of her chest and pull out the heart-shaped diamond. 'You and Jack. You just need to hold this with me. That's all. Ever so easy.'

'Nothing worth it is that easy!' yells Nikesh. They're all up at the edge of the stage now: Gift and Nikesh, and Harcus, Priss and Lucie, Tattie and Rex. I can see my mam and dad, Alan, the rest of the ghosts, everyone from the theatre on their feet and moving slowly up on to the edges of the stage.

'Do you think I would want this?' shouts Matthew. 'It's me, Jack – your brother!'

Jack turns to look at him and there's a moment where I can see the boy trapped inside, who built a theatre for his friends to help them escape, but then he vanishes and is back to being Araine's minion once more.

'You could have had all this too!' Jack says to Matthew.

'All what?' I ask him. 'What do you have, Jack, if you don't have your friends?'

Everyone to the side of me takes another step closer.

'Oh, Hettie, there they are, all telling you not to do this, but how unfair is that? They did! They got to say goodbye, and they'd deny that for you?' Araine holds out the heart and I move towards her.

'It's just a goodbye,' I turn and whisper to Harcus, 'I'll stop after that. Just one goodbye.'

He shakes his head. 'It doesn't work like that, Hettie. The spiders should never have offered it. They were just trying to help. They didn't realize that the bonds of love can warp into something so full of rage and anger, into that!' He points at Araine who is circling me and Jack now.

'Don't let her win. Don't let anger beat you!'

I make another move forward towards the heart. As I look up into it, the centre of the diamond begins to swirl; it fills with black clouds.

'Yes!' cries Araine. 'Just a little closer, just one tiny touch – you and Jack and me together, forever!'

'I'll have Matthew again!' Jack shouts, but it's as if Araine has set him to say it on autopilot; he doesn't seem to even know what that means or feels like any more.

I sit bolt upright.

Araine and Jack – they don't love those they've lost any more. You can't keep people close to you like that for this long without it eating you up.

I look at everyone I love. I promised them I'd be different this time.

Gift and Nikesh are holding out their arms to me, arms in which I've laughed and cried, and they've held me.

The ghosts, they've had all this extra time together – that's so unfair. But they're telling me not to.

I close my eyes to make everything stop; it's all too much and I think of my grandad.

My grandad loved lots of things, like bruised bananas, getting the last bits out of a ketchup bottle, my mam and, most of all, me. That's not me being big-headed: that's just a fact.

I don't have to have him there beside me to know what he would do. I can imagine him speaking to me, his smell, his voice. He's there, here in my heart, not in one made from a diamond.

I imagine Grandad by my side, and he nods at me.

Just a tiny little nod and I know what I have to do. I have to keep him in my heart, but I also have to let him go. That's the only way to live. That's what Harcus and the ghosts have been trying to tell me.

I don't know what's real any more, and what I'm imagining, but I sob and tears stream down my face as I hear my grandad say, 'Hettie Lightfoot, I love you best of all.'

And I reply, in my heart and in my head, *Even more than* – and I choke back the tears so I can speak. *Even more than my future?*

And, for the first time ever, my grandad's reply is no.

I'm sobbing now, breath catching in my chest. The audience could run for the doors, but they're not. They're staying. They believe in me to do the right thing.

Araine is too absorbed in herself to realize what's happening.

'Have you still got them in your pocket?' Grandad whispers in my ear and I realize it's not him speaking, it's me. He's in me: after all that time we got to spend together, he left the best parts of himself here, in me.

I can do this. But I can't do it alone.

I cry out to my friends, 'Help me!'

I don't speed towards Araine and the heart; I don't try to wrench it out of her hands with the pliers. Instead, I reach up to the cherry tree and hold tight to one of its branches, and I think about Grandad and how much I love him, and how much I need to let him go.

I take my hand away and I gasp. A leaf has grown where I touched it, blossom beginning to sprout.

'Come on!' I yell to everyone. 'This is Grandad's tree, this is Lucie's tree, and Nora's and Matthew's and Priss's. This is the tree for everyone we've ever loved and lost.' I can't speak any more because I'm sobbing too much.

Gift runs towards the tree, holds tight to a branch and says, 'This is because Ed Red loved ready-salted crisps and he'd always give me the last one and I miss him so much it hurts!'

When she takes her hand away, there are two blossom petals. She looks at them in awe, then at me, and I smile at her.

'Come on!' she calls, and everyone comes to the tree.

Alan grabs a branch. 'Ed, this is for leaving me your caravan. I promise to use it and have adventures and raise a pint to you wherever we travel.'

'*Noooooooooo!*' shrieks Araine as she realizes what's happening. 'No, no, no! That's not the plan. You need me. You need me to give him to you.'

I shake my head at her as the tree begins to bloom and she begins to tremble violently, making a crackling and popping sound.

'No, I don't,' I say. 'Because he lives right here.' I tap my heart. The half-lives and ghosts see what I'm doing and tap their hearts too.

My mam notices. Taps her heart. Catches my eye and smiles through her tears, mouths to me, *He does, Hettie, pet. He does!*

We turn to face Araine and Jack, the tree nearly in full blossom, all holding branches, tapping our hearts.

Araine begins to crumble, wither and dry up in front of me, and I step forward to take the heart from around her neck.

I'm grabbed by my wrist. Jack!

I reach into my pocket and feel the pliers my grandad gave me, the ones that Harcus gave to Jack, the ones that Lucie first used that lived in a now-empty space on a rack in two different workshops, and ended up here, with me, now. I try to hold on, but Jack easily takes them out of my hand.

It's all over: he's going to help her.

But he smiles at me and taps his heart. There is warmth in his eyes, and I can finally see the boy in him, the one that Tattie and Harcus and Snod loved with all their hearts. Matthew's little brother.

'You did what we didn't have the strength to do, and now we'll be free. Thank you. This is for Matthew and Nora,' Jack says as the tree flourishes into full bloom.

Araine lets out an almighty shriek as Jack leaps towards her and snips the heart from around her neck with the pliers. The diamond falls to the stage, as Jack and Araine both scatter into dust.

Then Gift is holding me tight.

Then all my Free Spirits, all Jack's Free Spirits, the ghosts, the automatons, my mam and dad, Alan, everyone from the old Arts Centre, they're all surrounding me, surrounding the cherry tree that's blossoming into life.

'Thank you,' says Harcus, his arm round Lucie. Tattie is holding Priss's hand.

I look behind them, and there is Lucie and Harcus's mam. I gasp. Beside them there's a young Araine, clutching hands tightly with Nora. Then there is Jack, young and happy, wearing short trousers, with his older brother Matthew standing next to him, his hand on Jack's shoulder.

Grandad isn't there. But he is here. I tap my heart.

'You did it,' says Harcus. 'We knew you would.'

'Together,' says Tattie.

'Not you too,' I say. 'I can't lose you.' Gift is on one side of me, Nikesh on the other.

'You won't,' says Tattie, and points to my heart. 'We'll be right there. With Ed Red and all the others that have gone before us.'

Nikesh and Gift hold me tight, the spiders scrambling towards the heart, as we watch the ghosts fade away to nothing and the ghost light finally goes out.

That night I'm lying in bed with Snod and Walls back in their spots by my wardrobe. They don't talk or move any more, but I chat away to them. I tell them all about Grandad and the things we got up to. It hurts to talk about him. But that's OK. Mam says it's meant to, it will get easier the more we talk about him, and we can do that as much as we want.

I wriggle to try to get into a comfier position, and Rex, who is keeping my feet warm, opens one eye and stares at me. It's as if he's asking me a question with his white eyebrow raised.

'Nope, my little ghost dog, I don't know how you're still here either,' I say, reaching down to give his head a pat. 'But we are going to have so many adventures together, starting with producing a new show! Nikesh is going to write it – *Attercop Theatre: A Ghost Story*.'

I lie back on my pillow and watch the spiders above me weave a canopy over my bed to keep me safe and warm. One scurries into the palm of my hand to curl up and fall asleep.

'Thank you,' I whisper to them all. 'Sweet dreams.'

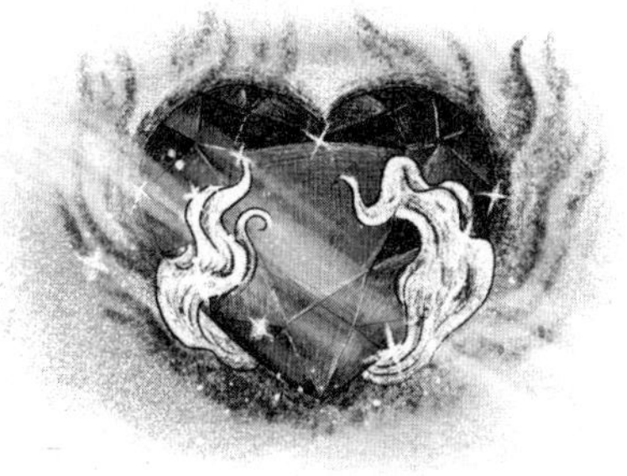

Epilogue

The archivist arrives at the theatre early, as she always does, and finds a parcel on her desk. Inside is a letter: an envelope full of papers, photos, a diary and two notebooks, and a box. She opens the letter first:

We hope this finds you as well as possible. We know we can trust you because you helped us once, and we know you love theatre as much as we do. The things you are about to read you may not believe, but we think you should. There was one little bit of magic left, and we used it to make a few alterations. It turns out models can be combined to bring out the best of them. We believe that theatre should be for everyone. Read on, then take the box to the stage and open it there. This will give you the means to carry on. We've made sure it's safe. Love, the Free Spirits.

An hour later, there are photos and papers strewn all over her desk, and she's pulled her hair down and put it up again countless times without realizing she's even doing it. She's read the diary twice and the notebooks once. It can't all possibly be true? She grabs the box and runs to the auditorium. When she opens the doors, she gasps.

The metal and silver have been combined with luxurious red velvet and gold. The boxes are now made of wood and there are names carved in swirls underneath them. She goes closer to read.

In memoriam: Harcus and Lucie
Lightfoot and their darling mam
Araine and Nora Redwood
Jack and Matthew Redwood
Tattie and Priss Lightfoot
Edward Redwood

Everything has a higgledy-piggledy feel that brings it all perfectly together. She laughs in wonder, then goes towards the stage.

It can't be! There's a ramp leading her up, and when she gets to the top there is a cherry tree, in full bloom, growing out of the centre of the stage. Beside it is a Victorian-style lamp post. She knows that it can't possibly be real, at the same time knowing it absolutely is.

She sits under the tree and opens the box. Inside is a heart-shaped diamond. A spider drops gently on its silk thread from the branch above and settles on her hand.

'Hey there, little creature. The notebook says this is now safe. Thank goodness for that. But we can sell it, and make this place open to everyone.'

The ghost light on the stage suddenly glows brightly, and the archivist nods.

'We'll leave you burning, just in case the ghosts ever want to come home.'

Acknowledgements

Dear reader, if the acknowledgements are your best bit, like they are mine, and you always come here first, like I do, fellow kindred spirit, I hope these don't disappoint.

This book started out as Hettie's story, a girl who loved theatre and found acceptance and her place in the world. Just like I did. With encouragement from my incredible editor Ruth, I delved into the other characters' stories too, and this book is so much stronger for it – thank you for believing in Araine and Jack and my ability to weave their lives together. Thank you so much to my copy-editor Jane and absolute legendary editorial manager Wendy for helping me a tremendous amount in all the historical details I hadn't expected to need to know, as well as such insightful wordy wisdom that lifted the book to new heights. Any historical inaccuracies are mine and mine alone (sometimes on purpose to help the story along).

Other Puffin superstars are genius editor Linas, incredible senior designer Alice, and PR legend Sarah. There are many others who work ridiculously hard to make books sparkle and I hope to meet you all and thank you in person one day. Thanks so much to Nat who took a chance on this story. And to Gillian and Valentina for saying yes to another arty adventure – your illustrations always make me cry happy tears.

I couldn't have written this book without the theatre staff who allowed me to come backstage, let me into their secrets and ask All the Questions: Darlington Hippodrome, Theatre Royal Drury Lane in London, and the Georgian Theatre in Richmond, North Yorkshire.

I'm very grateful to have found my love of theatre at school. Thank you to the teachers who gave their own precious time to put on shows when it wasn't on the curriculum. I think it saved a geeky girl like me, and I'm sure there are lots of other children who would benefit from finding their place there too. We need art in schools so that young people can thrive. Thanks to my fellow DAs at Bretton Hall where I learned to be a tree, and especially to my wonderful friend Liesel who carries my books across whole cities and helps me to be brave and go into bookshops to sign them.

I'm very fortunate to work in theatre with passionate, kind, inspirational folk. Thank you to all the incredible people I've had the honour of playing with, especially recently in *The Secret Garden, Chop, Dissolve, Burn* at Alphabetti Theatre, *Wintry Tales* at Live Theatre and *Night Classes* with Unfolding Theatre. And for all the support from Arc Stockton and Theatre Hullabaloo in Darlington.

Thank you to my agent extraordinaire, Molly, who does the best email titles.

Thank you to all the schools, festivals, organizations, awards ceremonies, booksellers and bookshops who've hosted and supported me and my books, and to the friendships made. They mean the world.

Thank you to the Scottish Book Trust for taking me on their Inclusive Stories Tour. It is making a MAHOOSIVE difference in highlighting disabled representation in children's books. To Fraser for not getting lost and sorting hotels when they couldn't count. And to Signe, who is at the helm of making great change happen and has brilliant shirts and the best taste in dogs.

I'm grateful to be able to write stories that include all sorts of characters, including those who are disabled and neurodivergent, like me. It's brilliant that young people are seeing more of themselves represented in books and plays. Thanks go to all those who went before me and made it possible, and to those to come who will make it even better. I have the privilege of doing oodles of school visits – the next generation is awesome.

Mega thanks to Aunty Janet, my AJ, who is the biggest super-fan the world has ever known. Thank you to Fran and Tom for pep talks when I got scared about tackling multiple timelines. Thank you to Cake for your maiden name – I probably should have asked before stealing it, but I thought it would be more fun this way.

Finally, all the thanks and love in the universe to Mum, Dad, Soph, Mads and Alex – I couldn't do this without you. And to Mark and HL, who are exceedingly understanding when I go AWOL to work and write, and give the best hugs when I get back.

PS All my characters are made-up. All except one – Rex the theatre dog. Thank you to Ali for allowing me to write him into this book. It would have been a very rubbish story if you'd said no.

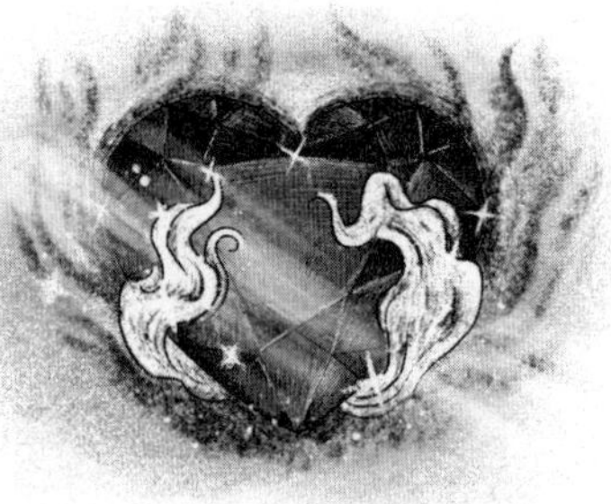

About the Illustrators

Valentina Toro is a disabled illustrator and children's book writer from Colombia. She has written several children's books published in Latin America and has also worked as an illustrator for publishers around the world. What she likes most about making books is that, in them, she can imagine amazing worlds, like the one in this story.

Gillian Eilidh O'Mara loves adventures and wandering, rich colours and flights of imagination, people-watching on public transport, cold North Sea air, bobble hats, big questions she can't answer and lying outside looking up and wondering what it's all about. She is a self-taught artist who learned while her babies slept, as well as a multi-award-winning social entrepreneur responsible for starting several community enterprises and a trustee of Unltd, a charity that supports social entrepreneurs across the UK.

Driven by a motto she picked up as a child that 'life is big – be all you can be', Gillian strives to bring a sense of creativity and thoughtfulness to everything she does and to see the wonder in everything and everyone.

Read more magical adventures by
LISETTE AUTON:

Alpha Lux was only a baby when she was found washed up beside a remote lighthouse. She was raised by a mermaid, and now the lighthouse is home for any disabled person who needs somewhere to belong.

But when Alpha realizes that her beloved family are in danger of being discovered by Outsiders, she must decide what kind of future she wants . . . and what she's willing to do to get it.

Mimi adores her wild, fun, full-of-life gran, but she's worried because Gran has started to forget things. Then cracks begin appearing around their home, and a mysterious black crow arrives – and only Mimi is able to see them.

Mimi is determined to solve the mystery. Luckily she has new friends to help: Titch and Nusrat. Together, they're the Stickleback Catchers, solvers of puzzles and seekers of adventure . . .